More Praise for

THE
WAY
IT
WAS

"Sinatra was mostly a private man having only a select few confidantes who knew anything about his personal life—among them his longtime manager Eliot Weisman. In his book, *The Way It Was: My Life with Frank Sinatra*, Weisman tells all on the late legend's sad final days." —RadarOnline.com

"A fascinating account of Eliot Weisman, who served as a manager, confidant, and advisor to some of the biggest names in entertainment including Liza Minnelli, Sammy Davis Jr., Joan Rivers, and the 'Chairman of the Board,' legendary singer Frank Sinatra." —*Parade*

"Pushes aside preconceptions about the iconic singer and celebrity.... Use[s] anecdotes and stories as a means of time travel." —*Gold Coast*

THE
WAY
IT
WAS

THE WAY IT WAS

MY LIFE WITH FRANK SINATRA

ELIOT WEISMAN
AND
JENNIFER VALOPPI

hachette BOOKS

NEW YORK   BOSTON

Hachette Books
Hachette Book Group
1290 Avenue of the Americas
New York, NY 10104

hachettebookgroup.com

twitter.com/hachettebooks

First Edition: October 2017

Hachette Books is a division of Hachette Book Group, Inc.

The Hachette Books name and logo are trademarks of Hachette Book Group, Inc.

The publisher is not responsible for websites (or their content) that are not owned by the publisher.

The Hachette Speakers Bureau provides a wide range of authors for speaking events. To find out more, go to www.hachettespeakersbureau.com or call (866) 376-6591.

"We'll Meet Again" words & music by Ross Parker & Hughie Charles. © Copyright 1939 Chester Music Limited trading as Dash Music Co. All Rights Reserved. International Copyright Secured.

Print book interior design by Timothy Shaner, NightAndDayDesign.biz

Library of Congress Control Number: 2017946386

ISBNs: 978-0-316-47009-4 (trade paperback), 978-0-316-47007-0 (ebook)

Printed in the United States of America

LSC-C

10 9 8 7 6 5 4 3 2 1

DEDICATION

This book is dedicated to my family: my wife, Maria;
my three sons Eric, Roy, and David; my daughter,
Carol Chenkin; my sister, Adele Weisman;
and my grandchildren, Josh, Ross, Samantha,
Sophie, Emily, and Harry.
May this book provide a lasting memory.

ACKNOWLEDGMENTS

I want to give special thanks to my daughter, Carol, who encouraged me to write this book and helped secure the publisher, which allowed me to make the idea of writing a book a reality.

A big thank you to my coauthor and partner, Jennifer Valoppi, who I have known for over 20 years and is the person who gave me the idea to write my memoir.

It may have taken me awhile to get going, but when I was ready you were there. There is no one else I would have done this book with. You understood the Boss and you understand me.

Special thanks to Steve Lawrence, Eydie Gormé, and Liza Minnelli. You were there when I needed you the most and you stuck by me.

To the Boss, you changed my life forever.

ONE

Frank Sinatra was not afraid to die. From the day I met him back in the 1970s till his passing at the age of eighty-two, he lived his life with strength, courage, and at times, even reckless abandon. The death of his iconic status, however, was another matter entirely.

It's been twenty years since his passing, and he knew he would leave a legacy for the generations. Nothing frightened him more than eroding the patina of his glorious run. Still, he forged ahead, refusing to be shelved with all the forgotten musicians of a bygone era. Nothing made him happier than staying relevant and in demand, till his last storied breaths, cultivated through years of holding those beautiful, elongated notes.

I was his manager and I like to think I played a small role in his enduring career.

Was he having memory problems toward the end? Sure he was, but he could handle that on a live stage with the audience in the palm of his hands.

Did he use those memory problems to his advantage, especially with me?

You bet he did. And so, I wasn't entirely surprised, as we rode in the back of a limo down Sunset Boulevard in 1993, when he said,

"What are we doing here, Eliot?" Had he forgotten the six months' worth of conversations, negotiations, and reminders? Not a chance.

"Boss, we're going to the recording studio," I said.

"This is bullshit," he said.

Still, he trusted me. When we walked into the lobby of the Capitol Records Building, he should have felt like a star taking a victory lap. Instead, I couldn't shake the thought that he looked like a kid who didn't want to go to his first day of school. The hallway to Studio A was lined with photos of Frank, Dean Martin, and Nat King Cole. They were the kings who built this circular palace that towers into the airspace at Hollywood and Vine.

He didn't even look at the photos, and I was too preoccupied to do so. There was only one thing on my mind, and that was to make sure he sang. I was nervous. My stomach was uneasy, and I knew it would be that way for some time to come.

The last time he walked that hall was 1961. He had ruled much of the 1950s and then led off the 1960s with one of the greatest bodies of work ever in popular music. It was there at Capitol that Sinatra collaborated with Nelson Riddle, Billy May, and Gordon Jenkins, and where they successfully birthed the concept album by grouping songs together to set a mood, from tender love songs to swinging dance music. He owned the legacy with years of hits like "I Get a Kick Out of You," "All of Me," and "I've Got You Under My Skin."

Shortly after, he started his own record label, Reprise, which was unheard-of for a singer to do in those days. He was the Chairman of the Board, the Voice. What did he have to be worried about?

I was startled and frightened when I saw the lost look in those Ol' Blue Eyes as we made our way to his old recording studio. It was filled with all of his favorite things: Tootsie Rolls, Wild Cherry Life Savers, Jack Daniel's, and a pack of Camels. I was hoping the familiarity would take him back to that time when he was on top of the charts and on top of the world.

This was *Duets*. I was executive producer of this album, along with Capitol's Charles Koppelman and Don Rubin. This was to be our piece of the Sinatra recording legacy—provided it was ever completed. This was his wife Barbara's piece of his recording legacy, too. He had gifted the rights to his previous recordings to his children.

The band was all there, seated and waiting for their cue. It was a combination of musicians who traveled on the road with us and studio players. The musicians had been paid for four days in advance, so there was a lot riding on this. Bill Miller was a familiar face on piano.

There were horn players, strings, and drums. Phil Ramone was producing. He was off to the side with the soundboards, anxiously looking through the glass that overlooked the studio. Hank Cattaneo, Frank's longtime associate, was coproducing. He had ridden in the limo with us.

Patrick Williams, who scored the music for hundreds of films and television shows, was conducting. He was the second-biggest star in the room. He was hired to do for the recording sessions what Frank Sinatra Jr. did for his dad in the live concerts. Patrick was standing in front of the musicians.

Sinatra was seventy-seven years old and it had been almost ten years since his last recording, *L.A. Is My Lady*. It was the first time I had ever been in a studio with the Boss, and his presence sent an undeniable wave of nervous excitement through the room.

Still, something wasn't right. He stood there in his satin Members Only bomber jacket and his demeanor was all wrong. This was the guy who owned every room he ever walked into. He looked confused, uncomfortable, and almost shy.

In more than two decades together, I had never seen him scared before. Once, we flew from Japan to Australia in a major storm. Everyone on the plane was terrified as we were jostled around in the winds and rain. I watched Sinatra sit casually sipping his Jack Daniel's, while I was sure we were going to die.

Another time, on one of our Italian tours, the pilot had to have one of the plane's two engines jump-started and said it might not make it to our destination. Sinatra told him to take off anyway, reasoning we could fly on one engine if we had to. We were not on a deadline; he was just a stickler for time, to say the least. Nothing fazed him.

He was the Boss, he was in charge—always. He directed with surety and everyone followed his cue. That's the way it was. So here we were, ready to make the boldest move of his career in years, and he was hesitant.

Duets would be a lucrative recording deal for any artist to pull off and would put him in front of a whole new generation. This was his moment. It was our moment. Everyone wanted it so bad. Everyone knew he could do this—everyone, that is, except Sinatra. Then he saw the soundproof booth, smack dab in the middle of the studio.

"What's this, a rocket ship?" Sinatra said. "I sing on the stage with the band."

The soundproof booth would have to be torn down and a small stage erected. The crew was called to start work on it. Magic would not be made that night.

I called Barbara, as I would do several times over the course of the coming days, and the three of us went to dinner at one of our favorite Beverly Hills hangouts, La Dolce Vita. By the next evening, there was a stage in place of the booth and we were ready to roll, but it turned out to be another false start. When Frank saw the room, he started pointing to his throat. He said he couldn't sing. I called Barbara from the car as we headed to dinner.

"Barbara, I have the Boss with me. He says his throat is not right so we are going to La Dolce Vita and we would like you to join us," I said.

"You're kidding me," she said. "I'll meet you there."

The first night, he had a legitimate complaint, but if he had had a problem with his voice he would have told me when I picked him up at his house, or on the car ride down, not when he stood in front of the microphone.

"You can do this," I said to Frank, as we sat at his favorite table. I ran through all the protections I had set up for him. If he didn't like the final cut, nothing would be released. He had no financial responsibility; Capitol paid for everything. Best of all, technology had significantly improved since the last time he was in the recording studio. If a note were off, now it could be fixed. He either didn't believe that or he didn't want to.

When Barbara walked in, he pointed to his throat.

"I have no chops," Frank said quietly, which meant he couldn't sing.

"Maybe you're a washed-up singer," Barbara said.

No one spoke to Sinatra that way.

It was late and the few patrons who were still there were finishing their meals.

I noticed people staring. There was no obvious ruckus, but they weren't gawking at a star, either. Loud whispers made it clear they were witnessing a quiet but fierce battle between husband and wife—one that would propel him to new heights, if we all survived the dinner.

"You're full of shit. You're yesterday's news. You didn't even ask for tea," she said, which was something he often did before he sang, especially if his throat was bothering him.

Sinatra went quiet. When he did that, you never knew what it meant. I'll tell you the whole story later, but suffice it to say that was a quarter of a century ago and the rocky start to the biggest-selling album of Sinatra's career.

Thankfully, Barbara had a gift for handling her husband. Of

course, he was a musical genius. For my part, I was trying to keep the most talented man I knew performing.

Audiences adored him and it was clear from the arenas he filled that his devotees were much more than the aging fans from his youth. Young people wanted to emulate him. They still do. My son Roy used to say, "Don't you owe it to the world to make another Sinatra album?" I guess he was right.

Sinatra knew I was looking out for his best interests in whatever we did together. He always made me feel he had confidence in me, perhaps not in so many words but in a thousand gestures. When he asked me to be co-executor of his estate, I said, "I'm honored, but why me?"

"Who the fuck else knows where everything is buried with this crowd," he said, "this crowd" being his family. He was well aware of the discord between his wife and his children, and Frank hated conflict in his personal life.

I believe I earned all of their trust to the extent that was possible, and that meant there could be relative peace. At least Barbara and the kids were on speaking terms for most of Sinatra's life. They may not have been saying nice things about each other, but they weren't saying them to each other's faces.

That fragile truce gave us a chance to write a new will, do several business deals including ties, cigars, recordings, and commercials, and increase his net worth substantially. The Sinatra name was a brand long before building your own brand became a national pastime.

The luster of the Sinatra name shone on everyone around him. If you had Sinatra as a friend, well, you didn't need much else in life. Sinatra made men. He certainly made my career.

When he parted ways with his former manager, Hollywood powerhouse Mickey Rudin, I wanted to help them put things back together. Rudin thought Sinatra's career was over and he had other, more important clients to tend to, but when Rudin died more than a decade after their parting, the headline in the *New York Times* still read, "Lawyer for Sinatra and Other Stars." Sinatra was everyone's biggest and brightest star.

If you had Sinatra as a client, his allure extended to all your clients. I never once had to use Sinatra's name to negotiate a better deal for another performer, but his influence was ever present. Whether it was Liza Minnelli, Sammy Davis Jr., Don Rickles, Steve Lawrence and Eydie Gormé, or one of a host of others, all the decision makers at the venues knew Sinatra was my client and were happy to make deals for everyone, in the hopes they had a shot at booking the Boss.

Before I was Sinatra's manager, I managed Liza. She stood by me during the most difficult period of my life and helped to restore my credibility in Hollywood when I was caught up in a devastating scandal that I will tell you about shortly.

Sammy Davis Jr. was in dire financial straits when I took him on. I was an accountant and money manager by training and we were working hard to straighten his finances out, when throat cancer cut his life short and we ran out of time. Sinatra loved to hang out with Sammy, we all did. He was all fun and no hassles.

The biggest disappointment of all my clients was also the man I believe I did the best job for—Don Rickles. He too was an old Sinatra friend who I took on at a low point in his career. We parted after decades together over a couple of percentage points on my commission and what I considered to be an unreasonable and un-Sinatra-like request.

Steve and Eydie, more than most of my clients, understood finances and knew that leaving my clients with more money than when I started was always my primary goal.

I considered all my clients to be my friends, and while money matters were my strong suit, I learned to play psychiatrist and protector as well. I knew my clients' likes and dislikes and when to push and when to pull back. That was especially important with Sinatra. I learned to read his moods and his body language. Sometimes he wanted to talk and sometimes he wanted to be reflective. Sometimes he just wanted the company.

I knew the cities he liked to perform in: New York, London, Miami, Chicago, New Orleans, and San Francisco. He enjoyed venues where he felt a sense of intimacy with the audience, 4,000 seats or less. When we played arenas, where there could be 20,000-plus fans, we switched from a standard proscenium layout with the stage on one end, to a theater in the round, so he could feel more closely connected to his audience.

If he didn't like a venue he would say, "Hey, Eliot, you got a camera?"

"Sure, Boss, what do you need?"

"Take a picture of this place, 'cause we ain't never coming back here."

Because Frank was such a stickler for time, his rule was that the venue could be no more than 20 to 25 minutes from an airport or hotel. Most of the time they were 30 to 40 minutes away, and I paid for every one of those minutes as he tapped his watch and said, "How many times do I have to tell you, you have twenty-five minutes to arrive at our destination?" Of course, he knew I had no control over the location of the best concert locales but he loved to harass me anyway.

One day I wasn't in the mood.

"You know, Boss, we need to do a hangar tour. We'll go from airport hangar to airport hangar and put up a stage and you won't have to drive anywhere."

"Great idea. Have the jackets printed up: 'Hangar Tour,'" he said.

He loved playing casinos because he didn't have to go to the car. He went right from the stage to the dining room and bar, where we would hang out into the wee small hours of the morning, as the song goes.

Now I'm almost eighty years old and I feel like Frank must have felt when he walked past all those pictures of his younger self that lined the halls of Capitol. While I'm not competing with myself in my prime, like Frank was when we recorded *Duets,* writing this book, and looking at my life through an eighty-year-old lens, has clarified the roads I took, the turns I missed, and the circles I ran in when I thought I was moving full speed ahead. Thankfully at this age, I have the good fortune that the memories from twenty-five years ago are more vivid than the memories of yesterday's aches and pains. And what a roller-coaster ride my life has been. When Sinatra retired, it was like coming around the final bend of the track. I thought I had had enough and was ready to get off, but when I did, I realized the world was not nearly as exciting a place.

My journey with Frank all started at the bottom of the roller coaster.

TWO

On a Friday afternoon in September 1977, I drove down the right-hand lane of Tarrytown Road in Westchester County, New York, about twenty-five miles north of Manhattan. I had a sick feeling in the pit of my stomach.

I wasn't speeding, and the road was relatively open. I noticed a car behind me, one to the left, and another one cut in front of me. As we reached the far side of a stoplight, all three cars slowed to a halt and I had no choice but to do the same. A man in a suit walked over to my station wagon and flashed a badge. "Step out of the car, please, Mr. Weisman. You're under arrest."

"For what?" I said, but I already knew. The day before, I had testified to a grand jury looking into the business dealings of the Westchester Premier Theatre.

"Leave the keys in the car," the agent said. "We'll take care of it."

He told me to put my hands on the roof of the car, and he proceeded to handcuff my hands behind my back. At FBI headquarters in New Rochelle, I was photographed, fingerprinted, and taken to a nondescript conference room with a long, dark table in the center.

There were four agents in the room. I was advised that my wife, Micky, and I had committed bank fraud by exaggerating my income by a few thousand dollars on a mortgage loan application. Then they spoke of stock fraud and obstruction of justice, a combination that could lead to possible racketeering charges against me. They brought out everything they could think of to heighten my fear, and it worked.

"You're a good guy," one of the agents said. "But you're looking at twenty years. You need to cooperate with us." I was thirty-seven years old. Fifty-seven meant I would be an old man.

"We have two hundred hours of tape recordings," another agent said, "one hundred hours of phone recordings that include you. We can't promise you anything, but if you cooperate we can recommend the judge go easy on you."

I rarely spoke on the phone. "If you have a hundred hours of me," I said, "I certainly want to hear them. Can I make a phone call now?"

"When you're done with processing," an agent said.

The processing dragged on for hours.

I sat silently as they played wiretap after wiretap of familiar voices of men talking about skimming profits and selling tickets for seats that weren't on the books of the Westchester Premier Theatre, which I built and oversaw as president.

The men who were speaking were not the kind you wanted to identify, much less turn into the authorities for wrongdoing. Disavowing any knowledge of them would be the best course of action, but of course that wasn't possible. They were both known and silent partners in the theater. Some were friends from the Lake Isle Country Club, one of the few Westchester clubs that welcomed Jews and Italians in the 1970s.

There were plenty of Italian names on the wiretaps—Gambino, Castellano, DePalma—but there was one man they really wanted to hear about.

"Do you know Frank Sinatra?" the agent said.

Now, you have to understand, I grew up in a neighborhood in Brooklyn where nothing was worse than a rat. You kept your mouth shut and didn't talk about other people's private business, especially not to the feds.

"Yeah. He's a limousine driver in New York," I said, which was true.

"Frank Sinatra, a limousine driver," the agent said.

"Yeah," I said.

Of course, I knew the Sinatra they were referring to. Frank Sinatra had been plagued by allegations of mob affiliations for most of his career. Rumors dated back to the days when J. Edgar Hoover ran the FBI and kept secret dossiers on celebrities. Over what would ultimately be a thirty-year time period, the FBI conducted numerous investigations into Sinatra and linked him to notorious organized crime bosses like Bugsy Siegel, Lucky Luciano, and Sam Giancana.

It was the photo with a host of mob bosses, including the so-called boss of bosses, taken at the Westchester Premier Theatre that the FBI was determined to use to finally tie Sinatra to organized crime. It didn't matter that I had no personal knowledge of Sinatra's connection, or lack of it, to the mob. I only knew that the wiseguys, like much of the world, adored Sinatra.

As the feds played the tapes and I listened to people repeatedly incriminating themselves, I realized how little I knew about the business I had created. It was difficult for me to understand how I had come to be in this uncomfortable chair in a dingy office room in FBI headquarters. It was Friday night, and I knew there would be no arraignment, which meant no bail, until probably Monday morning, so I sat and listened. When the agents left the room, ostensibly to give me time to think about cooperating, I drifted back to a time when life was filled with hope and promise and the Westchester Premier Theatre seemed like a stroke of brilliance. Nothing in my life had prepared me for this place. I had a good education, a beautiful family, and a great life. I had always tried to do the right thing. If my mother had been alive, I would have had a hard time explaining to her what I was doing there.

My father, David, was an accountant who represented among others, the songwriting duo of Rodgers and Hammerstein and the artist Marc Chagall. He had a 1 percent stake in the Broadway show *South Pacific* and that enabled us to move from a two-story Brooklyn brownstone to a nice house in New Rochelle, not far from the FBI building I now found myself in.

Growing up on the streets of Brooklyn, I loved to play stickball and baseball. My father played piano, and I dabbled in tennis because both he and my mother, Edna, loved the sport. Edna was an athlete and was once the New York State amateur tennis champion. Most of all, she was my buddy. She was competitive and willful. The old adage that *winning isn't everything, it's the only thing* was the credo mom and I lived by long before I ever heard Vince Lombardi say it.

There's an advantage to being the oldest child of a woman in her early thirties. You can remember her when she was at her most beautiful. My sister Adele, who is eight years younger than I, doesn't have the same wealth of memories I do. As a boy, I remember my mother, always fit, in perfect health, in her white tennis skirt and blouse. I remember the joyous smile when she was on the court of our local tennis club hitting the ball back and forth with a wooden racket. Playing tennis made her happy. Baseball was my first love, but I loved playing tennis with Mom and Dad. So it was all the more difficult when my mom was diagnosed with breast cancer. In the late 1940s, that was often a death sentence. Doctors performed a mastectomy and removed some of her lymph nodes.

I was angry, scared, and mostly helpless. My father didn't drive, so at barely thirteen years old, I would drive the family car to the local Safeway on the weekends to shop while Mom recovered. It was one of the few things I could do for her. I would organize the grocery list in my head by the pattern through which I would walk through the aisles. To this day, I love to go food shopping. I suppose it makes me feel like I am contributing to the family.

As Mom recovered, I watched her struggle to move her arms, hoping to regain her mobility and strength, but she could never again reach up to pound down on her powerful serve. Someone suggested she take up golf.

That summer we vacationed in northern New York State, at the Sacandaga Inn in the Adirondack Mountains. It was a rustic, sleepy town filled with summer cabins, water sports and lush greenery. I was standing on the driving range as a golf pro instructed my mother. I watched a woman I considered to be a tremendous athlete struggle to hit the ball. She swung and thumped. The ball rolled ten yards off the tee. She swung again and sent the ball fifteen yards off on a hard right. It was hard for me to believe that my athletic mother couldn't make direct contact with a ball that was standing still. I giggled. She swung and missed. I let out a laugh.

"The ball's not moving, Mom," I said.

She sneered and swung, and the ball skipped off to the left.

I laughed out loud. I couldn't help myself.

"Mrs. Weisman, may I have your club, please?" the pro said to my mother.

She handed it to him and he grabbed the driver by the head, then walked over to me. "Go ahead. Give it a try," he said.

I gave a cocky smirk and walked to the tee as my mother stepped away.

Too easy, I thought. "I'm afraid I'll hit that house over there," I said, pointing off into the distance.

"Don't worry," the pro said. "Just hit."

"Okay, but I'm not responsible if I break a window or something."

I held the club like a baseball bat and wound up with all my might, like a batter going for an easy home run with the ball slowed to a dead stop. I missed and swung around full circle and fell to the ground. On the second swing, I almost threw my shoulder out as the club planted hard into the sod.

I was hooked. Mom and I played every day. I spent the rest of the summer at the driving range hitting balls until it was dark. I played until my hands were calloused and blistered. I never touched a tennis ball again. It was only a nine-hole course, so we would play nine and start all over again. Mom was better than I was, but one day I had the best of her. I had just parred two holes and I was ahead.

She was on the green, focused on a twelve-foot, left-to-right putt. "Don't miss that putt," I said.

Without breaking her stance, she looked up and glared at me. "Fuck you," she said, as she proceeded to stroke the ball and we watched it roll into the hole.

It may have been the first time I ever heard my mother say that and it was certainly the first time she ever said it to me. It still makes me smile. I loved her unabashed competitiveness.

My dad worked all day and someone had to give my mother the necessary injections to help her recover. Dad was pretty squeamish, so I gave my mother her shots. I hated watching the needle pierce her flesh, but I was willing to do practically anything to keep her alive and out of the hospital.

Arnold Palmer became my idol, and although I had aspirations to become a golf pro, my father wouldn't hear of it. I ended up at the Wharton School of Business at the University of Pennsylvania, and was a freshman when Mom died. It was a difficult time for all of us, especially my sister.

I called home as often as I could, which between my class and study schedule was about once a week. Adele always tried to put on a brave face, but I knew how much she missed Mom. I missed her, too.

I was happy that at least Adele had our housekeeper, Chris, to provide somewhat of a maternal influence. For all Chris did in taking care of my mom when she was sick and then taking care of my sister, she was more like family to me than hired help.

The rest of my phone time was spent with Maxine, whom everyone called Micky. She was my high school sweetheart and we were married my senior year of college.

Maxine was proud of my academic credentials, that I majored in accounting and business law. I had a degree in economics, which gave me the ability to adapt to most any business situation. I went to work for one of the big eight national accounting firms, just like I planned.

Life, however, was not going according to plan for Dad and he struggled with his work after Mom died. He surprised us all when he left his accounting firm and tried to go it alone with a tax and investment practice that specialized in tax audits. He had always been part of an organization and had no idea how to handle the numerous facets of running an office. When his billings dropped significantly and he was clearly in need of help, I worried he wouldn't be able to send my sister to college and keep up his lifestyle. I was looking for a transition, too, so I decided it was a good time to see if I liked working with my father.

Dad loved the idea and promptly renamed the company Weisman & Weisman. Our offices were adjacent to the Paris Theatre, across from the Plaza hotel, off Fifth Avenue in Manhattan.

Dad was a great tax accountant but I could tell by the way he delegated the workload that he was a lousy administrator. I took over all the hiring, firing, and basic business functions of running the office.

When my college friends started to become successful, I turned them into new clients. I also brought in clients from the two country clubs I joined.

The truth is, I didn't care for accounting. So, I started the Copia fund, a small hedge fund, on the side. Meanwhile, over the seven years I worked with my dad, his hundred-thousand-dollar-a-year business had grown to a half-million dollars a year. When I knew it was secure, I convinced my cousin to join the business and I gave him my half of the firm. I moved on. Eventually I joined a Wall Street firm and invested people's money as a broker.

My little sister, who studied at the Juilliard School, was now graduating from a college called Beaver, which I always thought was a ridiculous name for a woman's college. (Thankfully, it's now called Arcadia University.) When I asked her what she wanted to do, she said, "I don't know. Maybe I'll be a teacher." Adele was a city woman. She liked culture, arts, and entertainment. She wasn't about to be a teacher in the suburbs, and New York City wasn't a safe place to be teaching. There were constant reports of teachers being roughed up by students.

"Are you fucking crazy?" I said. "Are you looking to get killed?" That put an end to that discussion.

I asked my friend Charles Roden to give her an opportunity in his stock brokerage firm. She went on to graduate with an MBA from New York University and today she is a successful personal money manager.

Micky and I had three kids: Eric, Carol, and Roy. We lived in a nice house in the Westchester County suburb of Scarsdale. We had a good life. I played golf whenever I could at Lake Isle Country Club. I was the club champion three times.

One day, the caddie master said, "Hey, Mr. Weisman, a new member heard you were a good golfer and would like to play with you. Can I introduce you?" That introduction would change the course of my life.

Greg DePalma and I played the back nine. He wasn't a good golfer but he was a lot of fun and we had a lot of laughs that day. He said he was in the jewelry business and I had no reason to doubt him. He told me, if I ever needed a gift for Micky, I should let him know. He was married to a Jewish girl. They were roughly the same age as my wife and I, and we began to socialize together.

A short time after we became friendly, he invited Micky and me to go with him and his wife, Terry, to the Westbury Music Fair, on Long Island, to see Tom Jones in concert. It was 1971. The two women rode in the back while Greg and I chatted in front. Parking at the theater was overcrowded and difficult. I stepped out of the car and said, "Are you kidding? This is a dump."

Then I saw people selling $50 tickets for $200 in the parking lot. Westbury was a covered theater in the round and I couldn't imagine why anyone would want to see someone perform that way. Half the people were looking at the entertainer's ass.

Nonetheless, all twenty-eight hundred seats of the theater were filled, Tom Jones was great, and the audience response was better than great, it was wildly enthusiastic. As we drove home, I said, "Wouldn't it be great to build something like this in Westchester?"

"You don't have the balls," Micky said.

THREE

The weekend following the Tom Jones concert, DePalma talked about building a theater as we hit balls on the driving range. Tony Cabot, a fellow club member and respected New York producer and composer, was also there. The world-famous Rainbow Room featured his music for much of the 1960s and '70s, so he was our resident expert on the musical landscape of the area.

"Hey, Tony, we were out at Westbury last weekend. It's a cow pasture out there," I said. Westchester was a more affluent community and our friends loved live entertainment. "What do you think about building something like that out here?"

"You'd be rich," Cabot said.

"Would you be the musical director?" I said.

"Absolutely. It's a stone-cold winner."

And so it began. Other guys around the club would hear us talking on the golf course and everyone was getting excited. I asked the guys at my brokerage firm. "It makes sense," they said. People loved going to the theater. Westchester residents were rich enough to afford the tickets. The acts would play six nights a week. It would be a state of the art proscenium theater, not a theater in the round like Westbury. A lot of entertainers wouldn't play a theater in the round.

DePalma introduced me to Richie Fusco. Richie said he was in the clothing business and manufactured women's dresses. Between DePalma's friends, my friends, and Lake Isle members we raised $250,000 in seed money.

The Westchester Premier Theatre would have two restaurants. It would be state-of-the-art. I could *see* Shirley Bassey on my stage. I went looking for real estate.

Most everything I looked at wasn't suitable; it wasn't big enough and didn't have enough room for parking. Then I found the perfect location, right off the parkway. The problem was that the U.S. Environmental Protection Agency had placed restrictions on a fifteen-foot-wide brook that ran through the property. The people who owned the land were understandably happy to make a deal. I called my uncle Herman Weisman, a well-known New York lawyer, and took him to see the property.

"Eliot, you're crazy. Don't do it. When you start putting in pilings there is going to be runoff and it's going to kill the wildlife in that brook."

I called another expert. He told me, "If you fill it properly, with pure fill, it will be fine." I preferred that answer and I bought the land with investors' money.

In the summer of 1973 we did a public offering at $7.50 a share and raised $2 million. Now I could see every performer I ever loved on my stage, Frank Sinatra, Sammy Davis Jr., and Dean Martin being just for starters. The stock plunged to $2.50 a month after the opening.

FOUR

On September 30, at the end of the 1973 baseball season, the New York Yankees beat the Detroit Tigers 8–5 and fans stormed the field to get their hands on any memorabilia they could find. It wasn't because the game was so extraordinary, but because the beloved House That Ruth Built had fallen into disrepair and was about to close down for much-needed renovations. Some fans had come with pliers and hammers to unbolt the seats, which they carted home on the subway. Others ripped the sod from the field and pulled out the lightbulbs from the scoreboards. The Yankees moved to Shea Stadium along with the Mets for the 1974 and 1975 seasons and the football Giants moved to the Yale Bowl in New Haven, Connecticut.

The debris that was left was carted off by dump trucks looking for anyplace to dispose of the trash. They found DePalma and he charged them $75 per load to dump their garbage on our property. The refuse from the old Yankee Stadium became the landfill for the Westchester Premier Theatre.

The landfill was, needless to say, far from pristine, and the EPA determined we were secreting dirty water into the brook. They closed us down for eight months, until we fixed the violation. We had to add three steps to the back stage door, because the land had sunk an extra foot and a half due to the improper landfill. We were over budget and two years past the expected deadline, but when it was finished, it was gorgeous.

Ralph Alswang, who designed the Gershwin Theatre in Manhattan, was our designer. The lobby was blue, with a bar in the center and red and white striped candy carts at either side that sold penny candies like Mary Janes and licorice out of white paper bags. Alswang would complain, "You're ruining my avant-garde theater with candy carts."

"Stay out of our moneymakers," DePalma would say.

There was Premier East, a sit-down club-style restaurant, and Premier West, where a buffet dinner was served. They were run by my friend Billy Losapio. He was the youngest brother of Gregory and Sergio, who had their own restaurants in White Plains. I brought Billy in for his loyalty and understanding of the restaurant business and local community. Billy was also very savvy to the local wiseguys who went through the neighborhood restaurants.

"You've got to be careful," Billy warned. "These are not the type of guys you are used to doing business with."

The theater itself was done in shades of red. In order to fit thirty-five hundred seats, we designed the two ends of the seating at ninety-degree angles, around a half-moon-shaped stage. It seemed like an optimal use of space, but the end result was that the people in the two ends saw mostly the performer's profile.

On March 24, 1975, we opened the Westchester Premier Theatre to a sellout crowd. It was the biggest accomplishment of my professional life to that point. All our friends came. Women showed up in cocktail dresses, bell bottoms, and furs and men wore jackets and ties, a step up from the popular leisure suit of the day. I was in my best suit and Micky was absolutely beautiful.

Diana Ross, a huge international star, was performing. All the local papers covered it and we were the talk of the town.

Walking through the packed house was a thrill and everyone involved could feel the excitement. Still, there was a part of me that couldn't wait for the night to be over with. Behind the glamour and sparkle, I couldn't shake the feeling that something was about to go terribly wrong.

In retrospect, I should have put the theater in Chapter 11 the day it opened, but given the circumstances I found myself in, there's no telling how that might have turned out. The truth is, Westchester Premier Theatre was in trouble from the start.

Over the next few days, as I looked at the gross profit margins from the food and liquor, I realized the numbers didn't add up.

"Something is wrong," Billy said when he looked over the books. "These gross profit percentages are crazy." We were expecting at least twice as much.

I took a walk over to DePalma's office, next to the box office.

"Hey, Greg, we had a 15 percent profit on the liquor last night. That's really low. How's that possible at the prices we're charging?"

"It's opening week," he said. "We're buying people drinks and there's a lot of spillage."

When the pattern stayed consistent over the next couple of weeks, I became convinced things were going south and that this wasn't going to be an easy fix. I knew I had a problem but I was thirty-seven years old, with the arrogance of youth and the ambition of someone who wanted to be somebody. Though I didn't grow up poor in a financial sense, poor is often a state of mind. My wife's parents were wealthier than we were and I wanted to at least be able to give her and my children the lifestyle Micky had grown up with. It's not an excuse, but perhaps it's an explanation for why I didn't hightail it away from the Westchester Premier Theatre when I realized I had little control over what was going on. There was another reason that weighed heavily on my mind.

I went back to Greg's office.

"This is ridiculous. The gross profit on the liquor is 50 percent of what it should be," I said.

He looked up from his desk. "Mind your own business," he said.

DePalma was intimidating. He was a bit taller than I and in reasonable shape, but it wasn't his physical stature that bothered me. A few years earlier, DePalma had asked me to take a ride out to Rosedale, in Queens. The Italian-American Civil Rights League had purchased a plot of land to build a camp for underprivileged New York City youth and he wanted to stop by a gathering that was being held there. The league was formed to combat negative stereotypes against Italian-Americans and boasted tens of thousands of members, many who came out for their rallies.

Cars were parked all over the grass of the 250-acre plot of land. There were probably a couple of hundred people socializing. We had driven my light blue Coupe de Ville Cadillac, which had a phone in it. Car phones were rare in the 1970s and required an extra, larger radio antenna for reception. The phone made me more efficient and I considered it a necessary extravagance. The phone, a plain black handset, was mounted on the front console of the car and had no dial or keypad. When you picked up the receiver a mobile operator answered. You gave her your number and the number you were calling and she made the connection.

DePalma and I were talking to some people near the car when a casually dressed guy with thinning hair wandered over to it. He looked around and then called out to DePalma.

"Hey, Greg, can I see you for a minute," which did not sound like a question.

It was a short conversation. When DePalma came back he said, "Eliot, I need you to do me a favor. I want you to give your phone to my friend over there. He's going to send some of his buddies to take it out of your car and I'll replace the whole thing next week."

"What?" I said.

"I need you to do this, Eliot."

I watched two men in slacks and sport shirts nonchalantly dismantle the phone and antenna with nothing less than professional speed and efficiency.

Later that night, DePalma called me and said the man he gave my phone to was Joe Colombo, the founder of the Italian-American Civil Rights League and the head of one of the five New York crime families. I canceled my number. DePalma never replaced the phone and I never asked. I bought a new one.

So when DePalma told me to "worry about my side of the theater," meaning the business side, and he would worry about his, meaning the operations, I backed off.

I did what I could do. I worked on booking the best and biggest acts I could find, including Sammy Davis Jr., Engelbert Humperdinck, Tom Jones, Liberace, and Cher.

I was hoping the theater would grow in popularity and we would entice more season ticket holders. It was a lot of long shots and a constant source of anxiety but at this point I thought the worst thing that could happen was that the theater would go broke. In retrospect, that would have been the best thing that could have happened.

Of all the performers, no one generated as much publicity as Frank Sinatra, but it had nothing to do with his singing.

FIVE

I n 1976 and 1977, Frank Sinatra did more than thirty mostly sold-out shows at Westchester, including several shows with Dean Martin. I, along with everyone else who worked there, was a Sinatra fan.

"Mr. S., if there is anything you need, just ask me," I remember saying as we shook hands for the first time.

I would go backstage before and after the concerts to say hello to Sinatra and his crew and make sure everything was going as planned. Jilly Rizzo, a restaurateur and Sinatra's longtime friend, confidant, and bodyguard, was usually there. Jilly was a tall rectangle of a man. He was six feet three inches, with broad, square shoulders. You could identify the outline of his body from a block away. He was always tan, wore distinctive aviator glasses with black and gold frames, and had come to head Sinatra's security, after his son Joey took over the popular Jilly's Bar on West Fifty-Second Street in Manhattan. Jilly grew up on the mean streets of the Lower East Side and knew how to take care of himself. He had known Sinatra since the 1950s and I could tell by the relaxed nature of their relationship that they shared a special bond.

Mickey Rudin, Sinatra's thickset, boisterous attorney, would fly in from Los Angeles. His brash, rough-around-the-edges style and

Harvard degree made him a star among entertainment lawyers. He even had small parts in a few films. Rudin was quick-witted and usually wore a suit and tie.

They would go to dinner after the concerts, and often Sinatra expanded the group to include some locals and occasionally DePalma and me. I had to wake up early in the morning, so I went only if they were eating nearby. We usually went to one of Losapio's brothers' restaurants, Gregory's or Sergio's. Over time, we all became friendly and I was always available if Mr. S. needed me.

One night backstage, Jilly told me Sinatra had had a fight with his girlfriend Barbara Marx, a beautiful blond former Las Vegas showgirl who had been married to Zeppo Marx, the straight man of the Marx Brothers. Sinatra threw her clothes into the hallway of the Waldorf-Astoria Towers, where he stayed when in New York. After she collected her things, Jilly took Barbara to the airport and she headed back to the west coast. I had no idea what to make of the story. It was none of my business and I figured if Jilly wanted me to know more, he would tell me. I didn't ask questions.

A few days later, I was backstage in the reception area outside Sinatra's dressing room, talking with the group that would be joining him for dinner. Sinatra called me in. He was putting his shirt on for the show.

"Hey, Eliot."

"Yeah, Mr. S. What can I do for you?"

"During the show, three songs from the end, take the limo and go pick up Jackie Onassis at her apartment on Fifth Avenue. Bring her over to Separate Tables and I'll meet you there."

"Sure, Boss."

It didn't take much to conclude that he had a limited selection of people in that room available to send, and I guess he figured I was the most presentable. This was certainly the most important thing Sinatra had ever asked me to do.

He told Jilly to tell the rest of the group to be on their best behavior.

I was a Kennedy supporter, and I should have been excited to meet our former first lady, Jacqueline Kennedy Onassis, but this was for Sinatra. It was work and I had to stay focused. By the time the driver pulled up to her place, she was waiting in the lobby. She was very elegant.

"Mrs. Onassis," I said. "Mr. S. asked me to escort you to the restaurant."

I was a little nervous. She was calm and soft-spoken. She made me feel relaxed. We made small talk in the limo about the theater and Sinatra's concerts. We arrived at Separate Tables, a casual Italian restaurant owned by Sinatra's friend Lou Pacella.

Sinatra was always an impeccable gentleman. He stood up for women when they came to the table; he lit their cigarettes, held doors, and never swore in front of a lady. But you could tell by the way he treated Jackie O. that she was special, a cut above the rest. She was refined, even demure, and of course there was a whole mystique to her life of celebrity and tragedy.

We were all seated at a rectangular table and they were seated next to each other in the middle. Sinatra was unusually attentive and reserved.

He had met her when she was first lady and it has been reported that many years later, after the death of her second husband, Greek shipping tycoon Aristotle Onassis, Jackie O. and Sinatra had a brief fling.

This night, the other guys and I could all tell Sinatra was smitten. There were eight or ten of us, and only one other woman besides Jackie O. Everyone was on guard and, as Jilly had warned, on their best behavior. Unlike our usual raucous dinners, no one spoke loudly and there was not a curse word all night. Of all the dinners I would come to have with Sinatra, this was the most boring.

I think Sinatra wanted to lighten things up. So, after dinner we left for the Rainbow Room, the famous rooftop restaurant and club at Rockefeller Center, where Sinatra's pal and sometime opening act, comedian Pat Henry, was performing.

We had a few cars with drivers waiting for us. Sinatra, Jackie O., Jilly, and I took one of the limos and the others followed behind. Sinatra and Jackie O. sat in the back and Jilly and I were in the two seats that faced them. There must have been a press leak, because by the time we pulled up to the entrance on West Forty-Ninth Street, there were several photographers waiting.

Jilly jumped out of the car first and asked the paparazzi to please refrain from taking photos and clear the way so everyone could go into the building. Jilly was *not* the Secret Service, so it's not surprising that in the next instant, cameras and fists were flying.

Jackie, who did not want to be photographed in the middle of a melee, bolted for the brass revolving doors.

When Sinatra, Jilly, and I entered the building, Sinatra looked around the lobby.

"Where is she?" he said.

Jackie had made her way through the lobby and down the hallway of brass-inlaid black terrazzo floors, to the bank of elevators that went directly to the Rainbow Room. She was waiting there with the white-gloved elevator attendant. We rode silently to the sixty-fifth floor.

The scuffle changed the dynamic of the evening. I don't know exactly what was going through Sinatra's mind, but I believe he was worried when he walked into the building and couldn't find her. He was used to taking care of women. Or perhaps he thought she didn't want to be photographed with him. Whatever it was, he was also tired, and as the night went on, he seemed to lose interest in her. We watched Pat Henry's show and after a drink or two he asked me to take Mrs. Onassis home. Sinatra and Jilly went back to the hotel in a separate limo. During the car ride, Jackie told me she ran off because she was scared. A few days later, when I was hanging around backstage, Sinatra told me he wished he had never sent Barbara home.

Sinatra had his chances with many women, and despite enormous pressure from his children to go back to his first wife, Nancy, in retrospect it is clear to me that he truly loved Barbara.

He never said no to her and there was nothing she wouldn't do for him. They reconciled, and within months, on July 11, 1976, Frank Sinatra and Barbara Marx were married.

A few months earlier, Sinatra was in the middle of ten sold-out performances at the Westchester Premier Theatre. One night, DePalma called me and said, "Carl is coming to the show tonight."

"You mean our barber?" I said, thinking he meant the man who cut our hair in Eastchester.

"No. Big Carl is coming to the show."

Bad idea.

"Big Carl" was how everyone who knew him and wasn't with law enforcement referred to Carlo Gambino, the Sicilian-born head of the Gambino crime family and the reputed "boss of bosses" of the crime syndicate. My associates in the theater were small potatoes compared to Big Carl.

"Sorry, Greg. I can't make it. I have to do something with Micky and the kids tonight."

That was a lie. It was a gut reaction but I believe this was the best decision I ever made in my life.

The next day, DePalma called me. "What a picture we got last night. You should have been there."

Immediately my palms began to sweat. "What's the picture?"

He rattled off names and I ticked off titles in my head. It was a who's-who of mob big shots: Paul Castellano, the man who would eventually succeed Carlo Gambino as the head of the family; reputed mobster Tommy Marson; Carlo Gambino, the "boss of bosses"; Aladena "Jimmy the Weasel" Fratianno, who later turned state's evidence and went into the witness protection program; Salvatore Spatola, a convicted heroin and cocaine trafficker; reputed capo Joseph Gambino; Richard Fusco, who became consigliere of the Colombo crime family; and of course DePalma. And there was Sinatra, right in the middle, with his arms around DePalma and Marson.

"You have to get rid of that photo," I said.

"What are you talking about? I made a hundred copies."

"Don't give them out."

"I'm only giving them to the guys."

"I have to call Rudin," I said.

I reached Rudin at the Waldorf Towers and told him this was a bad picture to have floating around and he agreed. He told me he would reach Sinatra and call me back within the hour.

"Sinatra said it's only a picture. He takes pictures with fans all the time. This is no different," Rudin said. "And he was **annoyed** that I brought it up."

To Sinatra, taking a photo, having a drink, or meeting with whomever he wanted was deeply rooted in his sense of what it meant to be a free American. To him, that photo was one of many photos with some admiring fans. To the FBI, that photo was reason to ramp up another Sinatra investigation.

As I sat in the FBI headquarters almost a year and a half later, I thanked God I had the good sense to go home that night and stay out of that photo. Every once in a while you can look back at your life and see the fork in the road—the choice you made that landed you where you are and the alternative choice that would have led somewhere very different. This was my fork.

As I sat listening to hours and hours of wiretaps, it was clear that I was not a target of the investigation but rather a not-so-innocent bystander of the FBI probe. While I never participated in the illegal profit skimming, I did know, at least in part, what was going on, but I felt powerless to do anything about it.

There's no doubt in my mind that my life and the FBI's perception of my life would have been very different if I had been in that picture.

SIX

There he was, the beloved Frank Sinatra, casually laughing, standing in the middle of eight of the most notorious alleged criminals in the country, with his arms around two of them. It looked like a happy bunch of thugs hanging out with their famous pal. The media loved it, and the photo was inescapable as it made newspapers, magazines, and television. For weeks, you couldn't go anywhere without seeing the damn thing. It brought more notoriety to the Westchester Premier Theatre than all the publicity we paid for and more. While Sinatra saw it as an innocent photo with fans, taken backstage after a performance, it gave the impression, especially to the U.S. Department of Justice, of a cozy meeting between organized crime big shots with Sinatra squarely in the middle.

The photo continues to have a life of its own and still surfaces in every book, article, and Internet search about Sinatra and the mob.

Despite numerous FBI investigations into Sinatra, no charges against him ever materialized. A few years later the Nevada Gaming Control Commission would ask Sinatra about allegations of skimming profits from the Westchester Premier Theatre. He responded, "I have never in my life, sir, ever received any illegal money. I have had to work very hard for my money, thank you."

The gaming commission cleared him of charges of ties to organized crime and granted him a gaming license.

I was not so lucky. Both Sinatra and I suffered from associating with the wrong people. Those associations were now bringing my life crashing down all around me. I was caught up in a sweep of indictments with nine other defendants, including DePalma, Fusco, and Marson, from the photo. I came to learn from the government that DePalma was a made man in the Gambino crime family. Also indicted was Lou Pacella, from Separate Tables. Pacella, the government claimed, was an organized crime member who arranged for Sinatra to perform at the theater and in exchange received cash under the table.

I was prosecuted for bank and stock fraud and racketeering. The bank fraud charge was the government making good on its threat regarding the minor income discrepancy on my home mortgage application. The media outlets revived the photo and it was everywhere again.

The federal government alleged a "pattern of racketeering activity" and skimming off revenue. I never skimmed a penny, but money siphoned off from ticket and souvenir sales was the major reason the theater went into Chapter 11 bankruptcy. It was the bankruptcy that triggered the indictments a few months later.

From the day the FBI picked me up, I knew I would have to leave the theater, either by choice or mandate. I don't remember which it was. Dick Clark took over the operations and I was out of a job.

Government prosecutors did everything they could to pressure me into cooperating with their investigation. It was falsely reported in a local newspaper that I had cooperated with authorities, which was not only untrue but potentially unhealthy, considering the mobsters involved in the investigation. I can only assume that was a planted story designed to have me running to the government for cover. I didn't have the magic bullet that would bring down the government's "bad guys," which included Sinatra and Rudin. It's not something I would have done even if I had, and those close to me knew that.

While I didn't run to the government for cover, I did, in a sense, run to Mickey Rudin. As soon as the FBI released me after questioning, I stopped by a pay phone on the way home to call him. It was obvious from the tapes that the FBI was looking to pivot from those handling the theater, to making a case against Rudin and Sinatra. I didn't think they were culpable but I wanted to let them know what was going on. I flew out to Los Angeles and stayed at the house of my old friend, and Don Rickles's manager, Joe Scandore. I met Rudin at a hotel coffee shop and told him the FBI was looking to connect him and Sinatra to unreported money for souvenirs, or ticket sales. I had another, more personal motivation. The entertainment business was loaded with organized crime figures and Rudin knew people much higher up on the food chain than I did. I wanted him to spread the word that I was not ratting anyone out. He thanked me and I left and went home. We spoke from time to time via pay phone.

Before the theater went into bankruptcy, I worked very hard to make sure all the entertainers were paid in full. I did not want a reputation for stiffing performers and I neglected other payables, to ensure that the people who drew our crowds were paid. That earned me respect in the music industry. I was also seen as a "stand-up" guy who would not falsely drag famous names into the mix, despite enormous pressure, in order to cut a deal.

Steve Lawrence and Eydie Gormé were the first people I called when I needed work. Long before Sonny and Cher's popular variety show of the 1970s, Steve and Eydie were a husband-and-wife singing duo with their own television show that dated back to 1958. They played the Westchester Premier Theatre the year we opened, 1975.

It was a Saturday and they had two shows. In between songs, Steve did a short comedy stint. During the first show he was on a roll. The crowd laughed hysterically and he ate it up. As a result, the show ran fifteen minutes over. That backed up the parking lot from people leaving the first show and those arriving for the second show and it set DePalma off.

Steve and Eydie were still on the stage when DePalma found me in the hallway by the dressing rooms. "Your Jewish friends are messing up the crossover in the parking lot and it's causing a traffic jam!" DePalma yelled, as the opening salvo in what became a very heated discussion.

"Don't worry about it. We'll start the second show twenty minutes late," I said, but DePalma was still fuming.

When Steve and Eydie left the stage I took them to their dressing room and locked the door. I stayed backstage with them in between shows while they had something to eat and DePalma calmed down. I was always protective of the performers. It takes a lot to put yourself out there in front of thousands of strangers and I respected their courage and confidence.

Steve and Eydie were very thankful for how I took care of them and were happy to give me work when I needed it. Most of their booking deals were a guarantee against a percentage of the box office. So, someone had to reconcile the box-office receipts to ensure they were being paid properly. I knew how to reconcile the box offices and I made the venues account for every ticket. I went on the road with them for a bit and eventually handled their bookings. With a source of income, I could breathe a little easier.

In all, there were two highly publicized trials that lasted for months and I was lumped in with DePalma and other organized crime figures. The photo was always the focal point of media coverage. Nick Ackerman, who had served in the office of the Watergate special prosecutor, was the assistant U.S. attorney handling the case for the government. Ackerman was aggressive and relentless and the trial felt like an exercise in keeping the truth out. At one point the judge admonished the government for withholding exculpatory information.

The *Washington Post* reported Ackerman was known for "shooting from the hip" and said that he even claimed the chairman of the board of Warner Communications, Steve Ross, was the "real culprit" in the Westchester probe. Ross said the accusation was "outrageous" and no charges were ever filed against him.

These were among the most frightening days of my life. Each day I sat in the courtroom, flanked by nine other defendants, at least half of whom the government had identified as crime family members. I tried not to tremble. I never knew what was going to come out of Ackerman's mouth. He continuously surprised me with new and increasingly vicious allegations. I was sure the snake that bit him died.

Rudin and I talked from time to time, always via pay phone, and one day I called him and told him I really needed more work.

"Liza needs a road manager," he said, "but you're not going to make a lot of money."

"I have kids. I need money for food," I said.

Rudin opened the door for me and I started working with Liza. I had met her at the theater but didn't really know her. I assumed he told her he needed a favor and she agreed to bring me on.

For four to five days a week I was either preparing with my lawyers or sitting in front of the judge listening to the most damning accusations about myself. Then on the weekends I would walk out and step into a waiting limo to meet Liza, wherever she was in concert. I spent the car ride trying to make the mental transition from being beaten down and treated like a criminal to being in charge and treated like someone important. It was a crazy mental process and required a tremendous attitude shift to do my job properly.

Liza knew what I was going through and watched me struggle. I think she felt sorry for me. It also quickly became apparent that I was overqualified for the road manager job and I was given a shot at handling some of her bookings. Liza and I bonded and she, along with Steve and Eydie, stayed with me through many of the ups and downs to come. I will be forever grateful.

Meanwhile, Jimmy "the Weasel" Fratianno, one of the other men from the photo, was called as a witness for the government. In order to discredit him, my lawyer, Norman Ostrow, ran through a list of the people Fratianno had killed. Instead of backing down, Fratianno recounted with pride, in gross and shocking detail, the brutal murders of more than ten people. The jury was visibly shaken and horrified, as was I. It made a lasting impression that I'm sure was responsible for the first trial ending in a hung jury.

In the end, a young insurance agent said he could not convict anyone based on Fratianno's testimony. He was the sole holdout against conviction.

The prosecution didn't give up. By the second trial, some of those with mob ties, including DePalma, Fusco, and Pacella, copped pleas. Marson, who was as wide as he was tall, had his trial severed for health reasons.

Fratianno's testimony had been so disturbing, the government chose not to bring him as a witness in front of the jury the second time.

The trial shook the sleepy New York State community of Scarsdale and the constant media attention caused my wife and children to lose friends. There were parents who didn't want their kids playing with mine.

I believe that under normal circumstances, without the celebrity connection, this would have been considered a simple white-collar crime and I would have received a slap on the wrist, or at least not done any significant time. Because of the association with criminals with celebrity-like reputations, however, the government pressed the prosecution with full force.

It was downhill from day one. During voir dire, as the lawyers were questioning the potential jurors, a woman was selected whom I was vehemently against. Her son was a prosecutor turned criminal defense lawyer, and to me it looked like his job switch made her angry and that made her biased in favor of the prosecution. Nonetheless, she was on the jury and ultimately became the foreman. In my mind she sealed the prosecution's case.

I was sentenced to a devastating seventy-eight months in prison at Sandstone Federal Correctional Institution in Minnesota. The six-and-a-half-year sentence exceeded even my most dire prediction and was two and a half years longer than what DePalma copped a plea for. On top of it, Sandstone was thirteen hundred miles from Scarsdale. With children in school and no direct flights, how would I see my family? I could barely breathe.

How could this be? Did the judge believe the prosecution's claim that I was withholding information on Sinatra and Rudin? Was this another effort to push me over the edge and force me to cooperate? I was going to prison, while a guy like Fratianno, a grotesque murderer, was starting a new life in the witness protection program. I wallowed in my grief for a few hours and then decided I had to move forward. I had to find a way to overcome the worst moment of my life.

As I waited to turn myself in, my attorney called. Ostrow said a colleague had told him I should go see former judge Harold Tyler, who was a principal in Patterson Belknap Webb & Tyler, one of the most influential law firms in Manhattan.

"He was a former assistant U.S. attorney. He was appointed by President Kennedy to a seat on the U.S. District Court, and just came off a stint as deputy U.S. attorney general. He knows the players and the system. He's very politically connected," Ostrow said.

Obtaining a meeting at a law firm like that would . ot be easy. Convincing them to take my case, and give it the attention it needed, would be even harder. There was no problem on either point.

Tyler also had a close personal relationship with the judge on my case, Bob Sweet. Tyler had advocated for Sweet to become a judge, which meant Tyler couldn't represent me in court. So Tyler introduced me to the team that would work with me, led by a young Rudy Giuliani. Giuliani would go on to work in the U.S. Department of Justice, become mayor of New York City, a consultant in the Trump administration, and head of a security consulting firm. Michael Mukasey was also part of the team. In 2007 Mukasey would be appointed the eighty-first attorney general of the United States by President George W. Bush. Before that, he was chief judge of the U.S. District Court for the Southern District of New York and eventually returned to private practice.

I had come across the perfect team. The overwhelming sense of hopelessness was easing, and while there would still be a long road ahead, I was confident I had found the right path.

As for DePalma, his path was to move in and out of prisons for years, until he eventually died in jail in 2009, as a ranking capo.

SEVEN

It has been almost four decades and it is still difficult to think about the heartache of leaving my wife and three teenage children and turning myself into authorities in January 1981. My family, education, and work ethic put me completely at odds with what would be my new surroundings, but I knew I had to adapt and survive.

I was processed at the Metropolitan Correction Center in Manhattan. My first thought was, *How will I communicate with the outside world?* I had a business to continue to run, and without communication, I wouldn't be able to support my family.

The MCC was part of the Federal Bureau of Prisons. It was a temporary holding unit before inmates were sent to prison to carry out their sentence. As I mentioned, I was designated to be sent far from my family, to the harsh climate of Sandstone, Minnesota, but was allowed to stay at MCC during my appeals process.

MCC had no bars and my small cell was a room with a bed, toilet, sink, mirror and a door that locked from the outside. I was terrified. I'm surprised I didn't jump out of my skin when I was tapped on the shoulder. A fellow inmate introduced himself on the first day.

"Walk slow, drink a lot of water and mind your own business," he said. He went on to tell me that my laundry, bed-making responsibilities, and the waxing of my floor would all be taken care of. I didn't know what to make of him at first but I thanked him and kept my mouth shut. Courtesy of DePalma, perhaps? I never knew for sure.

My unit at the MCC had one free phone on the floor, which could be utilized at certain times of the day for five minutes. That would never work for me and my business.

Then I saw two beautiful pay phones mounted on the wall with a Manhattan exchange, which inmates could use most of the day, provided they had enough coins.

I knew I could reach anywhere in the world with a dime.

I called my assistant, Jean Dearstine, and told her to have a Manhattan telephone number installed in Scarsdale, which the phone company was happy to do for a fee, and then install a router. That way I could place a call to my office, which in reality was the laundry room at my Scarsdale home, and Jean could route the call to whatever number I gave her, whether it was New Jersey, San Francisco, or London. I gave Jean as much money as I could afford to pay her, which was not a lot, but she was dedicated and loyal and I was extremely grateful for her help.

Less than two weeks after I arrived, on January 20, 1981, Ronald Reagan was sworn in as president of the United States. I couldn't imagine, sitting there in prison, that very soon I would come to meet him.

Meanwhile, I was busy on those phones as much as I could be and booked tours all over the country and Europe without anyone ever knowing where I was calling from.

The most precious resource I had was my weekly allocation of a roll of dimes from the commissary. I would go through the roll in a couple of days, so I counted on family and friends to bring me dimes whenever they visited. Again, I was booking acts for Liza and Steve and Eydie.

While it was a bewildering time and my whole family was fearful, with a steady income stream we all felt a little better. Jean would move into the house and watch the kids while my wife went on the road with Liza. Micky had a pretty good idea of what to do as a road manager and she protected my interests financially, if not on the personal side. Unbeknownst to me at the time, she started an affair with one of Liza's road musicians.

I had no contact with Sinatra, but as I had more and more successes, Rudin gave me a shot at handling some of Sinatra's bookings out of jail. I would do the work, Jean would convey the details to Rudin, and Rudin would put the final bookings on his stationery and give it to Sinatra.

The MCC was located in the same complex that housed the U.S. attorney's office, and I was only an elevator ride away from the office of prosecutor Ackerman. Ackerman had only one photo on the wall—a framed shot of Sinatra. I took it to be a reminder of a constant interest in bagging the bigger fish, certainly not an homage to an entertainer.

I agreed to review the tapes of the wiretaps with Ackerman, as long as he would help me with my reduction of sentence, provided I convinced him I had no information about Sinatra and Rudin that would tie them to the mob. I was always wary of Ackerman but it felt good to be trusted by him and I was happy to have something to do. One of the worst parts of doing time was just passing the hours.

Most days, working with Ackerman meant listening to the endless hours of wiretaps of the theater phones and related parties. Of particular interest was an FBI recording of DePalma running through a checklist of who collected cash from the souvenir sales from the shows Sinatra and Dean Martin did together.

At the end of the Frank and Dean engagement, DePalma had called and told me he took a bag of money and offered it to Sinatra. I had no idea how much money was in it. He told me Sinatra said, "Are you kidding me? You guys are broke. Split it up between yourselves." Sinatra was entitled to a share but this was money that was off the books.

On a subsequent tape, DePalma was talking about splitting up the cash that Sinatra refused.

"I gave five to Mickey," DePalma said.

"What does that mean?" Ackerman challenged. "Obviously Mickey Rudin."

I was caught by surprise. Five thousand dollars was a minuscule amount of money for Mickey Rudin and I can't imagine he would have taken it. On top of that, my livelihood depended on him.

"That's Micky my wife," I said spontaneously.

Prosecuting my wife had initially been used as a threat to intimidate me into cooperating, but she was never charged. Now that I was in jail, her involvement was over. Rudin was helping me to feed and clothe my kids. Enough was enough. I didn't want to become embroiled in a new controversy and trial.

During these lengthy sessions with Ackerman, he realized I was very knowledgeable about box-office procedures and had figured out how scams involving the underreporting of ticket sales worked. He asked if I would explain the process in detail to some FBI agents. I agreed as long as it was a general conversation not related to specific incidents.

This became a turning point in our uneasy relationship. As time went on, the tone between us changed. Ackerman let me work out of the law library at the U.S. attorney's office. A U.S. marshal picked me up each day at nine thirty in the morning and took me back at four o'clock in the afternoon. When I wasn't working with Ackerman, I could use the phones in the library and conduct business, as well as have visitors. They knew I wasn't dangerous.

I booked Steve and Eydie for eight nights at Carnegie Hall. On the morning of the first show, there was a knock on my cell door. It was an FBI agent, who informed me there was a death threat on the couple at the historic venue.

"What are your thoughts on how to handle it?" he said.

"Get Steve Lawrence on the phone," I said. "Tell them what you plan to do and how you are going to protect them."

Ninety percent of the tickets were already sold, so I knew they wouldn't want to cancel the performance, if they felt safe.

"We will completely sweep the hall with metal detectors and go through the place with dogs in the afternoon. We will also have agents in the hall from the bottom floor to the top during the entire run of the show. You can rest assured nothing is going to happen."

I waited an hour before calling Steve myself, to give him time to speak with the agent.

Steve and Eydie decided to continue on with the show and we laughed about the insanity of the FBI coming to me in jail with this problem. The FBI did exactly as promised and the performances went on without incident. It was an indication, to me at least, that Ackerman, the FBI agents, and I had developed a mutual respect for each other.

When it came time for the reduction-of-sentence hearing, in the spring of 1981, Giuliani argued for my immediate release. Judge Sweet looked to Ackerman for a response and he stayed true to his commitment. Ackerman said that I had been very cooperative, to which the judge replied, "This is the guy you wanted me to throw the book at?"

My sentence was reduced from 78 months to 36 months, which was still a three-year sentence. As for Giuliani, this was the last argument he made before going to the Department of Justice.

I was told you're only allowed one shot at a Rule 35 sentence reduction hearing. Somehow my lawyers wrangled a second shot a few months later.

In the summer of 1981, Michael Mukasey argued my case and my sentence was reduced even further, to thirteen months. I was incredibly relieved. With time served, I was released from MCC in October and spent four months at a halfway house on the Upper West Side of Manhattan.

Though Ackerman had tried to bury me in the beginning, in the end he was good to me. We even stayed in touch, and one day he told me he was considering going into theatrical law. I arranged for him to have a job interview with Buddy Hackett's law firm and he was hired. All's well that ends well, I guess.

The halfway house was off Broadway, a town house that would sell for millions today. A small group of us lived there. It was comfortable enough and I was grateful to have some semblance of freedom. Some nights after the late news, the government employees who ran the house would tell us to go home and check back in the morning. I would go back to Scarsdale and my crumbling marriage. By now I knew that my wife was in a relationship with one of Liza's musicians and I half-understood. I told Micky I wanted to put our family back together again, but she said she needed more time to think about it. I couldn't give her that time. Maybe it was my ultimate fear of being rejected or maybe I was trying to let her off the hook easy after all we had been through together, but in any case we parted amicably and remained friends.

My life had been ruined by the unsavory characters I knew, and I understood that if I was ever going to rebuild my life and become successful, I had to separate myself from anyone and everyone remotely connected to the theater and my old life. I had to relocate.

While in the halfway house, I was also allowed to work at my home office in Scarsdale. I even received special permission to attend Liza's New Year's Eve performance at the Diplomat Hotel in Hollywood, Florida. The juxtaposition of going from a halfway house to a limo to see a client was once again startling, but I could feel my life coming back together. In the meantime, I had gone from weighing 223 pounds to 160 pounds and was in the best shape of my adult life. It was the first time I ever wore a pair of jeans and thought I looked decent.

Liza did a double take when I walked backstage. We hugged. It was one of the most important moments of my life. I was back and I felt welcomed.

"Everybody should go to jail and look as good as you do," she said.

I told her that come February 12, the day of my release, I'd be on the road with her. Perhaps more than anyone else, Liza, Steve, and Eydie helped me rebuild my reputation and my life. They were never afraid to be seen with me, and that restored my credibility.

On February 13, 1982, I was on a plane to Florida. I wanted to live where the weather was mild and I could easily fly to New York and Los Angeles yet stay far enough away from the part of my life I wanted to put behind me.

I wasn't sure if Florida was far enough, but it was adequate. A friend helped me secure a town house at the Inverrary resort, in Broward County. It was a popular spot, home to Jackie Gleason and the Jackie Gleason Inverrary Golf Classic. I rented there for a year and have lived in Florida ever since.

My assistant, Jean, who had been so instrumental in my life, came with me. She was in love with Gary Labriola, who had been an innocent gofer for DePalma. So I took him under my wing and made him Liza's road manager. Jean and Gary eventually married and she told me I was the father she never had. I even walked her down the aisle.

Meanwhile, I made more money in 1982 than I ever had in my life to that point.

EIGHT

By 1982, I was living in Florida, stripped of my professional licenses, with a failed marriage and three children to support. The entertainment industry was flourishing and I was working with some of the hottest, most in-demand acts in the live-performance, middle-of-the-road genre, which encompassed a wide range of traditional popular music, including easy listening, smooth jazz, soft rock, and show tunes. I had the best female singer live on the boards in Liza Minnelli, the best husband-and-wife team in Steve Lawrence and Eydie Gormé, and the king of them all in Frank Sinatra. It was an incredible opportunity to start my life anew and I was determined not to screw it up.

On a cool, early April afternoon, I stood outside the limo on the tarmac of a private airport in Pittsburgh thinking about how lucky I was. I watched Sinatra's jet, the *Lady Barbara,* taxi on the runway. I could see him through the window. I wondered what he would say, what I would say? This was the first time I had seen Sinatra since my life began to unravel.

I was there at Rudin's request and happy to have been asked. At this point, Sinatra thought of me as his road manager. Rudin wanted to protect Sinatra, so he never told him about the extent of my work, and there's no doubt in my mind that Rudin continued to help me out, at least partially because he was afraid of what I might say to the feds. He also knew that Sinatra liked me and that I could handle whatever job was thrown my way.

Normally Sinatra was the last to step off the plane, but this day he came off first. As he descended the steps, he pointed his fingers at me like a gun and simply said, "Thanks." He had many ways of showing gratitude, as I would come to learn, but this was the only time he ever directly said thank you, in all our years together.

Sinatra was an avid newspaper reader and had repeatedly seen my name in the press, accompanied by that infamous photo of him and the guys from Westchester. I assumed he knew what was all over the media—that he and Micky were the target of the investigation. He believed I was a scapegoat for an overzealous prosecutor going after famous names. It was a sense of wrongful persecution that he personally felt keenly and that we both shared. I already knew at this point that Sinatra was a loyal and dedicated friend to everyone he cared for. He hated to see someone taken advantage of and he loved to fight for the underdog and stand up to bullies.

So I wondered, had he helped me convince Tyler and his all-star legal team to handle my appeal and secure that rare second shot at a sentence reduction? I'm sure Sinatra had nothing to do with it personally, but he was a master of making a comment to a well-placed friend and producing results. I don't believe in coincidences and I didn't win the lottery. Someone was helping to orchestrate my good fortune.

He approached the car.

"Hi, Boss. It's great to see you. Did you have a good flight?"

As he came closer to me I thought about how good he looked with his Palm Springs tan. We shook hands. Then he embraced me, like I had occasionally seen him do with close friends. It was a gesture I appreciated. He didn't have to say a word. I could feel his compassion for me and his sincere gratitude. In the car we discussed business as if nothing unusual had occurred. Everything else was left unsaid and it would be many years before we discussed my time away.

That first night together, I stood in Sinatra's dressing room at the Civic Arena before the show. He was sipping tea, as was his custom, when he handed me a small, unlined, white piece of paper.

"You did the right thing by moving to Florida. If anybody tries to bother you, if you ever have a problem with anyone, here's a number. Use it."

Handwritten on the note was "Matty" and a phone number. I folded it up, put it in my wallet, and forgot about it. It was not a number I ever intended to call.

NINE

There was a war of sorts going on in the talent agencies. The big three, William Morris Agency, International Creative Management (ICM), and Creative Artists Agency (CAA), all wanted to make deals for their clients and move on to the next deal. They collected their 10 percent but did little if anything to manage the client or the engagement.

They didn't monitor how many tickets were sold and they either didn't care or didn't understand that the success of each show was a critical link in the chain of a client's success. Let's face it, careers are built on sold-out performances, not empty houses. Not surprisingly, with this kind of care, clients were unhappy, and it was a revolving door of talent going from one agency to another when their multiyear contracts expired. I started doing the things for my clients that the big agencies weren't doing for theirs.

I did what came naturally to me. I took the booking and talent management skills I learned from the theater and all the things I knew from my accounting and financial background and used them to benefit my clients.

Frank, Liza, and Steve and Eydie were the stars on which I built my talent management company, Premier Artists Services. I received 5 percent of Sinatra's earnings and 10 percent of Liza's, as well as Steve and Eydie's management fees. Liza wanted to do thirty-five to forty live shows a year, and I while I was not handling her film work, I had to be prepared to change her schedule at the last moment if a movie project came through. We spoke on the phone at least three times a week and managing her affairs required a lot of effort, so Rudin was happy to hand over the responsibility and take the burden off him.

For the first few years, I saw Frank mostly on tour. We would go on the road four to five times a year for anywhere from several days to a couple of weeks at a time. When I wasn't traveling with Sinatra or Liza, I was with Steve and Eydie. Being on the road with all my clients created a familial bond.

I believed that the relationship between artist and manager was extremely personal and based on mutual trust, respect, and success. It was about my commitment to addressing their needs and capitalizing on their talent. If either party wasn't happy, we shouldn't be working together. I had had enough of lawyers at this point and wasn't about to go to court to keep a client who didn't want me to manage them. As a result, I never had a formal agreement with any of my artists. It was unheard-of in talent and management agencies not to have a talent contract. But that was fine with me. After all, the way I managed careers was also unheard-of at the big agencies, as I was doing things for my clients that no one in the industry was doing.

The talent agencies found the clients bookings, negotiated the contracts, and collected their commission. To me, that was the easy part. The real work was beyond the booking. I truly managed their career; I strategized about the right venues for each client and how best to ensure those venues were sold out. I was very protective of their careers and made sure their dates went well, they were paid, the money made it to their bank account, and whatever was left over was invested.

Frequently, people in entertainment don't have the time or interest to look at numbers; they just want to perform. When artists don't pay attention to their money until it's too late, either they have tax problems or their bank account is empty. If you spend a hundred cents on every dollar and don't put anything away for retirement, you end up broke. I've seen it happen many times with entertainers and athletes. So I worked with all of my clients to make sure they had qualified people who could help and protect them.

As my relationships with artists grew, I made sure they were living within their means, saving money, had adequate insurance, and were working with competent accountants, investment advisors, and money managers. Plan, organize, staff, and direct. It was basic business from the Wharton School.

I also took care of the people who worked for me. My assistant, Jean, had stuck with me through thick and thin, so I gave her all the profits due to me from the souvenir sales for my acts. It was the least I could do.

The entertainment business is a very small industry and everyone talks to everyone else. If I wanted to book Sinatra I rarely called a theater or arena to ask for a booking. I called a few colleagues at the various talent agencies and venues and casually let out word that Sinatra was thinking of going out on the road. The next day I would have ten calls from people looking to book him.

Meanwhile, managing Sinatra gave all my clients leverage, which I used to their advantage. It was very difficult for a venue operator not to accommodate my requests for other artists, if they had any hopes of Sinatra gracing their stage. If I signed Sinatra at a location and called to book Steve and Eydie or Liza there, too, the person in charge was likely to be agreeable both on dates and in negotiations. Sinatra's impact always gave me an edge. While I never had to threaten to pull Sinatra, everyone knew it was in their best interests to work my artists into their schedule even if it meant moving someone else.

When the agencies called me to solicit representation of Steve and Eydie and Liza, I told them I was booking their dates as well as managing their careers.

"You can't do that," one of the big three agents said.

"Why not?"

"That's illegal."

"Ill-eagle sounds like a sick bird to me," I quipped. "California has a lot of crazy laws and I don't live in California." My lawyers said I was well within the scope of the law in handling both functions.

From my early days at Westchester Premier Theatre, when I practically lived backstage before every performance, I could see up close the nerves and angst of the artists. After all, taking center stage requires a unique personality and resilience. I couldn't lay myself bare like my clients did. A bad show or a less than enthusiastic audience could be devastating, perhaps only topped by performing to empty seats.

I have a tremendous respect for anyone who has the courage to stand in the spotlight and perform with all their heart. There is something special about an artist who performs live. No mistake can be covered up or redone. Movie stars can do three or four takes. Live performance is one shot. The pressure is enormous and that's what makes so many of them a little nuts.

While a less-than-perfect show can send some entertainers over the edge, success can also be a downfall for talented people. They achieve a level of acclaim and then they have to keep up that pace. Success always depends on the next job offer or project. The entertainment industry is a young business and they might be in the hands of a newbie at an agency, production company, record label, or film that has no idea who they are or what they've accomplished.

Frankly, they don't care. The artist has to be humble with people who don't have their talent or knowledge, and they need to stay focused and remain true to who they are. When you are famous, people offer you everything, and the second you are not, they drop you. That's where a good manager comes in, but even that is not always enough.

The entertainment business is as much a psychological game as anything else—for performer and spectator. So, just as I didn't want my performers to see empty seats, I didn't want their audiences to, either. No one wants to pay money to go to a concert that people aren't clamoring for.

I meticulously followed the box office on a monthly, then weekly and daily basis. Every date, I had someone reporting box-office sales to me. If there was a problem, I could spot it early and try to fix it by increasing promotions. If we were close to a performance and the balcony was open, I donated the seats to charity. If a client had trouble selling out arenas, I booked them in smaller venues that they could easily sell out in a few hours. A few sold-out performances and I would put them back in the arenas. There's nothing like being unable to purchase a ticket for one show that makes you want to buy quickly for the next. Everyone wants what they can't have.

It became very clear to my clients that I was concerned about their long-term financial well-being. We were in this together to make money and I wanted to make sure everyone left me better off than when they started.

These are simple principles, I know, but they helped me build a personal appearance agency that would rival the biggest and best.

TEN

S tarting a new life meant many things. I was forty-four years old, constantly on the road, with a sense of personal loneliness and abandonment. I had been in prison less than a year, but when I came home, the world I inhabited had changed. Fortunately, all things can be made new again.

On Labor Day weekend in 1982, the Monmouth Park racetrack was buzzing. The New Jersey track had a country club atmosphere, with impeccably landscaped grounds and red geraniums that hung over the privately rented boxes with a view of the lavish floral parterre.

I was seated in the front, finish line table, overlooking green and white striped umbrellas and the shiny, muscular bodies of Thoroughbred horses. I was there because Eydie loved the races and had asked me to do what was practically impossible: book a primo table for the final racing day of the season. It wasn't easy but I did it. Then, at the last moment, she canceled so she could rest up for her next performance. I wasn't about to let that table go to waste, so I decided to take a date and go anyway.

I could see the tension in the jockeys' bodies as they readied themselves at the gate atop the graceful steeds. I followed every twitch of the mane of the horse I had chosen to win, place, or show.

Horse racing for me was serious business. Socializing was for after the race was over.

Sonny Werblin was seated to my right and Leon Hess to my left. The clubhouse was a sea of colorfully dressed women in elaborate, wide-brimmed hats and men in jackets and ties. There's a reason horse racing and gambling have gone hand in hand for thousands of years. It is exhilarating to watch a Thoroughbred perform and know that no matter how long it has trained and practiced, there are still plenty of places to stumble. Like any live performer, some horses can't get out of their own way. They are flawless in practice but choke when it's time to deliver. Some days they aren't feeling well and no matter how talented they are, they produce subpar results. I could see when a horse wanted to win; they put everything out there on the track but couldn't beat the lead nose. I understood their pain.

Then there were the Thoroughbreds that were determined to win, no matter how bad a day, or what challenges fell in their way. They were hypnotized by the track, exhilarated by the starting gunshot, and egged on by the screams of the fans. I could almost see it in their eyes all the way from the clubhouse.

As I carefully studied the racing form looking for a name or detail that would scream out "winner," I heard a woman's voice.

"Mr. Weisman?"

I looked up.

"I'm Maria Chiarella. David Hart asked me to stop by and see how you're doing."

Oh my God.

Now I understood how Sinatra felt when he first laid eyes on Ava Gardner in the late 1940s. There are many stories about exactly when and how he first met Ava, his second wife and the woman widely considered to be the great love of his life, but he told me he was walking through a revolving door at the Pierre hotel as she was walking in. She was so breathtakingly gorgeous that he followed her around, circled back inside, and introduced himself.

I spun in my imaginary revolving door and glanced at her hand to see if she had a ring on her finger. She didn't. How could that be? Then I thought, *Does she have a boyfriend? There has to be something wrong with this woman. She's gorgeous and she doesn't have a ring on her finger?* I had a date with me, so I had to play it cool. I also had to know more about this girl. That night, while Steve and Eydie were performing, I went to David Hart's office. He had set me up with the tickets at Monmouth, and knew Maria.

"What's the deal with her? Why isn't she married? What's wrong with her?"

"She's a great girl."

"Why no ring?" I said.

"She's just out of a long-term relationship. She's a former Miss New Jersey Hemisphere contestant and her picture is plastered all over the area on billboards promoting the track," Hart said.

"Sinatra is opening next week in Manhattan. Offer Maria two tickets to any show. It's a thank-you for taking such good care of us at the track."

Sinatra was in New York for an engagement at Carnegie Hall. He had returned from Monaco, where he and Barbara vacationed with Princess Grace and Prince Rainier. Shortly after he arrived in town, he learned that the princess, Grace Kelly, his dear friend, had been in a horrible accident with her daughter Stephanie. Princess Grace was driving an eleven-year-old Rover 3500 from Roc Agel, the family's farm, through the rugged, hilly terrain above Monaco. She missed a steep hairpin turn and the car somersaulted 120 feet down an embankment. Stephanie was expected to recover but they weren't so hopeful about Princess Grace.

Sinatra and Grace Kelly had been friends since they costarred in *High Society* in 1956, and the Sinatras frequently visited the royal couple at their palace in Monaco. He spoke of Grace with the same sense of reverence and respect for her talent and character as when he spoke of Ava. I knew he cared deeply for her.

Barbara said that Sinatra offered to cancel the Carnegie Hall engagement but that they decided he would continue on with the concert dates and Barbara would go to Monaco with her son Bobby.

By the time Barbara landed, Princess Grace had died. When Sinatra heard the news, he withdrew into silence. For close to an hour, I thought we would lose the concert. Part of Sinatra's enduring appeal was his swagger. His confidence and the way he carried himself and moved were as natural and determined as his language and song. Eventually I could tell by his stride if he was happy, agitated, or angry or if his stillness was sadness or he wasn't feeling well. That night as he sat in his dressing room before the show, I didn't know if he would have the strength to go onstage. He seemed despondent. Then, when he heard his cue, like any great professional, he began to prepare.

Sinatra always had a bottle of Jack Daniel's in his dressing room for friends, but he never drank alcohol before a concert. He drank tea with lemon and honey as he vocalized. He slowly pulled on his Dunhill tuxedo, always pants first, and then the Turnbull & Asser shirt. His movements grew more determined, as if he were coming back to life. His valet helped him with the perfect black silk bow tie, which fastened with Velcro in the back. He poked his finger into the orange silk hankie that showed his face and torso, arms folded, silk-screened in white on the bottom right-hand side of the pocket square. "Love, Frank Sinatra" was written in his handwriting. He would occasionally hand the hankie out to an appreciative audience member. He ran it through the fingers of his other hand and folded it once, tucking it into his breast pocket, points down, so the image was no longer visible.

Sinatra walked to the stage and paused for a breath. I could see he was again in full command. He absorbed the adoration and the applause and went to work. He was a master of his game and there was no amount of distraction that could take him away from his responsibility to his fans. The stage made the world right.

He never spoke to me about Princess Grace's death, but from time to time during the course of that engagement, I would find him staring off into space. While I am sure he mourned his dear friend in his own way, he never let it affect his performance.

Meanwhile, several days later, Barbara was back from Monaco and Maria took me up on the offer to see Sinatra in concert.

The night of the show, I pulled Gary to the side. I arranged it so that if she showed up with a parent or girlfriend, she'd sit in Barbara Sinatra's box. If she showed up with a man, some other box.

Maria showed up with her girlfriend Linda, but instead of Barbara, she found Ava Gardner in the box, with a dark scarf wrapped around her head, one end of it flung dramatically over her shoulder. Ava was only sixty years old but she required assistance from two security guards to settle into her seat and one end of her mouth seemed slightly askew. She was quiet and elegant, and still very recognizable.

Maria introduced herself. "It's an honor to meet you. You're so beautiful," she said.

"Thank you, and so are you," Ava said. That's the kind of compliment a girl never forgets.

Barbara was sitting in the front row, floor seats. Maria and Linda spent much of the night whispering and wondering whether Barbara knew that Ava was in the box.

After the concert, I invited Maria and her friend to dinner at Romeo Salta's, one of my favorite Italian restaurants and one that I thought would impress a girl named Chiarella. It worked. When

Maria quickly lit her own cigarette with a Bic, I said, "A girl like you should be using a gold lighter." She flashed that beautiful smile.

We had a few drinks and a lot of laughs that night, and when we spoke again a few days later, we made plans to see each other when I returned from my travels.

"I'm going on tour with Liza to South Africa and the Riviera in a couple of days. When I come back, let's have lunch—alone this time," I said.

ELEVEN

Liza Minnelli was not the greatest singer. She was not the greatest dancer. She was *the greatest* all-around female live performer I have ever seen. She was not even the greatest beauty, but when she connected with those eyes to wherever you were sitting—from the front row to the balcony—by the end of the third song the audience was firmly in her grasp.

Like her mother, the actress and singer Judy Garland, and her father, the film director Vincente Minnelli, Liza was an icon and an American treasure. She was on the short list of a dozen true stars, such as Rita Moreno, Audrey Hepburn, and Marvin Hamlisch, who won the "grand slam"—an Emmy, Grammy, Oscar, and Tony award—the four major awards in television, music, film, and theater, respectively. She brought power to everything she touched.

While I was not involved with Liza's film, theater, or television career, I found her award acceptance speeches telling. In 1973, when she won an Oscar for Best Actress in the film *Cabaret,* she said making the film was "one of the happiest times" of her whole life. When she won her second Tony Award, for *The Act,* in 1978, she said in her famously breathless way, "The thing that I like to do most in my life is to work and to work hard and I think the thing that I like second best is when somebody said, you did a good job."

In many ways those statements sum up the complicated quality that defines a star. They love what they do and they *need* the applause. They *are* their performance. They are their own product. The spotlight is where they shine. It's where they are happiest, and the adulation is what they live for.

Liza never wanted to use her mother's fame for her recognition, and she didn't have to. Unlike her half sister, Lorna Luft, who attached herself to her mother's music, Liza wanted to be and *was* a standout in her own right.

In my opinion, Lorna had a better voice than Liza, but no one had Liza's charisma. She had that elusive "star quality" that everyone in the entertainment business looks for. It's hard to define and even harder to create. It's the ability to quickly pull the audience in. There's an electrical quality to it, and I still get goose bumps when I think of some of Liza's great nights onstage.

Garland died of an accidental overdose in 1969. A doctor warned me that when someone is born to a drug-addicted parent, they are born an addict and will struggle their entire life with those demons. Liza had drug and alcohol issues and she has been very open about her battles with addiction and her stints in rehab.

So I worked not only with Liza, but also with those closest to her. I tightened the circle around her to ensure, the best I could, that she was exposed only to positive influences. Composer John Kander and lyricist Fred Ebb, one of the most successful Broadway duos in history, were among Liza's closest confidants and producers. They, along with her personal assistant, Roni Agress, and Roni's husband, David, who was Liza's lighting designer, truly cared for Liza and wanted her to be well. Having put Labriola as Liza's road manager also helped me keep an eye on things. Anyone on her team who contributed to or encouraged bad behavior was fired. While I can't say we kept her drug and alcohol free, with the help of her friends we at least kept her drug and alcohol use to a minimum for a decade.

Addictions can also take a huge toll on finances. When Liza and I started working together, her net worth was literally zero. She was spending as much as she had in assets. I was determined to help her build up her bank account. She was frugal about all the wrong things. She wouldn't buy a candy bar at an airport if she thought it was too expensive, but she spent lavishly on other aspects of her lifestyle, especially partying.

The South African tour was the beginning of the financial rebuilding process.

Thousands came to see Liza perform in eleven shows in Sun City, an opulent gambling resort built by Sol Kerzner (who went on to build, among other things, the Atlantis Paradise Island Resort in the Bahamas). Sun City was in Bophuthatswana, a multiracial yet economically segregated community in the northwestern region of the white-ruled Republic of South Africa. A *New York Times* reporter met us at the plane, but I wouldn't let Liza be interviewed. These were the days of apartheid and I didn't want her to become engaged in a political scandal.

Sinatra had opened the 6,000-seat Sun City "Super Bowl" a little over a year earlier. Since then, entertainers like Paul Anka, Cher, Shirley Bassey, and Olivia Newton-John had made their way there, on the assurance that they wouldn't play to all-white audiences.

As I watched the white team leader order the black stagehands around with almost no respect or regard, I couldn't help but think they were treated like slaves. Seeing it firsthand, I fully understood what apartheid meant. When I told Liza what I witnessed and later discussed it with Frank, it was obvious we would not return. In fact, I never took any of my clients back there.

From Sun City, and before heading back to New York, we went to the Italian Riviera. I was sitting on the balcony of my hotel room overlooking the turquoise waters of Italy's Liguria region when I noticed the bottle of water on the side table. It was clear glass, with a photo of the Mediterranean Sea surrounded by the picturesque mountains of the region. Written across the front was "Chiarella."

I had never before heard of water by that name, and although I don't believe in omens, there was a part of me that took it as fate. It was an excuse to call Maria. She was no relation to the water company, but we laughed about it.

We met for lunch at one of my favorite classy restaurants in Manhattan, the Four Seasons, in the Seagram Tower on Park Avenue. Maria came sans girlfriend, and as we sat around the large square fountain surrounded by huge potted trees, I waited for her to pull out a cigarette. When she did, I lit it with a gold Dunhill lighter I had purchased for her on my way to the restaurant. "Merry Christmas a little early and no more Bics," I said.

TWELVE

The John F. Kennedy Center for the Performing Arts is an enormous marble, rectangular structure located on the banks of the Potomac River in Washington, D.C. It was created as a memorial to President Kennedy, who was a lifelong supporter of the arts. It is the cultural center of the nation's capital and has been frequented by every U.S. president since it opened to the public in 1971.

On opening night of Sinatra's Kennedy Center performance, President Ronald Reagan, who was in his first term, and First Lady Nancy Reagan visited Sinatra in his dressing room.

I could tell by the warm embraces and hugs that both Ron and Nancy were very close to Sinatra, old friends. Sinatra had relationships with presidents dating back to Franklin Delano Roosevelt and, of course, Jack Kennedy. A lifelong Democrat, he defected to the Republican Party in 1970, when he backed incumbent Ronald Reagan for governor of California. Over the years, he raised hundreds of thousands of dollars for his campaigns and Reagan even roasted Sinatra on *The Dean Martin Celebrity Roast* in 1978. Sinatra coordinated the talent for his presidential inauguration in 1981 and both Reagans had attended his wedding to Barbara.

Nancy was one of the few people who had a direct line to Sinatra, and he to her. I don't know how often they spoke, but I know they didn't want to have to go through all the standard channels for their conversations.

When the Reagans walked into Sinatra's dressing room, he told everyone to leave except me. I was a bit startled, but stood by.

"How are you, Mr. President?" Sinatra said.

"Good, good," he said.

"Mr. President, this is our *friend* Eliot," Sinatra said.

"Oh, Eliot, it's nice to finally meet you. Are you okay?" President Reagan said.

"Yes, sir," I said.

"Good," President Reagan said as he shook my hand.

I never knew what to make of that brief conversation and I knew I wouldn't get an answer if I asked. I also knew there was no advice Sinatra wouldn't seek if he thought he could help a friend.

THIRTEEN

Being a star is an intricate cocktail of talent, persistence, resilience, and a strong support system. Being an exceptional manager means working hard and being an advisor, confidant, and part-time psychologist. Sometimes I felt like I needed a shingle with multiple degrees.

There will always be bumps in the road. I tell young artists, success is about your ability to overcome the bumps. A failed audition, a bad recording session, or a concert that's not sold out are all obstacles that can derail an artist. I cared about my clients' lives, so I was particularly sensitive to those bumps and wanted to help the artists conquer them. I wasn't always successful.

Maria introduced me to her friend Ben Vereen, a truly amazing talent. He won a Tony Award on Broadway for *Pippin,* was on top of the world at one point, and then struggled to find work even as an opening act. He deserved better than that, but like so many entertainers, addiction set him astray. It was the bump in the road that became a mountain and I couldn't help him overcome it.

I have always credited Steve, Eydie, Liza, and, of course, Sinatra for my show business achievements. They, along with Sammy Davis Jr., were my core acts. Over the years I also represented Don Rickles, Joan Rivers, Paul Anka, Julio Iglesias, Marvin Hamlisch, Engelbert

Humperdinck, LaGaylia Frazier, Aaron Carter, and the French singer Charles Aznavour when he was performing in the United States.

Each artist was unique and carried with them a unique set of baggage. Part of being a good manager meant knowing what made your clients tick. Being in the live performance business was all-consuming and entertainers often must neglect huge chunks of their life in order to focus on their performance. A certain self-centeredness is required to be able to do your job and that means spouses, children—even adult ones—often pay a high price. Performers spend a lot of time on the road. Add divorce into the mix and the divide grows.

As I became closer to Sinatra, I also drew closer to his family. I imagine it is tough being the child of an icon, especially when you are talented, and it pained me to see the tension between Sinatra and his only son, Frank Jr. I watched them both tighten up at the mere sight of each other. Junior rarely came around, even when Sinatra played Los Angeles. On the occasions they were together, their body language and approach to each other made it clear they were not entirely comfortable. They were always polite and well-mannered, always gentlemen, but I never once saw them engage in typical father-and-son banter. They were awkward with each other and they seemed to keep their distance. The strain was particularly clear to me because Sinatra was so warm and friendly to his daughters, especially Nancy Jr. and his grandchildren. He always gave them a big hug and a kiss, yet with Junior, sometimes it was a handshake or if it was a hug and a kiss it was brief.

There's no doubt that in general, Sinatra tended to be more protective toward women than men, and perhaps that had something to do with it. There seemed to be a lot of mutual respect between him and Junior, but not the warmth of a close parent-child relationship.

Junior was an extremely talented musician and performer, but his concerts lacked excitement. To say that he didn't have his father's style and charm is certainly true, but then again, nobody had Sinatra's charisma, except maybe Elvis in a different way. Junior toured and did all of his own original material and I felt his show didn't have the artistic value the consumer was looking for. As a result, his concerts were not making a lot of money. I thought I could help change that.

Junior knew his father's music and execution as well as anyone who ever sang Sinatra, and it was clear to me that audiences wanted to hear him sing "Come Fly with Me" and "I've Got You Under My Skin." I thought if I could represent him and convince him to incorporate his father's songbook, we could create a very successful and financially lucrative tour.

I invited Junior to lunch. We met at a restaurant at the Beverly Wilshire Hotel, on Wilshire Boulevard near Rodeo Drive in Beverly Hills. I had seen him socially on several occasions, but this was the first time we were out alone.

After some small talk I said, "You know, Junior, I watched you perform at a gala fund-raiser in New Jersey, the Monmouth Park Ball. You were great, but the audience came to hear you sing 'Fly Me to the Moon.'"

"I can't do that," he said. "I don't sing my father's music."

I wasn't entirely surprised. Liza felt the same way about her mother and wasn't about to sing "Over the Rainbow." Still, I believed Junior would be a hit a with his dad's music.

"I can see you singing 'One for My Baby.' You're a terrific musician. You would be great and I know I can secure you a lot of solid bookings. This can work for you."

"No," he said. "I'm not going to have an audience look down on me because I don't sing Sinatra the way he does. I don't want to hear the critics, either." I never knew Junior to be particularly sensitive to criticism, but it was clear he wanted to avoid the inevitable comparisons. Still, I persisted.

"Everybody sings Sinatra. Who better than you? It's your legacy. The music belongs to your family. You are the only one who will be able to keep this music alive onstage."

"I won't ride my father's name and popularity," he said. "Maybe after he retires, but not now."

It was my professional opinion that I could not create a successful tour if he was not willing to sing his father's music, and I certainly didn't want to position myself in his career and have it be a failure.

"I don't get it, Junior. Why do you have so many problems with your father? You seem to have such a hard time communicating with him."

He paused and looked at me. "How would you feel if you never had dinner alone with your father until you were thirty-seven years old?" he said.

That was a powerful statement and I contemplated it for some time after that meeting. Both father and son were passionate about their music, but I believe they lacked a certain bond with each other and that kept them at a distance both psychologically and musically. I hoped that someday I could help heal that rift.

Music is about emotions. Great songs tell a story. It takes talent to deliver the story with passion, dignity, and style. A superstar has to hit home runs all the time. You also need gifted songwriters, arrangers, and musicians. There is a reason some of the greatest professionals wanted to work with Sinatra. Whether it was Quincy Jones, Sammy Cahn, Jimmy Van Heusen, Billy May, Nelson Riddle, or Don Costa, they knew that working with Sinatra increased the likelihood of their success. He announced the names of the songwriters and arrangers on the concert stage. He respected their talent. They knew he would do their music justice. They didn't want to let him down, because they knew he would not let them down with the performance.

Some singers think singing with passion means being loud and hitting the high notes. Sinatra half-spoke much of his music. His appeal was his authenticity, both as a person and in the interpretation he brought to a song.

There was the skinny young Sinatra singing "Nice Work If You Can Get It" as his voice and body swooned, when he sang "Oooh, where two hearts become one. Who could ask for anything more?" He had the gleam in his eyes of a young man falling in love. That was me once, and probably you.

The middle-aged, finger-snapping Sinatra sang "I've Got the World on a String," and you knew he did. He blew and rolled the imaginary dice as he pleaded, "Luck, if you've ever been a lady to begin with, luck be a lady tonight." We all wanted to be him.

No matter where you were from, you understood when Frank sang, "These little-town blues." New York was a metaphor for anywhere when he sang, "I want to wake up in the city that doesn't sleep, to find I'm king of the hill, top of the heap."

Finally, it was the older Sinatra, who had put on a few pounds, singing "My Way."

"My Way," with its defiant and personal lyrics, was an anthem to generations. Audiences loved it because they related to it. It was recorded hundreds of times, by everyone from Celine Dion to Sid Vicious of the Sex Pistols, and was so popular in Asia that it had to be taken out of karaoke bars because fights broke out over less-than-perfect performances.

"Regrets, I've had a few, but then again, too few to mention," was a statement everyone who achieved some level of success could relate to. Everyone wants to look back on their life and proudly say they did it their way. He closed virtually every show with that song, to thunderous applause.

It has been widely reported that Sinatra's daughter Tina said he "loathed" that song, that he considered it "self-serving and indulgent." I don't know how Tina came to that conclusion. Trust me, if Sinatra didn't like the song, it would not have been in the show. When he walked off the stage each night, he told me if he didn't like something. He did not enjoy performing "Strangers in the Night," despite the fact that it sold more singles than any other of his songs. As a result, it was rarely in any show.

The "My Way" lyrics were written by Paul Anka, for Sinatra and about him. It was his life. It was also my life and it was probably yours. Anka had been a star since the 1950s and wrote hits like "Put Your Head on My Shoulder," "Puppy Love," "Lonely Boy," "Diana," Tom Jones's biggest hit, "She's a Lady," and Michael Jackson's "This Is It." I represented him briefly during the mid-1980s and I never saw him do a bad show. Anka was a strong singer and performer and a rare and outstanding talent among songwriters. He was five feet six inches tall, funny, strong-willed, very macho and definitely insisted everything be done his way. He had a great eye for art, which proved to be a good investment for him, but he didn't trust many people, which left very little room for a manager, so our manager-client relationship was short-lived.

For "My Way," he took the melody from French singer Claude François, who wrote it as "Comme d'Habitude" (As Usual), a song about the end of a love affair. Anka heard it while vacationing in France and approached François and his cowriter, Jacques Revaux, and acquired the rights to the music. As the story goes, Anka was out to dinner with Sinatra in 1968 in New York when Sinatra told him he was quitting the business because he was sick of it and said "you have to write something for me." Anka went home and wrote the song as if Sinatra were writing it, and put it to François's melody.

Sinatra had been down-and-out before. He was written off by Hollywood and then won an Oscar. He was the subject of fifty years of mob investigations and refused to change his life or his friends. He understood "I ate it up and spit it out." The closing line of that song is often cited, "The record shows I took the blows and did it my way." True, that was Sinatra, but the preceding lines spoke more to me about who he was. "For what is a man, what has he got, if not himself, then he has naught, to say the things he truly feels and not the words of one who kneels." Sinatra knelt to no man, and Anka captured that magnificently. The "final curtain" was a reference to what was supposed to be Sinatra's last performance before retiring in the early 1970s, but the line also made it one of the most requested songs at funerals. Anka and Sinatra made history with "My Way."

Anka also wrote a song that Sinatra recorded in the 1970s called "Let Me Try Again." It was written for Sinatra's comeback concert at Madison Square Garden. It was about him coming back after retirement and saying, "Let me try once more." I was personally fond of that song and used to ask Sinatra to put it in the show. I always believed his version had the opportunity to be another "My Way." I never understood why he refused to add it in or even give it a try. One day as I listened to the lyric, "Think of all we had before, let me try once more. We can have it all you and I again," it occurred to me it reminded him of Ava.

Now Barbara was the focus of his personal life, and she was nearly always on the road with us. Sinatra was at his best on the road. He loved being on tour but also loved to push my buttons. If we were on the road too much he would say, "What are we, broke?"

We took some time off and I was back home, working at my office in Florida, when Sinatra's personal assistant, Elvina Joubert, or Vine, as she was known, called. Vine was a middle-aged, no-nonsense, African American woman with short brown hair and a trustworthy smile. She took care of Sinatra on a day-to-day basis.

Vine was his caretaker and companion for forty years and I frequently looked to her to ascertain the Boss's mood.

"The Boss wants to speak with you," Vine said. "I gave him the calendar and he doesn't see any dates."

Sinatra picked up the phone.

"What, are we retired? There's nothing on the calendar."

I had been waiting for this opening.

"That's because you fired the conductor," I said, half-joking.

"Well, fix it," he said.

I waited a beat. "Why don't we ask Junior to conduct?"

"Are you crazy?" he said, but he thought about it for a moment. "You'll regret that."

"It would be good for you to have your son out there on the road with you."

"You've never done me wrong so far. If you think that's the right move, I'll try it."

I immediately called Junior.

"I hope you don't have a busy schedule, because your father just hired a new conductor and it's you."

There was silence for a moment.

"Eliot, that's great," he said calmly.

"Do you have any conflicting dates?" I asked.

"No, I don't have any conflicts."

I had some show tapes sent to him and scheduled an extra sound check, but the truth is, Junior didn't need it. It was a seamless transition that I think meant a lot to both father and son. I know it meant a lot to me to see Junior out there on the stage doing a fantastic job.

Once we hit the road together, he was his father's conductor until Sinatra retired.

FOURTEEN

Frank Sinatra lived life on his own time. He wanted to come and go as he pleased and he wanted to do it in great style. As a result, he rarely tolerated a commercial airline schedule. There were five of us who regularly traveled together; Frank and Barbara, Jilly, Vine, and me. Occasionally we would buy out the first-class section of a 747, if we had to fly halfway around the world and couldn't secure a private jet. Sinatra preferred to have his own jet, flown by his longtime pilot, Johnny Spots.

Johnny was an even-tempered, skilled pilot, always dressed in slacks and a white shirt. He had a good sense of humor and easily handled Sinatra's demanding and occasionally last-minute travel schedule.

Maintenance on a private jet, which might sit in a hangar for months at a time, was a cash burner. Eventually I convinced Sinatra that it was more prudent to lease planes for Johnny to fly. Until that point, we traveled either on the *Lady Barbara,* which was a Lear, or on a Gulfstream that Sinatra bought with a friend from Palm Springs.

One morning, I was riding in a Lincoln Town Car that was ushered onto the airport tarmac by security. I was early for our flight, but Jilly was already there and joined me on the Gulfstream.

There was a sofa situated cross-wise at the back of the plane, along with four light tan leather seats that swiveled to face each other so a table could be set up for meal service. There were two more seats behind those. "Good morning, Johnny," I said to the pilot. "I hope it's a good day for flying. I'm not up for a bad one."

"It's good enough," Johnny said.

"Doesn't sound good to me," Jilly said.

Usually we had a flight attendant, but at the moment it was only me and Jilly. "Don't sit down," Jilly said. "I want to show you something."

He led me to the back of the plane by the bathroom, and pointed to the floor.

There was a bump under the rug right behind the last seat.

"Do you want to see something?" Jilly said. "Pull the rug back."

I did. There was a black rectangular box, approximately a foot and a half long, ten inches wide, and six inches deep. The lid had been removed, and nestled inside the fitted case was something that looked like either a long gun or a short rifle.

"That goes everywhere with us," he said.

I looked at Jilly in astonishment. I don't know much about guns and have never owned one myself. It looked dangerous.

"What is it?" I said. "I mean, I know it's a gun, but what the fuck?"

"It's an Uzi submachine gun, made in Israel. It was designed in the 1940s and prototyped in 1950. Golda Meir gave it to him."

"Thanks, Jilly. I needed one more thing to worry about."

I didn't know the details, and I knew better than to ask Jilly. He would tell me what he wanted me to know when he was ready, and not before. Sinatra had a license to carry a concealed weapon for most of his life but I was pretty sure a submachine gun didn't fall into the category of approved concealed weapons. Traveling with it internationally would be a major disaster for everyone if we were caught, especially for me, a convicted felon.

I don't know what my face looked like at this point, but Jilly laughed.

This was one more thing to add to the list of things that could go wrong, though I never asked Sinatra why it was there. Over the years, I came to learn the story behind the weapon, and not surprisingly, it started with how passionate Sinatra was about supporting the rights of those who couldn't stand up for themselves. Whether it was speaking out for civil rights, supporting Martin Luther King Jr., or demanding equal rights for Sammy in segregated Las Vegas in the 1960s, Sinatra abhorred racism. Sinatra was also a supporter of Israel and many Jewish causes and charities. He was a champion of the underdog, and as Junior once aptly put it, "Israel is a nation of underdogs."

In 1948, Israel declared its independence and the state of Israel was formed. The already ongoing conflict between Israeli and Palestinian forces intensified when armies from Lebanon, Syria, Iraq, and Egypt joined forces and the Arab-Israeli War broke out. The United States recognized the de facto government of Israel but maintained an arms embargo against all parties.

Teddy Kollek, who would become the mayor of Jerusalem, was the leader of a group that was smuggling weapons to Israel. They were operating out of a hotel near the Copacabana in New York, where Sinatra was performing. Kollek became friendly with Sinatra, and though he didn't know him well, one day he asked him for help.

Kollek had to move funds to a captain aboard a ship in New York Harbor to have weapons delivered, but he was under FBI surveillance. He needed someone who wouldn't be followed, so he asked Sinatra to deliver the package filled with cash. Sinatra agreed. One night after his show he took a ride to the harbor and handed over the payment. For decades the story was kept secret to all but a few.

Golda Meir was elected prime minister of Israel in 1969 and I have no doubt Sinatra liked the tough, straight-talking "grandmother of the Jewish people." She thanked Sinatra for all he did for Jews everywhere and said she wanted to give him something special. The Uzi was a good-luck charm of sorts. I don't know if it was ever loaded, but it traveled with us.

Soon, we were in the heart of the Mediterranean and for Sinatra, being on ancestral soil held a special place in his heart. He loved the Italians and there seemed to be heightened emotion to everything we did, especially in the summer of 1987. That was our second trip to Italy together in a year, but it was Sinatra's first Italian tour. From the beginning, there were a series of occurrences that both rattled and amazed me. In many ways, everything that could go wrong did.

We were traveling with Barbara and her son Bobby, with dates in Bari, Rome, Verona, Genoa, and Santa Margherita. Jilly was with us, too, of course, along with Vine. Rudin's office had booked us into two villas, a few miles apart, outside Milan. The Sinatras, Bobby, and Vine were in the palatial estate and Jilly and I were in the other, smaller villa.

We all met for meals in the dining room of the Sinatras' villa, an Italian Renaissance castle with a gated entrance and intricately manicured grounds. The room was formal, with a forty-foot polished wood table adorned with sterling silver candelabras and frescos on the walls. A small section of the far end of the enormous table was always set for meal service, with the Sinatras seated next to each other at the head. The living room was filled with silk upholstery and paintings that for all I knew were created by the Old Masters. The bedrooms and bathrooms were small and cramped, typical of Europe's historic structures. There was a staff that included a chef, but Sinatra was used to staying in presidential suites at luxury hotels, with butlers, restaurants, and immediate service. The limited menu and slower service required a mental adjustment for Sinatra.

That night, we had dinner under the light of the giant candelabras at the grand dining room table, with the patio doors open and a cool breeze coming through. It felt like a family holiday as plate after plate of pasta, risotto, vegetables, and a variety of meats were served, along with copious amounts of special local wines.

Barbara organized where everyone slept, and when she deemed the second-floor master suite too small for the two of them, she took over the adjoining room that originally had been set aside for Vine, to give Sinatra more space. She put Vine downstairs. Vine took care of all of Sinatra's day-to-day needs, from making sure his clothes were ready to laying out his medications. There was no intercom in the house and if he woke up in the middle of the night and needed something, he didn't want to be standing at the top of the stairs yelling for Vine. So, when it was time to go to bed, Sinatra said he didn't feel like climbing the stairs and instead slept in a small room next to Vine's downstairs. Jilly and I went back to our less-than-luxurious rooms in the smaller villa.

The cool breeze was long gone by the next morning at breakfast, when Jilly arrived sweating and cranky.

"Eliot, who the fuck booked this place?"

"You need to call Mickey Rudin," I said with a shrug.

"I can't believe the Old Man isn't climbing the walls. There's no air-conditioning in this place. Did you see the room he's sleeping in? It's a fucking closet."

I too was annoyed at the accommodations, but mostly I was worried about what the Boss might do when he had had enough. He could say let's move or let's go home. Either way, the other shoe was about to drop. We knew it was just a matter of time, so we waited. We made it through another day.

The following morning, Sinatra walked into the living room. He was casually dressed in slacks and a shirt and, by the sound of his voice, was now clearly irritated.

"Get me my suite at the Hotel de Paris. We're going to Monte Carlo."

We were packed up and out the door before lunch.

As our car pulled away, I looked out the window at the tall Italian cypress trees that lined the winding driveway.

"Hey, Eliot," Sinatra said. "You got a camera?"

"Sure, Boss. What do you need?"

"Take a picture of this place, 'cause we ain't never coming back here."

FIFTEEN

The Hotel de Paris was a lavish, five-star hotel located feet away from the grand entrance of the Place du Casino, Monaco's legendary gambling establishment, made famous in James Bond films. The ochre marble entrance to the casino was majestic, but for the most part, Sinatra was past his gambling days. The hotel was everything you would expect of a playground of princes, oligarchs, and billionaires. The stunning foyer was filled with crystal chandeliers and relief sculptures on the walls and ceilings. The suites were equally luxurious, furnished in brocades and tassels.

The terrace of Sinatra's suite had panoramic views of Monaco. We sat on the balcony, sipping coffee, overlooking two-hundred-foot yachts lined up in the exclusive harbor. We could see the fountain at the main entrance to the casino. It was luxury living at its best and came with the requisite luxury price tag. Sinatra was pissed about his previous housing and Rudin was not happy with the impact this move would now have on our bottom line. The change of accommodations required more than a change in the location of our luggage. It meant the travel arrangements would have to be revised. This was to be our new base for all the concert venues and it became the catalyst for everything that would soon go wrong in the Sinatra-Rudin relationship.

We would take off and land in Nice. The trip to the Nice airport was nineteen miles on a hilly, winding, two lane road, with breathtaking views of the sea. It was only nineteen miles but it could take an hour in traffic and Sinatra hated being in a car for that long. A decade earlier Prince Rainier had built a small heliport with a single helipad so you could chopper to Nice Côte d'Azur Airport in nine minutes. For Sinatra, that was the only way to go, provided there were blue skies.

For our first concert in Bari, the weather was clear, so we took the chopper to the plane to visit. Jilly was excited about the trip. He grew up in lower Manhattan but his family was from Bari, so this was big for him.

Practically everywhere in the world we went, Jilly had friends, and Bari would prove to be no exception. From the plane I saw the small port city of Bari on the Adriatic, in the Puglia region of southern Italy. We came in for the landing and I realized that if there was one Italian more famous than Frank Sinatra in Bari, it was Jilly Rizzo. As we taxied on the runway, we saw dozens of locals, fishermen, and old women in peasant dresses holding signs saying "Benvenuto a Casa, Jilly," or "Welcome Home, Jilly."

"What's this, your fan club?" Sinatra said. Jilly smiled.

We disembarked and Jilly stood on the steps waving his hands like a mayor on a float in a parade. Down on the tarmac, Jilly greeted his friends and there were plenty of hugs and kisses. He didn't linger for long.

"What, are you a politician now?" Sinatra said in the car.

Jilly didn't say a word. He wasn't teary-eyed, but you could see by his expression that he was very touched by the outpouring of friendship. I think he was even happier that the Boss witnessed it all. Frank knew that Jilly had friends everywhere, but having him see it firsthand was a source of great pride for Jilly and an affirmation that he was a valuable asset to Sinatra.

If you knew Jilly, chances are you were crazy about him. I never met a person who knew Jilly who didn't love him, except possibly Barbara and of course those who had wound up on his bad side. Frank didn't go anywhere without Jilly, so he was always around. He even went to a private White House reception with them, the day after President Reagan's inauguration.

At one point, Jilly said to Sinatra, "Let's get out of here. We can't make any money here," and then he turned to the president and said, "Hey, Mr. President, when you're in New York come by Jilly's and let's have a drink."

Sinatra cracked up. He loved to tell that story. President Reagan had known Jilly for years and wasn't offended, but you can imagine that Barbara must have been appalled. I believe that she really liked Jilly, but he didn't fit into the social elite that she wanted her and Sinatra to associate with. Over time, she began to cut Jilly out of the social picture, which was terribly hurtful to both Frank and Jilly. Frank went along with it because he didn't want to rock the boat, so when we were on tour it was especially important to Sinatra that he was always with his most trusted friend and confidant. Sinatra loved Jilly specifically because he wasn't fancy, and he loved to needle him and remind him of his humble beginnings.

"Hey, Jilly," Sinatra said as we drove through the streets of Bari. "Whatever happened to that kid you threw through the window when you were bartending in the Village?"

"Come on, Frank. The kid was fine. What was I supposed to do? There's a bunch of wiseguys at the bar and the kid was being disrespectful."

"Procrastinator, he called you," Frank teased.

"I carry a dictionary now," Jilly said.

Frank laughed.

Yes, as the story went, in his younger days, Jilly threw a guy through a window because he called him a procrastinator, and Jilly, not being an educated man, assumed it was an insult. What he lacked in education he made up for in loyalty and veracity. In addition to being in charge of Sinatra's security, Jilly was a reliable sounding board. He didn't gossip and Sinatra knew that when he told Jilly something it was between the two of them. Sinatra appreciated his discretion and felt he could be himself around Jilly. He felt protected emotionally and physically.

Sure, Jilly was capable of rough stuff, but if you weren't there to cause trouble or bother Sinatra, Jilly was as respectful and as kindhearted as they came. One look at Jilly and you didn't want to mess with him. The truth was, he was a teddy bear on the inside but looked like a grizzly on the outside. Even I felt protected with Jilly close at hand. I was always happy to have him around and knew he was there to help out in most any jam.

SIXTEEN

Verona has been among Italy's most important artistic centers since the Middle Ages. Shakespeare set two plays there, *Romeo and Juliet* and *The Two Gentlemen of Verona*. A half a million tourists visit the so-called Juliet's House every year, though there is no solid connection to what is considered a fictional character. The medieval town on the Adige River also houses the Palazzo Barberi and a huge outdoor Roman amphitheater, the Arena di Verona at the Piazza Bra, which has been around since the first century.

The Arena is among the best preserved of antiquities and hosted 15,000 spectators, though it was originally built for 30,000. On a clear night, with its exceptional acoustics, the experience was magical.

Unfortunately, as late afternoon approached on the night of our concert, dark storm clouds rolled in. The choppers couldn't fly because of the low cloud ceiling, so we went to the airport the old-fashioned way, by car.

When we arrived in Verona, it was raining, and by concert time there was a sea of umbrellas. People were drenched sitting in uncovered outdoor seats.

The downpour posed an additional problem for the production. Water and electricity don't mix. You never know if there is going to be lightning in a rainstorm and I had no idea if this huge, ancient structure was equipped with lightning rods. I was concerned about Sinatra holding a live mic and being electrocuted, but the sound technicians said it was safe and that he should stay under the small overhang that protected the orchestra.

"What do you want to do, Boss?" I asked as we stood backstage.

"You've got two choices," he said. "Tell everybody to go home or give me the microphone and we all get wet."

"Let's reschedule," I said.

"You're gonna send these people home after they've been sitting in a typhoon for an hour? Give me the microphone," Sinatra said. "It's showtime."

From the moment he walked onstage, on time as usual, in his trademark tuxedo, it was clear the audience had come to play. As he launched into the opening number, they sang along. And for the rest of the night, that Italian audience, many of whom I'm sure did not speak a word of English, sang every word of every song with him. Sinatra loved it. He could have stayed under the stage overhang, but he didn't. If the rain was good enough for his fans, it was good enough for him, so by the second song he was soaking wet. It was an unforgettable experience.

He stepped off the stage, at the end of the full ninety minutes, encores and all, with a huge smile. He was energized and happy. He knew he had done a superior job and the audience got what they came for. That kind of crowd devotion was what he craved. "That was great," he said.

"Sure was," I said as I handed him a towel.

He dried off as best he could. Sinatra's tuxedo was like a wet rag, but he refused to change until we boarded the plane. Unfortunately, the car didn't go more than twenty feet when the tire went flat. We quickly switched to one of the police escort cars. Jilly rode shotgun and Sinatra and I sat in the back laughing at the juxtaposition of talking to Jilly on the law enforcement side of the wire cage divider.

"How does it feel to be in jail, Jilly?" Sinatra said.

"You're on the side with no door handles," Jilly said.

On the plane, as Sinatra walked directly to the back to change out of his wet clothes, he yelled up to the pilot, "Fire 'em up, Johnny. Let's go."

I heard the left engine turn over and start. The right engine sounded like it wasn't turning over. It was still pouring rain. Johnny came out of the cockpit with a serious look on his face.

"Mr. S., we have a problem."

"It's your problem. Fix it," Sinatra said as he slid one arm into his tour jacket. "I'm not getting off."

"The right engine won't start," Johnny said.

"So what? You have the left engine."

Johnny called for a ground crew and an interpreter and they jump-started the right engine while Sinatra, finally in dry clothes, settled in to a beige leather swivel seat with the rain beating against the windows. He had a glass of Jack Daniel's on the table in front of him.

Johnny came back again. A sense of frustration permeated his usually calm demeanor.

"Mr. S., we have the engine running, but if we lose the engine in the air, we may not be able to restart it."

Sinatra would hear none of that. "This plane can fly on one engine for forty-five minutes. Let's get out of here. Wheels up."

I was not happy. My heart was in my throat, but the 290-mile flight back to Nice became the least of my fears.

Sinatra was exhausted and had had a couple of drinks. Between singing in the rain, the car breaking down, and flying on one engine, his patience had worn out, he was tired and not in a good mood. Drinking didn't help.

"Go find out how much longer till we land," Sinatra said.

I went to the cockpit and asked Johnny.

"Fifteen minutes."

When I told the Boss, he said, "Tell him he's got ten."

Jilly laughed, and while Sinatra was serious, he wasn't stupid. He knew there was no way we were landing in ten minutes. A good sense of humor was a prerequisite for traveling with Sinatra. I just wanted to touch down before the engine died. I said a silent prayer of thanks as the wheels hit the ground.

Sinatra stood up from his seat and walked toward the front of the plane as a middle-aged, female customs agent in full uniform walked on.

"Sit down, sir," she said, our passports in her hand. "I'd like to inspect the plane."

"What's the problem?" he said.

"Do you have anything to declare?"

"No, we don't have anything to declare," he said. Sinatra was still standing and looking at me as if to say, What the fuck is this?

"Sit down, please, sir."

Oh no. I didn't like the way this was going. I didn't know for sure if the Uzi was on the plane, but I assumed the worst. If she found the Uzi, this was not going to end well. I had visions of ending up in jail till I was an old man.

I don't know if she knew who Sinatra was or if she didn't care, but she was acting cocky and I was afraid Sinatra was going to talk back and then we would have a big problem. I began to sweat. She surveyed the plane, and as Sinatra approached his seat, I kept her talking.

"Excuse me, miss," I said. "We just finished a two-hour concert in the rain and Mr. Sinatra is very tired." I stood up and slowly walked her to the door of the plane.

"We would really like to get off the plane. We've only been gone for a couple of hours and we didn't bring anything back. Would you like to take a photo with Mr. Sinatra? I have a Polaroid here and would be happy to take your picture," I said.

At that point, she realized who Sinatra was and her tone of voice softened.

"Yes, I'd like that," she said with a smile.

Sinatra approached and put his arm around her. I took two photos, in case my hand wasn't steady the first time.

SEVENTEEN

We spent our nights at the Hotel de Paris, at the restaurant Le Grill, overlooking the sea, or Le Bar Américain, an elegant jazz bar with leather club chairs and dark wood. Some nights Barbara would have food prepared in the kitchen of the suite for everyone. "I'll have the veal, pounded," Sinatra would say as he demonstrated his preference by banging his elbow twice on the table.

Barbara would join us for dinner after the shows, as would Bobby. Bobby had a wide social network in Monte Carlo. In addition to Frank and Barbara's friends, who were mostly associated with the royal family, Bobby had a group of younger friends whom he would sometimes meet up with after dinner.

One night at Le Grill, we were seated next to the nightclub impresario Régine Zylberberg. She was a colorful character who loved to sing, dance, and curse. She was small in stature but big in personality. She could be rude and feisty. She spent her young life hiding from the Nazis and went on to create the modern-day discotheque with Paris's Whisky à Gogo. She also opened Jimmy'z, a hot nightclub in Monaco known for drawing American, Italian, and Parisian jet-setters.

Someone from her table came over looking to take a picture with Frank. Jilly explained that Mr. Sinatra was eating and turned down their request. As the night went on, their table became louder and louder, making comments about how they were snubbed. Someone started snapping photos and Sinatra became increasingly miffed. Then someone threw something at our table and it almost hit Sinatra. I never saw what it was, possibly a piece of bread, because Jilly stood up and without a word, in one move, flipped their table over.

In an effort to keep things from spiraling out of control—assuming they hadn't already—and knowing it could always escalate, I told everyone in our group to leave. We all quickly returned to our rooms, including Jilly.

Bobby decided to go on to a local club, and as luck would have it, Régine and her friends were there. Insults were traded and Bobby called us. Frank told Jilly to make sure Bobby was safe and bring him back to the hotel.

There was a whole group standing at the bar when Jilly arrived. Bobby told him some words were exchanged with one of the guys and Jilly told the man to back off. When he didn't, a fight ensued, Régine started yelling, and Jilly picked her up and hung her by the back of her dress on a coathook. He left her kicking and screaming.

Back at the hotel, Jilly and Bobby told us what happened and we knew we needed to hightail it out of Monaco, especially when we learned the police were on their way to the hotel. Jilly, as I mentioned, had friends everywhere, and that included some of the hotel staff, who helped him slip out undetected by using the catwalk that ran alongside the sewer lines.

The rest of us walked out the front door. After a brief explanation to the police that the tour was over and we were on our way home, we arrived at the Nice airport to find Jilly waiting with his face buried in a newspaper. We all had a good laugh on the plane.

Monaco continued to be a favored spot for the Sinatras and there were never any further incidents with any of our group. As for Régine, Sinatra never forgave her, and when she invited him to her Miami club during the Ultimate Event Tour, his response was an unmitigated, no fucking way.

EIGHTEEN

The summer of 1987 was life changing for me. Maria and I had been dating for five years, and she moved to Florida to be with me. Not long after, she said, "It's now or never." I came home with a ring that night. Then I called Maxine, my jeweler in New York, and asked her to find me a beautiful stone.

While I was on tour in Italy, Maria started planning the wedding. The more we told people we were getting married, the larger the wedding grew, to include more than three hundred people. As I was hearing the stories long-distance, it sounded like work to me. All my clients were coming and I was going to spend my wedding night working the room and taking care of everyone. It was not what I had in mind. This was my opportunity to rebuild the family that I missed so much. I didn't want this to be an event where I had to make sure everyone was happy.

Maria agreed and we went with plan B: I called my dear friend Lévon Sayan, Charles Aznavour's manager. Aznavour was a French Armenian singer, songwriter, and actor who had sold more than 180 million records in eight languages. He was a national treasure, often called the French Frank Sinatra, and was known for his magnificent house in Galluis, France, which he had recently sold to Sayan. Sayan too was an Armenian Frenchman with a round face, jovial smile, and hearty laugh, a result, I suppose, at least in part from his training as an operatic tenor. We frequently worked together in Europe and the United States.

"Lévon, what are you doing this summer?" I said.

"Why? What do you want to do?"

"I'm getting married," I said.

"What does this have to do with me?"

"I was thinking that fantastic house of yours I keep hearing about would be a great place for my wedding."

"Wonderful," he said, in a way that made me believe he really meant it.

It would be a small, family-only wedding. We would take everyone we loved the most. We would start in Paris, marry in Galluis, and bring everyone with us on our honeymoon in Florence. Somehow it would make up for all the years I missed being with my children.

Afterward, Maria and I would break away for some alone time in Lake Como. Surely that would be more meaningful than a major production for three hundred people and counting, though not necessarily any easier.

Maria handled everything herself over the course of two months, and with the help of Sinatra's travel agent she took care of passports, flights, hotels, and transportation for nineteen of our family members and very close friends. All my clients had busy travel schedules, and while we were sure they would go just about anywhere in the United States for my wedding, we made it clear there was no expectation for them to travel all the way to Europe for a small family gathering.

We picked July 11, 1987, a convenient Saturday that fit in with our travel schedule and summer plans and also happened to be the Sinatras' anniversary date. I've always had an affinity for the numbers 7-11—two winners when shooting dice—so it seemed perfect.

Galluis is a small village in the French countryside filled with greenery, flowers, and an occasional wild animal, like a deer or jackrabbit. It reminded me of some of the beautiful golf courses I had played in the past. There was a small road leading up to the Sayans' hilly estate and not a neighbor in sight. There were potted plants, baroque décor, and a fabulous wine cellar.

The day before the wedding, Lévon and I were relaxing in the garden, smoking a cigar and enjoying some great champagne. Someone handed me a wire that came from Sinatra. It was a one-word Western Union telegram that said, in capital letters, DON'T. I laughed. Then the chaos began. Furniture was moved, a tent was erected, a walkway created, and I realized I was really about to become Maria's husband.

The next day, the local mayor married us in a civil ceremony at city hall. Then our longtime friend Father Raphael joined a neighborhood rabbi to perform the main ceremony. It was a perfect evening. Maria walked down the aisle in a Princess Diana–inspired, ivory lace gown with a huge skirt and the big poufy sleeves that were so popular in the 1980s. It had rows and rows of tiny bows and seed pearls and was created by Peruchio, one of Halston's designers.

The weather was ideal. My three children, my sister and her husband, and Maria's parents and siblings were all there with their children. People ate, drank, and danced to French music that none of the Americans recognized. Doves actually flew out of a six-tiered cake.

The sky was still fairly light at ten o'clock. It was a magical night.

NINETEEN

I was taking on the role of husband the second time around, with renewed hope and enthusiasm. I was determined to spend as much time as possible with my bride, despite a rigorous travel schedule. When it was feasible, Maria joined me on tours and became part of the extended traveling family. My personal life changed and my professional life was about to undergo a major alteration as well.

The Italian tour was considered a tremendous success. The concerts were sold out, the reception was warm and welcoming everywhere we went, and the audiences were enthusiastic. What more could we want? At least that's what I thought. The change in our accommodations from the villa to the Hotel de Paris, the move, and travel distances all added up and the tour was in the red. When Sinatra discovered that he did all that work and lost money, he was furious. Rudin never even paid me.

While trouble brewed between Sinatra and Rudin, I was focused on our next stops, most notably at New York's Carnegie Hall. The hall is among the most prestigious and famous concert halls in the world and is a reverential space for many performers. Frank Sinatra was awed by the history of Carnegie Hall. "Do you know how many ghosts live there?" he would say, referring to the many great artists who had performed on that stage. I wondered whether he ever stopped to think about the history he made, but he was too busy making it to properly reflect on its significance.

Carnegie Hall is an intimate space. There are only 2,804 seats in the main auditorium, spread out over five levels. For an artist who is used to performing in large arenas, standing on what is now called the Ronald O. Perelman stage, in the Isaac Stern Auditorium, is like singing in someone's living room. The audience can see you sweat.

Carnegie Hall was built by Andrew Carnegie in 1891, on Seventh Avenue between Fifty-Sixth and Fifty-Seventh Streets, in what at the time was an underdeveloped section of upper Manhattan. As he placed the cornerstone, Carnegie said, "It is built to stand for ages, and during these ages it is probable that this hall will intertwine itself with the history of our country."

Some of the world's greatest musicians have performed on its stage, including Gustav Mahler, Leopold Stokowski, and Maria Callas, not to mention Louis Armstrong, Billie Holiday, Judy Garland, and the Beatles, the greatest artists across all genres. Woodrow Wilson, Mark Twain, and Booker T. Washington also appeared at Carnegie Hall, putting it at the heart of America's intellectual past. With its soft white walls, red seats, and superb acoustics, many performers have dreamed about gracing its stage.

Sinatra was honored to perform along with pianist Vladimir Horowitz and conductor Leonard Bernstein at the reopening of Carnegie Hall in 1986 after a $30 million renovation effort. The hall had been returned to its former glory but with modern improvements.

Sinatra loved the renovated space and was looking forward to his eight days of concerts in September 1987. So I was surprised to see him nervous and edgy on opening night. Watching a man who didn't flinch at flying in a plane with a faulty engine tense up before a performance had me completely perplexed. Was it his respect for the venue? Did the thought of taking the stage in this special space make him nervous? I had never seen him like this before and wasn't sure how this was going to go.

To make matters worse, we were all on edge. Barbara wanted Sinatra to stop smoking, so a week or so earlier, while we were sitting in his dressing room at Bally's Grand in Atlantic City, he had announced that he was quitting and no one could smoke around him. I passed on the edict and everyone in proximity to him tried to quit, at least for short stints. The whole orchestra and crew, including myself, went cold turkey when he was nearby, which wasn't easy for anyone, especially me, considering I had been smoking since the 1950s. It became obvious that the combination of nicotine withdrawal and his respect for the hall was weighing on him.

Sinatra wanted to change into his tux early, so I kept him company in his dressing room. I watched as he carefully took off his pants and turned them upside down to hang them. I heard something drop so I looked to the floor. And what do I see there? A pack of Camels and a Zippo lighter that fell out of his pants pocket. Today I think it's funny, but at the time we were all suffering with the Boss's no-smoking rule and I was cranky.

"What? Are you kidding me?" I said.

He gave me a look like a kid caught with his hand in the cookie jar. As you can imagine, that was not a look that frequently made its way across his face.

"You're making us all crazy and you're still smoking?" I said.

"I really don't smoke that much anymore," he said. "I've really cut back."

For his whole life Sinatra had loved to smoke, but from that point on, he smoked only on very rare occasions and not in front of Barbara or when we were with a group. I eventually quit cigarettes as well, though I still enjoy an occasional cigar.

Meanwhile, he couldn't have picked a more stressful time to give up an old habit. His unhappiness with the results of the Italian tour was the constant undercurrent of all that was going on. On top of it, there was no love lost between Barbara and either of the Rudins. After all, it's one thing when your wife doesn't like your lawyer; it's another when she doesn't like your lawyer's wife. Barbara Sinatra and Rudin's wife, Mary Carol, had known each other for years and always seemed to be in competition. Barbara was a stunningly beautiful woman and Mary Carol was very attractive. Both were well known in the best Hollywood circles. They had the finest jewels and clothes, though few could outdo the baubles Sinatra bought Barbara.

They ran in different social circles, as much as that's possible among the small cliques of Hollywood's elite, and neither seemed to make an effort to include the other. Mary Carol was Beverly Hills establishment and treated Barbara as a newcomer. Barbara, for her part, was Mrs. Sinatra and ruled the roost wherever she went. While I never heard Barbara speak ill of Mary Carol, whenever her name came up, she never spoke well of her, either.

Mickey had his own opinions of Barbara, and would say the marriage, the fourth for Frank, would never last. Not only did he believe it to be true, but he also seemed to want it to be true. In various phone conversations we had, whenever Sinatra's family affairs came up, he always aligned with the kids. It was well known in intimate circles that the children didn't think the former showgirl was good enough for their father and they wanted Frank to go back to their mother, Nancy Sr.

Rudin, meanwhile, was working with Sinatra's accountant, Sonny Golden, to have Sinatra transfer some key assets to Nancy Jr., Frank Jr., and Tina. Specifically, Rudin told Golden to initiate the process of transferring Sinatra's "name and likeness" to the children as well as some of his recordings. My understanding is that the plans to do so had been discussed between Sinatra and his children much earlier on, but it was a long and gradual proposition to work out all the details.

One afternoon when I was in Beverly Hills, I dropped by Rudin's Camden Drive office. He was in a meeting with Golden and the three of us talked about the bookings I had coming up for Sinatra. The conversation turned to Frank and Barbara's finances and Rudin again made a point of defining his alliances.

"Barbara has enough with all the jewelry Frank has given her. She doesn't need anything else," he said to Golden and me.

Barbara knew that Rudin was siding with the Sinatra kids against her, so she was understandably suspicious of anything Rudin did that affected her financial security. Likewise, Rudin and the kids were always leery of Barbara's motives. Years earlier, there had even been talk of Frank adopting Bobby, who was already an adult. That proposal was audacious enough to be shut down within a day or two, and while it was said to have been Sinatra's idea, it served to fortify their mistrust of Barbara.

Given the history, it wasn't surprising that when Golden told Barbara about the proposed asset transfer, it launched a firestorm. At some point she hired Arthur Crowley, who was famous for, among other things, securing a $20 million divorce settlement for Johnny Carson's third wife.

While all this was going on, to my knowledge Sinatra stayed quiet, preferring to let the confrontation play out until he had all the information and was prepared to make a final decision. He trusted his advisors, of which Rudin had always been the most important. As much as Sinatra hated being personally embroiled in conflict, he was happy to have Rudin, who seemed to thrive on showdowns, handle disputes for him, such as in 1986, when Rudin sued Kitty Kelley to stop the unauthorized biography of Sinatra and then sued *Barron's* for calling him Sinatra's mouthpiece. Both lawsuits were dismissed.

People have often wondered what caused Sinatra and Rudin to part after thirty-three years together. In my opinion it was three things: Rudin maneuvering against Barbara, the clashes between the wives, and finally, the tour. Nasty letters were exchanged between Sinatra and Rudin and finally Sinatra sent him a letter that said, "We have to part ways."

I called Rudin and begged him to go to Palm Springs and talk to Sinatra. As much as I was angry at Rudin for not paying me for the Italian tour, there was another part of me that was grateful to him for helping me arrive at my position in life. So I felt a sense of loyalty to him. I had no expectation of taking over for Rudin, and in my mind they had been together too long to let the relationship dissolve over a failed concert tour.

"Mickey, how can you just let it go? You're friends. You've worked together forever. I'll fly out and we'll drive to the Springs together. You can work this out."

"No. I don't need him," he said calmly. "I'll work for my other clients and make more money. What are you going to do?" Rudin said.

I had been working for Frank all this time, but it was through Rudin's office. Now he was asking me to choose between the two of them. I was not about to dissolve my relationship with Sinatra. I had way too much going on.

"I'm working on a Frank, Dean, and Sammy tour," I said.

"That's never going to happen. The best you'll ever get out of him is ten shows a year at a gambling venue. You will make a big mistake if you go with him. He's a has-been."

To me, that was the statement of a bitter, angry man. We had come off a sold-out tour and Rudin should have known better than most that Sinatra was still standing despite having been counted out before in his career. We both knew about the failing health of the aging star, and while I'm sure Rudin knew more than I did, I believed that if handled the right way, Sinatra still had some good years left. I was determined to prove Rudin wrong.

That phone call was the last friendly conversation I ever had with Rudin. The end of the Sinatra-Rudin relationship was about to mean a new beginning for me. After a decade of working with Sinatra, I went from receiving 5 percent of Sinatra's earnings to 10 percent overnight. Then Bobby Marx called my office.

"I spoke with Mom and she feels the two of us should come to Palm Springs. We're all happy the Rudin relationship is done, but Frank is worried about what's next. He asked Sonny, 'So who's going to book me now?' and Sonny told him you've been doing it since 1978," Bobby said.

True, I had been handling nearly all of Sinatra's bookings, with the exception of the gambling venues, for years, but those statements made me realize that Rudin had never told Sinatra about the scope of my work. Bobby and I met in New York and took a direct flight to Los Angeles on *MGM Grand,* a superluxurious commercial airline owned by Kirk Kerkorian, with a first-class section that rivaled most private jets. We drove directly to Palm Springs to meet with Frank and Barbara.

The four of us spent the afternoon discussing the management of Sinatra's career, as well as the tour that Mort Viner—Dean Martin's agent, from ICM—and I were working on for Frank, Dean, and Sammy, which was slated to kick off in a few months. They asked questions about my career strategy for Sinatra, as well as for details about my accounting and financial background. It was pretty intense but the occasional smile on Sinatra's face told me he was satisfied with my answers. I knew this job was as much about refereeing the family boxing match as it was about managing Sinatra. I made it clear that I would not take sides and would advise them on what I believed was in Sinatra's best financial interests. Toward the end of the conversation, with Frank sitting there, Barbara was confident enough in Sinatra's approval that she said, "Eliot, we would like you to be in charge of Frank's business affairs."

Of course, I said yes. I didn't know whether this would be a short-term situation or a long-term one, but I hoped for the latter and was very happy to be involved. It was agreed that from that day on, Sinatra would be my priority and I would travel on every tour with him. In the process, I would be brought fully up to speed on all of Sinatra's finances.

That evening, as we sat down to dinner in their home, Bobby started the conversation.

"My mom and the Boss wanted me out here with you to help them put together a plan to make sure everyone is protected," he said.

"Darling, is that correct?" Barbara said to Frank.

"Absolutely," Sinatra said.

That meant that while I was now in charge of managing Sinatra's career, they also wanted my input on the proposed transfer of assets. Barbara was understandably nervous that Sinatra's key assets were being given away and Sinatra was still waiting for final word from his advisors, which now included me along with Golden, before giving the green light to the deal.

Over the coming months, as I delved into the details of his finances, I was disappointed to see that Sinatra was cash-poor. He spent a lot of money and gave a lot of money to his kids. By far the most valuable assets he owned were the rights to his name and likeness, and the royalties from his Capitol recordings as well as a 20 percent ownership of Reprise Records, all of which were slated to go to the kids as part of the transfer.

Sinatra founded Reprise in 1961, when he left Capitol Records to allow himself more artistic freedom. That's the genesis of the nickname "Chairman of the Board." He sold the label Reprise to Warner Bros. in 1963 but retained a 20 percent stake. So, unlike most singers of the day, who only received the royalties for singing, Sinatra earned royalties as owner of the music and label, which grew to include other artists, such as Arlo Guthrie, Frank Zappa, and Fleetwood Mac.

As I gathered the necessary information, I never spoke directly to Sinatra about it. He had told me on several occasions when we were alone how much he hated confrontation between his wife and kids.

"I can't understand how everyone in this family always thinks they are being mistreated," he frequently said. So I spared him the details until I had a firm recommendation.

This gift meant that the kids would own his name and likeness, as well as his portion of Capitol royalties, Reprise Records, and his master recordings. Despite my initial reservations, on closer analysis it looked like a good idea. The valuation Sonny had obtained from the IRS was very low and my guess was that it would produce a gift tax that would be substantially lower than the eventual estate tax if they waited until his death. The larger estate tax would pose a huge liability for everyone when he died. I knew I had to convince Barbara that trying to stop the transfer would not be wise. I called her in Palm Springs.

"Barbara, I think you should let this go," I said.

"What happens to me?" she said. "Am I protected?"

"Let's focus on income he can earn now, that you can benefit from. He can make personal appearances, commercials and things like that, that won't be included in the transfer. Of course, he will continue singing and keep selling out."

With no guarantees, she was reluctant. Again, I wasn't sure if I would be in this advisory role for the long term, but in the back of my mind I knew that if the kids were being given the rights to his music catalog and name and likeness, I could make a good case for almost everything else going to Barbara, which I believed was fair. Barbara dropped her objections and the kids were poised to be firmly in charge of the Sinatra legacy, though some of the income would continue to belong to Sinatra until his death.

That night I went to bed worried about the future. I knew why she was reluctant. Heck, even I could see it. Everyone was concerned about Sinatra's health. His vision and hearing were on a downward slide and he was having memory problems. I honestly didn't know how many shows he could handle a year. On top of that, he had been on an antidepressant for as long as I had known him, and I was convinced it was contributing to his difficulties.

There were more than a few false starts and mishaps. Nonetheless, we kept forging ahead. I'm happy to say that not only did Sinatra go on to make a lot of money, but he went on to make the two biggest-selling albums of his career, all of which irked Rudin no end.

TWENTY

Sinatra had a couple of weeks off, so Maria and I joined Liza for an engagement in Rome.

Liza was booked for several shows at the Teatro Sistina, a striking midcentury modern theater located on the black cobblestone Via Sistina. It was built on the former site of the Pontifical Ecclesiastical Polish Institute, once used to train Catholic priests, so it was somewhat ironic that this trip would come to include a visit with the first-ever Polish head of the Catholic Church, Pope John Paul II.

We were relaxing at the Excelsior Hotel, with its recognizable dome situated between the Spanish Steps and the Borghese Gardens, when Pierro Carriagi, our animated Italian tour promoter, came to our suite. From the balcony of our suite, Maria and I could see Liza sitting on her terrace. She was dressed in her signature black, offstage attire, smoking a cigarette. Carriagi, who also worked with me for Sinatra, was hyper, sweating and yelling into the phone in Italian. He turned to me.

"Eliot, my people say the Vatican is calling."

"What for?" I said.

"The pope heard Liza was in town and he wants to meet her."

"Sure," I said. "I think she'd like that."

"Sure?" Pierro said. "Of course she would! This is the head of the Roman Catholic Church. This is a tremendous honor. He was a fan of Judy Garland."

Pierro went to Liza's room to break the news. Liza wanted my Italian wife to go with her, and Maria loved the idea. When Carriagi added Maria Weisman to the guest list, the Vatican called back.

"Who is Maria Weisman and why is she with the group?" the head of logistics said.

"Si, si," Carriagi said. "Maria Chiarella Weisman," he said, emphasizing Chiarella.

That pretty much solved that problem and deterred both Liza and my wife from requesting that I tag along. Their papal visit was set for the same day as the American League playoffs between and the Minnesota Twins and the Detroit Tigers and I was quite content to sit in our suite and listen to the game on the radio. So, though I wasn't there, both Maria and Liza happily recounted every detail.

Meeting the pope required all the formality of a head of state combined with the reverence and awe due a man known as the Holy Father and leader of his own tiny nation. Liza and Maria were nervous and excited. They went over what they would wear and Liza wondered aloud whether she should wear a "doily" on her head. They decided to wear black, with no "doily." Liza wore a black skirt suit and white blouse with a Peter Pan collar and black felt hat, with a rounded top and wide, round brim. Maria wore a black dress and pearls.

Pope John Paul II, who is now a saint in his own right, was the first non-Italian pope in four hundred years. He had miracles attributed to him, and though it had not yet happened at the time, he is largely credited with being a key factor in the fall of communism in Europe.

The limo took Carriagi and the two women up to the private entrance of the pontiff's living quarters in Vatican City. They cleared security and entered a cobblestone road so large it resembled an airplane tarmac. They were greeted by four high-ranking church officials who they believed were bishops, in long black robes with large cross necklaces that hung low on their chests. Liza did a perfect curtsy and Maria noticed that the bishops were wearing fancy, presumably Italian shoes.

The clergy walked with the trio to meet another man, who wore elaborate white robes and a tall, white miter, or bishop's hat with the pointed top. He gently took Liza's hand and again she curtsied. It was all very imposing.

The bishop in white led them down an opulent hallway with a red carpet, high ceilings, and impressive biblical art. They followed him up a winding staircase, past several of the pope's Swiss Guard, with their brightly colored gold, blue, and red striped uniforms, to a small papal waiting room at the end. The bishop explained they should wait there until they were called in to meet His Holiness.

There were two very large, ornately carved double doors that secured Pope John Paul's private office. When they opened, a smiling monsignor summoned Liza in. After Liza had spent some private time with the pontiff, Maria and Carriagi also entered.

Pope John Paul was gentle and charming. He softly reached for their hands, one at a time, and asked simple questions.

"I did love your mother," the pope said to Liza.

She was trembling.

"I did, too," she said.

"I've heard you have been married several times," he said.

She looked frightened. She hesitated, and before she could speak, the pope continued. "Are you married now?"

"Oh yes, to a wonderful man." She sounded like Dorothy in *The Wizard of Oz*. "You know, I can perform here anytime you want."

When the pope asked Maria where she was from, she told her life story in one run-on sentence. He smiled and went to the drawer of his very large, carved wood desk and pulled out small white boxes of rosaries for each of them.

One by one, he put his hand on each of their heads and blessed them.

They stood in silent awe, frozen in place. When they left, they were lost in the reverence of the moment, and returned to the hotel bubbling about the experience.

I was thrilled to see how excited they were and was happy to have had some time alone to relax. Minnesota won. I told them about how Sinatra also received a rosary from Pope John Paul, during an earlier visit to Rome. While I never knew Sinatra to be an outwardly religious man, he once told my coauthor, Jennifer Valoppi, that the pontiff gave him a very special gift during their meeting. Sinatra went to the Vatican with Barbara and Jilly, and he met privately with the pope. Sinatra told Jennifer that the pontiff gave him a piece of wood from Jesus's cross.

Jennifer was somewhat startled.

"How is that possible? You mean the Vatican has Jesus's cross?" she said.

"That's what he told me," Sinatra said. "It was part of Jesus's cross."

They were having the conversation at Sinatra's Beverly Hills home in the early morning hours one night after dinner. Barbara went up to bed and their friend Dennis Stein fell asleep on the couch. Jennifer and Sinatra were left alone drinking cognac and talking about God.

"That's the craziest thing I've ever heard. What does it look like?" she said.

"It's just a little shard of wood."

"What did you do with it?" she asked.

"It's in a little pouch hanging on my bed."

Barbara was already sleeping so she didn't ask to see it, but she did investigate a little further. According to Catholic historians,

Empress Helena, the mother of the first Christian emperor of Rome, Constantine, traveled to Jerusalem. She had a pagan temple that had been built over Jesus's tomb torn down. When they dug underneath, they found three crosses believed to be the ones used to crucify Jesus and the two thieves. The church says a dying woman was healed when she touched the third cross, revealing the True Cross.

I didn't know what to make of that story and I don't remember personally discussing religion with Sinatra or seeing him pray, but others close to him said in his later years he used to say nightly prayers of gratitude. I know he had a plaque in his office in Palm Springs that was a partial quote from a poem found scratched on a cellar wall by a Holocaust victim during World War II: "I believe in the sun, even when it's not shining. And I believe in love even when there is no one there. And I believe in God, even when he is silent."

Most of us who were close to Sinatra will always remember the trip he, Barbara, and Jilly took to the Vatican, not only for its importance but also because Jilly, in his own inimitable way, sent out a Christmas card that year with a photo of him and the pope. It said, "The Pope and I Wish You a Merry Christmas."

TWENTY-ONE

Frank Sinatra advocated for many things over the course of his life. He was a man of great integrity and intense personal conviction. If he believed in something, he was unafraid to stand up and speak out. Sinatra was never politically correct, instead fighting against racism and anti-Semitism and providing substantial financial assistance to friends who fell on hard times.

When a Las Vegas casino refused to allow Sammy in the front door in the 1960s, Sinatra famously said, "Let him in or I'm out." He provided financial help to boxers Joe Louis and Sugar Ray Robinson when they fell on hard times, and gave them use of his plane when they needed it for medical treatment. I borrowed his plane to pick up Liza in Minneapolis when she completed her first stint in rehab at the Hazelden drug rehab center.

He was an avid reader of the newspaper in every town and city we went to. When he read a story about someone in need, especially if it was a policeman or fireman, he would have someone call Golden and send anywhere from $5,000 to $25,000 anonymously. Frank's father had been a fireman and he had great admiration for their service.

He had the capacity for deep, fierce emotions and that often made him empathetic to both friends and strangers. When Gregory Peck presented Sinatra with the Jean Hersholt Humanitarian Award in 1971, he said, "No one within the range of him who has needed his support has ever been refused it. Ladies and gentlemen, a man who pays his dues, Frank Sinatra."

Sinatra was a roller coaster of emotions. His mercurial nature was part of his mystique. Over the years I learned to pay attention to whether he was ill or had fallen into a state of melancholy. While we never discussed it, I knew that when he suddenly became quiet and pensive, I should leave him alone. His intense mood swings also fueled his talents.

"I don't know what other singers feel when they articulate lyrics," Sinatra said in an interview with *Playboy* magazine in 1963, "but being an 18-karat manic-depressive and having lived a life of violent emotional contradictions, I have an overacute capacity for sadness as well as elation. I know what the cat who wrote the song is trying to say. I've been there—and back. I guess the audience feels it along with me."

I can't help but believe that if Sinatra were alive today, he would speak out about depression. In 2016, the U.S. suicide rate surged to a thirty-year high, with stunning increases regardless of gender and in virtually every age group, except for the oldest Americans, over age seventy-five. The increase for middle-aged women alone was 63 percent. While Sinatra was intensely private, if he had seen those figures and thought he could save lives by removing a stigma about depression and encouraging people to seek treatment, I believe he would have done so.

Some of our greatest artists and thinkers in all of history are thought to have suffered from depression and/or manic depression. Michelangelo, Charles Dickens, Ernest Hemingway, even Abraham Lincoln and Isaac Newton. I would argue that Sinatra was a talent of similar extraordinary ability.

As I mentioned, he was on a first-generation antidepressant for all the years I knew him. Elavil, or amitriptyline, is a tricyclic antidepressant that impacts neurotransmitters like serotonin in the brain. It was the first line of treatment in the 1960s and '70s, and over the years, doctors told me it was best for short-term use. Sinatra, though, had used it for many years, and that always concerned me, especially when I understood the side effects could include vision difficulties and memory loss. I was told by his doctors that long-term use of Elavil required a careful weening off of it, which could lead to anger, agitation, and violent behavior.

Sinatra himself was not fond of doctors, and persuading him to keep an appointment was always a struggle. I'm sure his refusal to undergo extensive medical workups contributed to the long-term use of amitriptyline and that in turn contributed to many difficulties in his performance.

I didn't know how long he would be able to handle a rigorous schedule, but I was working on what was expected to be a sold-out tour, so there was no turning back.

TWENTY-TWO

I am by nature a risk manager. My job was to figure out how to make sure the thing that can't possibly go wrong but does, is taken care of. I had to have a plan B, plan C, and plan D, which would serve as a backup to any last-minute emergency like losing key personnel, travel musicians, or musical charts. For the charts, I instituted a policy to insure that they were never more than two hours' flying distance away from any concert location. They were to be kept in Chicago, Florida, and Texas in addition to home base in Los Angeles. That, I thought, would have us covered.

Musical charts are essential to a performance; they are the road map for every song and for every musician. Sinatra worked with brilliant musicians, for example, Nelson Riddle, who put together detailed and elaborate arrangements that gave Sinatra songs their distinct and beautiful sound. When the arrangement was complete, each musician was handed his or her part in the form of a musical chart.

Let's say you are a pianist. You may be substituting for the regular pianist, which frequently happens with musicians. You might read superbly and you might even be able to cold-play a song, live onstage. Without the chart, you have no idea if the arranger substituted a new chord on a song you knew by heart.

Sometimes the hardest part of a performance is not so much the complicated section the performer has to play, but instead, simply knowing when to come back in after a twenty-measure rest. The conductor cues you, but he has to know exactly when to do that for thirty-three different musicians and then for approximately twenty different songs. Even if you've been playing something for years, you can have a memory glitch. Most people don't have perfect memories. You need all thirty-three musicians to play all the beautiful orchestral ins and outs perfectly. It can't be done without the charts.

The big opening performance of Frank and Liza at the Meadowlands Arena in New Jersey in December 1987 was meant to be just that—big and groundbreaking. It was arranged by my new company, a joint venture called Corporate Entertainment Productions, or CEP, where my daughter Carol Chenkin worked.

CEP was created to handle special events, marketing, and sponsorships within the Young & Rubicam family of clients. My son Eric worked out the details and became the day-to-day liaison between Premier Artists Services and Burson-Marsteller, a subsidiary of Y&R. Carol worked on a team that figured out creative ways for clients to reach a new and wider audience. So, for example, when Schering-Plough developed a new asthma drug, Carol found Dennis Rodman, who was at the time a newcomer to the NBA, to promote the drug as an athlete with asthma.

American Express, a Y&R client, was in the middle of its "Membership Has Its Privileges" advertising campaign. Part of the "privileges" was special access to concert tickets. AmEx members had first crack at the tickets before they went on sale to the general public, giving them the opportunity to choose from a special selection of seats reserved for card members. The idea was to give card members the edge, to send them to the "front of the line," so to speak.

I was looking for a way to give the upcoming Frank, Dean, and Sammy tour the edge with an American Express sponsorship. This two-night, Frank and Liza performance was the trial balloon designed to stir up excitement with the executives for the upcoming tour.

Opening night was on a Friday in December and we were sold out. Carol was running around backstage to make sure everything was set for the VIPs who were coming in early for a special, invitation-only cocktail party prior to the concert.

I was wandering through the concrete backstage halls, making sure everything was going according to schedule, when our production manager, Hank Cattaneo, tracked me down. I had introduced Cattaneo to Sinatra as a top-notch soundman after Sinatra complained about the audio quality at a couple of his concerts. Cattaneo handled sound and lighting for most all my clients and Sinatra loved him.

"We have a problem. We have no music," he said. He was calm, which helped to keep me from flying off the handle.

"What the fuck are you talking about?" I said.

"The charts were left in San Francisco," Cattaneo said.

"We have three hours till showtime," I said. "I put the music in three places in case we ever had this problem. If they're not already en route from San Francisco, where you left them, get them from Chicago."

"The guy who has them in Chicago is not reachable."

"So get them from Florida," I said angrily.

"We can't reach him, either."

I was dumbfounded. I thought I had planned for every contingency, but I hadn't planned for not being able to access the backup plans. Carol said when she saw me I was ashen.

The music charts for every musician and every song in the show were in two boxes. They were always carried by hand and were never supposed to be checked in as luggage. Cattaneo was in charge of the crew and I didn't ask who forgot them or how they could possibly have been left behind.

Instead, I went to the Boss. He was hanging around with Jilly in his dressing room. My stomach was in knots, but I tried to at least appear in control. I explained to him that the music had not arrived. I knew they couldn't do the show without the charts but I thought it was worth a shot.

"Mr. S., you've been doing this music for years. Can you give it a try?"

He practically bit my head off.

"This isn't just sheet music. These are the musical charts. There's no way this will work."

Sinatra never rehearsed, but he knew there was a lot riding on this concert. I asked him to go out on the stage and give it his best effort. His initial impulse was to go home, but he saw my desperation and agreed to try. He made it through one song and my hopes were high, then he started the second.

Sinatra was a perfectionist, so much so that he hated when someone told him something was perfect. To him nothing was perfect. Musicians say he had perfect pitch. Most musicians have relative pitch. They could play any note on the piano or any instrument and he could tell them what note they were playing. His incredible ear heard every sound.

That night there were string and brass sections and nothing hit right. It wasn't so much anything I could hear but he could hear it and it threw him off. It was all wrong.

In the middle of the second song he put down the microphone and walked off stage.

"You do the show. Maybe you're better than I am," he said to me. Then he turned to Jilly. "Come on, Jilly, let's get out of here. We're going."

Sinatra walked out and my night started. I had no plan but I knew I had to tell Liza, who was in her dressing room.

"Oh, honey," she said. "I'll do the whole show." She acted as if nothing unusual had occurred.

"Are you crazy?" I said. "I don't doubt that you could do a whole show by yourself, but more people came to see Frank than you." I may have offended her, but frankly, I didn't care. I was furious with her. Sure, she could have done the whole show by herself, but the nerve and disrespect of that remark, when Sinatra was sharing his profits with her and treating her like a daughter, burned at me.

"I'll call Fred Ebb and see what he thinks." As I mentioned, Fred Ebb, of Kander and Ebb, was one of her closet confidants and she regularly relied on his expertise.

"Are you really going to have the nerve to try and upstage Sinatra? You'll never work with him again," I said. I didn't have time to be any more upset than I already was. I was in crisis mode, so I ignored her and went about trying to figure out a way to manage the damage. Liza found me ten minutes later.

"I spoke to Fred and he says it's okay for me to do the whole show or at least go out and do my first half of the show."

"The answer is no, Liza. You can talk to Fred all you want. As your manager I'm telling you no." She finally agreed and I told her I was working to resolve the issues.

An hour or so later I saw Barbara walking through the backstage tunnel. I explained the situation.

"You can go home, Barbara," I said.

"Why?" she said.

"He left."

"You're kidding," she said.

"No, I'm not kidding. So, now I need to figure out what to do with nineteen thousand people." She shrugged her shoulders, turned around, and walked back to her waiting limo.

Do I give them their money back? What do I tell the special guests who arrived early for the cocktail party? I called the building manager of the Meadowlands to see if Sunday night was available to switch the performance. It was booked with another act, but I didn't stop there. I asked him to see if he could persuade whoever it was to reschedule their date and we would work out a financial arrangement to make it worth their while.

Within a half an hour I had the answer. The rock band Rush was scheduled and they graciously agreed to move their performance to Monday night. I was feeling a little better. I still had the announcement to make. I called Susan Reynolds, Frank's publicist. She was the media-savvy daughter of Lee Solters, the famed Hollywood press agent. Solters represented Sinatra for a quarter century, until Sinatra decided to have his daughter take over.

"It's same time, same place, different night," I said. Susan went to work contacting news organizations and fielding calls from the media, explaining the concerts would now be Saturday and Sunday rather than Friday and Saturday.

Now I had to face the cocktail crowd, filled with the heads of all the partner agencies in addition to the biggest advertisers. I stood behind the podium.

"Ladies and gentlemen, a funny thing happened on the way to the forum. We left the music on the loading dock."

There were whispers.

"I'm responsible for all the people and making sure everything is in place and I take full responsibility for tonight's cancellation. We have been fortunate in rescheduling tonight's performance for Sunday night." There were gasps. "We will make up whatever costs there are and throw the same private party on Sunday all over again. Please stay and enjoy the party."

Several media outlets came backstage and they were the toughest ones to convince.

"Is there something wrong with Sinatra?" one of the reporters asked. "There must be something wrong with him."

"No, nothing."

They didn't believe me.

"You canceled a sold-out concert," another reporter said. "He must be sick."

"If he was, I wouldn't reschedule for Sunday and plan to go on tomorrow night."

"Aw, come on. You're not going to let all these people go home if something isn't wrong with him."

"You can print what you want, but if you say he's sick, I'll make a liar out of you tomorrow."

I went back to the cocktail party and the ruckus had calmed down. Some were curious as to how I had managed to maneuver a Sunday night concert. I told them I was grateful to the arena management for arranging the deal.

The following morning, someone from the Meadowlands notified me that the music arrived from San Francisco. I was in bed when they called to tell me it was there. Relieved, I called Cattaneo.

"Listen, everyone better have a thick skin and be relaxed. I don't know how Sinatra is going to be today," I said.

While I didn't know what to expect, I knew it was a good sign that my phone wasn't ringing and Vine wasn't knocking on my door. We drove out to the Meadowlands together, and other than being annoyed at the traffic in the Lincoln Tunnel, Sinatra was as nice as could be. You would never have known that anything had happened. We had two great shows.

Sinatra was rarely rattled by problems. His attitude was "Just fix it, Pally." I did and we were never put in that position again.

TWENTY-THREE

In order to truly understand the Sinatra mystique, you have to understand the Rat Pack days, when alpha males were admired and applauded for hard drinking, womanizing, and having each other's backs. It was a fraternity of handsome, rich, middle-aged men who never lost their boyish charm.

It was Sinatra, Dean Martin, Sammy Davis Jr., Peter Lawford, and Joey Bishop. There were women, too. Angie Dickinson, Shirley MacLaine, and Judy Garland were all associated with the Rat Pack. But the heart and soul of the Pack will forever be Sinatra, Martin, and Davis.

To hear Sinatra speak of those days was like listening to an athlete talk about how he beat the odds and brought his team to glory, and then did it again and again and again. He changed with the times, though. By his early seventies he was a devoted and loving husband, but there was something special about those Rat Pack glory days. Wouldn't it be fun to recapture the spirit of those times? That's what triggered the idea for the "Together Again" Tour. It was not only a dream of mine, but an opportunity to re-create a time and place where I knew my boss had been the happiest.

At first, Sinatra conceived of it as an old-fashioned "whistle-stop" train tour. He asked me to find out what it would cost to rent a locomotive, three private cars, two dining cars, and a caboose. We both loved trains, so at first it sounded like an interesting idea.

Once Dean and Sammy confirmed they were on board, my company, PAS, started to plan the tour according to the train routes. When we looked closely at the U.S. rail system, available routes and normal rail schedules, I envisioned the Boss tapping his watch every time there was a delay. Trains were the old days, inefficient and quaint. Planes were modern, and we could control timing and logistics much more effectively. We rented two jets instead.

As I mentioned, Sinatra didn't rehearse, so the two nights we spent at Sammy's Beverly Hills home, with the three of them in their tour jackets, standing at the piano laughing, singing, and clowning around, brought out the fan in me. It was incredible to witness and much more about camaraderie than work—it was some old buddies having a good time and the closest thing to a rehearsal that I ever saw Sinatra do.

In March 1988 we launched the U.S. leg of the tour. We scheduled forty performances in twenty-nine cities with Frank, Dean, and Sammy and sold them all out. Fans clamored for tickets, some selling for hundreds of dollars over the face price. It was a scalper's dream. I wanted to call the tour the "Pack Is Back," but Barbara nixed the idea. She didn't want it to have anything to do with the days and nights of endless carousing. So it was dubbed "Together Again," but there was no getting around the Rat Pack reference in people's minds or in the media.

Opening night, rows of limos pulled up to the Oakland Coliseum. Many carried men in tuxedos and women in their finery, all ready to relive a time when "it was a very good year." If I thought this was going to be an audience of gray hairs, I was wrong. "It's Frank Sinatra's world and we just live in it," I remember a tuxedo-clad young man saying to a television reporter on his way into the coliseum. He couldn't have been more than twenty-five years old, repeating a line Dean Martin made famous many years earlier. Sinatra was seventy-two years old, Martin was seventy, and Sammy was sixty-two. Yet the average age of our audience was forty-five.

Sinatra, Martin, and Davis had first appeared together twenty-eight years earlier, in Las Vegas. It must have been a hell of a thrill to walk out on the coliseum stage and see fifteen thousand people rise to their feet for a standing ovation all those years later for the historic reunion. They each took the stage individually: first Sammy, then Dean, and then Sinatra. Sinatra and Sammy went off without a hitch, but not Dean. He was accustomed to playing small venues in Vegas, not large arenas. He seemed weak and frail in that big space and had a hard time projecting. He was used to keeping his handheld microphone low, in the middle of his chest, and people in the back of the coliseum at one point started yelling, "Louder, louder!"

The highlight was when they returned together to close out the two-hour show with banter, jokes, and a medley. Sammy, the youngest of the trio, gave them a "golden age cocktail."

"What the hell is a golden age cocktail?" Sinatra said.

"It's Geritol and prune juice," Sammy said.

"It gets you going and keeps you going," Dean said, which is a classic line, but not everyone heard it. Sinatra pushed Dean's arm so the microphone would be closer to his face and the fans could hear him.

They joked about Sinatra still being Chairman of the Board, and Sinatra responded, "I'm still chairman and we're still bored."

The audiences ate it up and the performance was a huge hit. Everyone was riding high, but Dean's ego was bruised. The spring in his step was gone.

The next stop was an arena show in Vancouver, and Martin did the majority of the clowning around in his typical, boozy performance mode, even though he was not drinking at the time. I could tell his nerves were wearing thin, though. He didn't say anything, but he didn't look happy.

After the shows, Sinatra wanted to relive old times. He wanted to go out drinking and smoking, but so much had changed from their days of skinny pants, brandy snifters, and piano bars.

"Hey, pally, where we going tonight?" Sinatra said to Martin after the Vancouver show.

"I'm tired, I'm going to bed," Martin said.

Sinatra couldn't believe it. He had also gone to bed early in California. Sammy always joined us for dinner and the obligatory late-night cocktails, but in Sinatra's eyes it wasn't the same without the whole team. From his perspective, the after-show fun was half the reason for the tour.

On top of being tired, Dean was still grieving from the death of his beloved son, Dean Paul Martin, a year earlier, in March 1987. "Dino," as he was once known, saw his own success as a teenage rock star with Desi Arnaz Jr., and then as an actor. The kid had a reputation as a playboy and even briefly dated Tina Sinatra.

He was only thirty-five years old when, as a captain in the California National Guard, he was piloting a fighter jet in heavy clouds and it disappeared from radar. They discovered that he had crashed into the rugged top of Mount San Gorgonio in the San Bernardino National Forest, outside of Los Angeles. Dino had been flying since he was a teenager and was considered an excellent pilot, so this was especially crushing.

Weirdly, Sinatra's eighty-two-year-old mother, Dolly, was killed in a plane that crashed into Mount San Gorgonio during a snowstorm, in 1977. It was yet another, albeit tragic, connection between Dean and Sinatra.

Martin was never the same after the death of his son. He wasn't interested in drinking and carousing and having long dinners. He was on heavy doses of painkillers and wanted to go to bed after the concerts. Dean just didn't seem to be up to it, mentally or physically.

Still, Sinatra tried to push him to have a good time. From Vancouver we traveled to Seattle, where Sinatra again tried to engage Dean in a little after-show carousing. It didn't work. Finally, Mort Viner called me and said, "You have to tell Sinatra to lay off Dean. He needs his rest. If he starts going out at night he'll never make it through the tour."

I told Sinatra in the limo, on our way out to dinner after the concert. He was concerned about his old friend and hadn't realized he was in that bad shape. On the other hand, he didn't understand why Martin had agreed to the tour, if he wasn't up to it. "This isn't any fun," Sinatra said.

Next were three shows in Chicago, and by the third show the audience was still having trouble hearing Dean. At one point Sinatra, fed up, stood onstage and told him to hold the mic closer. That was the final straw for Dean. He realized he was out of his element in such enormous spaces and his health wouldn't hold out. On Monday, the following morning, Viner called my suite at the Ambassador East.

"I'm in L.A. with Dean. He's in the hospital. We took one of the jets back last night."

"What's wrong with him?" I said.

"He has a problem with his kidneys. I think it's an infection."

"When will he be better?"

"Honestly, Eliot, this isn't going to work out. He's not strong enough. He's used to playing three or four shows in Vegas. The arenas are too much."

I understood. Viner was right. Dean wasn't strong enough. I knew exactly what the Boss would say. I sat in my hotel suite trying to figure out how the hell I was going to convince Sinatra to keep going and salvage the tour.

We had made it through four cities and still had seven cities left on the first leg of the tour, before winding up at Radio City Music Hall in New York.

I called Shirley Rhodes's room. Shirley was Sammy's personal assistant and confidante but she was really like family. She was cheerful and trustworthy. Her husband, George, was Sammy's conductor and had been with him for thirty years. After George passed away, Shirley stayed on with Sammy as his closest advisor.

"We've got a problem," I said. I explained the situation.

"Sammy is really counting on this tour to make him financially even," Shirley said. "Times are tough."

"The Boss will be having breakfast somewhere between eleven and noon," I said. "Sammy and I need to go see him together. Wake him up and ask him to come to my room around ten o'clock so I can brief him."

Shirley arrived first and then Sammy was in my suite, casual but fully dressed, by nine thirty. We were all in the living area. When I explained what happened, he went pale and I thought he would collapse. He slumped down on the sofa. Sammy had such an upbeat personality, I had never seen him like this.

"Take it easy," I said. "When we tell Sinatra Dean is gone, his first impulse is going to be, 'Let's call for the jet and go home.'"

"Why?" Sammy said.

"He's going to be sensitive to the fact that tickets were sold on a Frank, Dean, and Sammy tour and he's going to say without Dean it's not fair to the fans. We need to make a deal with him. Just stay confident and back me up."

I called Vine and asked her to call me when Sinatra was on his second cup of coffee. He always had a second cup while reading the newspaper and eating breakfast. I didn't want to attack him with a problem before he had a chance to relax and orient himself to the day. She did.

Sinatra was sitting in his robe at the dining room table of his regular suite. Chicago had better, more modern hotels than the Ambassador East, but Sinatra was a creature of habit and he wouldn't even consider changing. He took one look at both of us, those blue eyes piercing over the top of his reading glasses. "To what do I owe the honor of this meeting?"

I was nervous as hell but went for it. "Dean is not well, Boss. He's not well and he can't continue," I said.

"No problem," Sinatra said, leaning back in his chair. "Call Johnny Spots and tell him to get the plane ready. You can figure out what kind of press release you want to put together."

"Wait a minute," I said. "The reason we are here is because Sammy and I talked about this. You can both do the shows through Radio City and then we go on break and we will figure out what to do next."

Sammy was prepared and knew exactly what to do. "Yeah, Frank," Sammy said. "It'll be great. I can pick up a few songs if you want and we'll go on as usual. I can cover the Dean part of the medley, no problem. Everything is sold out. We can't let this go." He sounded absolutely confident, just like we planned.

Sinatra stared at us. "The tickets don't say Frank and Sammy. There are three names on the tickets, not two. We can't deceive the fans."

With Sinatra you had to be ready for anything and I was ready for this. "We'll announce that Dean is no longer with the tour and give refunds to whoever wants them," I said.

"How many refund requests do you think there will be?" Sinatra said. That question was a glimmer of hope.

"Not many. No more than one hundred a show, would be my guess," I said. "Do you think that's reasonable?"

"I'll go with a hundred, as long as it's not more," Sinatra said, looking over his glasses. "More than a hundred refunds and it's over, we cancel the tour."

"If it's more than a hundred I'll tell you."

Sammy and I left the suite smiling. "You're a fucking genius," Sammy said. "It's like you scripted the conversation."

"No, I'm just a creature of habit like he is."

Now that we had a deal, I was worried about tomorrow's concert in Minneapolis. If we announced the change today, people might be upset and cancel. Nonetheless, I knew the Boss wanted me to take care of it immediately, so I did.

My worries were unfounded. I think fifty tickets were the most we ever refunded at any given show. Sinatra asked for the number of ticket refunds every step of the way, so the pressure was on until we made it through the entire leg of the tour and arrived in New York.

Vine called me and said, "The Boss wants to see you and you had better hold on."

I had no idea what he could be upset about. He and Sammy had delivered a string of great performances and there had been very little backlash from Dean's departure. When I walked into the suite at the Waldorf, he was sipping his coffee in his robe and reading the newspaper with his glasses on. He never looked up.

I was being frozen out, so I just sat down at the opposite end of the nine-foot-long dining room table and waited. Whatever it was, for him to behave this way was a bad sign.

Finally, he looked up.

"What are you doing here?" he said, acting as if he didn't know.

I thought I'd lighten the mood. "I figured you wanted someone to have a cup of coffee with." I smiled, he didn't.

"Grab your camera and get a picture, 'cause this is it. I don't want to do this anymore." He went back to eating his breakfast.

That surprised me. The shows were going well. There was a lot at stake, in the many millions of dollars, and since I managed both of them it was a direct hit on me as well. "Wait a minute," I said. "What are you talking about? After this we have a break. There's plenty of time to figure out who can replace Dean before we continue on the tour to Europe."

"Who are you going to get? Vic Damone?"

"No." I started to list off some names of older male singers.

"There's no male singer who can fill in on this gig. It's over," he said. He went back to reading the newspaper. I knew I couldn't let him shut this down. I had to keep the conversation going. My head was spinning. There was one other solution that I hadn't shared with him, but it was a very long shot.

A few days after Dean dropped out, I had called Liza to feel her out about joining the tour. When she picked up the phone she said, "No." I hadn't even asked the question but she knew it was coming. I asked why.

"Fred Ebb said it would ruin my film career. Gene thinks I should be a rock star. A rock star can't be performing with Frank and Sammy."

"Gene?" I said.

"Gene Simmons."

"From KISS?"

"Yes."

I expected her to consult with Fred Ebb, as usual. But Gene Simmons, the long-tongued, makeup-clad lead singer of KISS, known as the Demon? That made no sense to me. I knew they were friends, but I hadn't realized she was taking career advice from him. Had he really convinced her that a rock band was in her future? Gene Simmons was now obviously among the latest influencers in Liza's life, and Liza could be easily influenced.

"After all you've done, all you've accomplished, at the age of forty-two you're going to be a rock star?" I said. It seemed absurd, but she seemed convinced.

So, while I knew Liza had no intention of being a part of this tour, I needed something to keep the Boss from pulling the plug.

"Maybe there's no male singer, but what about a female singer?" I said.

He looked up.

"What about Liza?" I said. We both knew Liza's energy filled venues all the way to the cheap seats. She was a tour de force and would add a whole other dimension to the show.

He took his glasses off, pointed his finger at me, and said, "If you get Liza, you've got a deal."

I left his suite and started to sweat. It was just after noon. I went to the bar at the Waldorf and had a Bloody Mary and thought about how I would handle this. I happened to have a meeting scheduled with Liza to go over her bookings that afternoon. It was now or never.

Liza's apartment in the Imperial House, on Manhattan's Upper East Side, had the four-paneled Andy Warhol portrait of Liza in the entranceway, which always reminded me of just how iconic her face was.

Liza had other Warhols in her apartment, including one of her mother, Judy Garland, and her stage and film director father, Vincente Minnelli, who was responsible for such greats as *An American in Paris* and *Gigi*. Show business was in her blood. Liza was a great actress. She was nominated for an Oscar in 1970 for *The Sterile Cuckoo* and won an Oscar in 1973 for *Cabaret*. She had amazing performances in *New York, New York, Arthur,* and many other films. I knew she could act, but the audience always knew it was Liza who thrived on live performance. She was not a chameleon. She had one of the most distinctive faces in show business: dark, doe eyes with the impossibly long eyelashes, enormous smile and the dramatic short, fringed hairdo. She couldn't or didn't hide her face in a character.

We reviewed her booking schedule, but I bided my time and didn't say a word about the tour. As I was leaving, I finally addressed it. "As your personal manager I would be remiss if I didn't tell you that by not joining Sinatra's tour you are leaving four to five million dollars on the table." I figured the best way to convince her was to quantify it. The money would speak for itself.

She looked up at me with those eyes, as the reality settled in.

"Where do I sign?" she said. She smiled and I felt a huge weight lift off my shoulders.

There was no time to waste. It was Saturday afternoon, and Monday was a day off, which was an opportunity. Before I left the lobby of her building I called our publicity firm in Los Angeles and told them to fly our photographer to New York to shoot promotional material for Frank, Liza, and Sammy on Monday.

When I told Frank and a very happy Sammy that Liza was on the team, someone said, "Now that's the ultimate event."

TWENTY-FOUR

There was something special about the promotional photo for the Ultimate Event; Liza in a sexy, black, very short negligée-style dress, her right hand holding Sammy's while her left arm was wrapped around Sinatra's tuxedoed arm, his hand over hers. They were a team, they were friends, and, it was obvious, they were stars.

We were sold out everywhere we went, breaking box-office records in the United States, Japan, Australia, and Europe. Sinatra liked the name but was sure someone in the press would take a shot at us for having the nerve to call it the ultimate anything.

"Since when are you afraid of what the press would say?" I said. That was the end of the discussion and no one ever questioned the title again.

Sinatra kept everyone on their toes, and for the most part, he was on top of his game. Since he never did sound checks or rehearsals, he thought it was odd that Liza and Sammy spent so much time going over each note, movement, and section of dialogue.

"What do they need rehearsals for?" he'd say. "Don't they know the words?"

To Sinatra, it was just *him* going out there on that stage and he didn't need to practice being himself.

In the Frank, Dean, and Sammy tour, Sinatra took 50 percent of the box-office net and Sammy and Dean each were paid 25 percent. He had a special affinity for Liza and her talent that I believe was at least partially because of her mother. So, when it came time to bring Liza on board, Sammy retained his 25 percent and Frank split the balance with Liza. Frank and Liza each received 37½ percent, making her an equal partner. Still, Sinatra was unquestionably the Boss and everyone marched to his drumbeat.

Liza and Sammy stuck together and leaned on each other. Sammy was always the first onstage. Often Liza waited in the wings, talking with him, until it was time to go out.

"Is he getting instructions?" Sinatra would say.

If the front row of a venue wasn't full, I would plead for ten more minutes and negotiate down to five. I didn't want any performer to go onstage and see empty seats. Sometimes it would work and sometimes it didn't.

We were filming the concert the night of the reopening of the Fox Theatre in Detroit. The house wasn't full at eight o'clock.

Sinatra was standing backstage. He looked at his watch.

"It's two minutes after eight. I want a downbeat at eight-oh-five." Sinatra said.

"Frank, we need the front row full," Sammy said.

I agreed, we needed to wait.

Sinatra blew up. "It's showtime," he bellowed. His voice was like a hurricane that blew in and pushed everyone into place. Liza flew up the stairs to her dressing room, her long, limber legs taking two stairs at a time. Sammy hustled out onstage. We all laughed about it later. Everyone knew the impact of a Sinatra command, especially Sinatra, and we all happily obliged. The clock was always ticking.

In the middle of one show, Sinatra was onstage when he stopped and turned to the conductor, Frank Jr.

"I'm just waiting for a downbeat, not a bus." He turned back to the audience and then glanced over his shoulder. "Where you working tomorrow?" he said.

The audience laughed.

"I can say that joke to him because he's my son. Take a bow, Frankie."

Junior made a comical, fearful face and the audience laughed harder. That was Sinatra's way of acknowledging his son's good work. It was an "I'm proud of you," Sinatra style.

Sinatra was not the kind of star to demand the green jelly beans be removed from the bowl, but he did expect everyone to be on time, always. When he thought the group was moving too slow, he had tour jackets made that said "Hurry Up & Wait."

He sometimes took punctuality to the extreme. If you were on his plane and didn't play by the rules, you could expect to be left behind. He threatened to take off anytime someone was late. And it didn't matter who it was. Once, he left without Elizabeth Taylor, when her then fiancé, Dennis Stein, couldn't coax her out of the bathtub. When he was performing with Pia Zadora, he almost made the helicopter take off without her husband, Meshulam Riklis, on board, because Meshulam was late.

"Next time we take off without you," Sinatra said.

The only problem was, it was Meshulam's helicopter.

I remember in the early years of my touring with Sinatra, he made Red Buttons cut his opening act short in Seattle because the show was booked for eight thirty rather than eight o'clock, and between flying and car time, he would miss his self-imposed curfew to be back in Palm Springs. He was adamant about being home before midnight. So I gave all the officers in our police escort hundred-dollar bills to expedite our ride to the airport.

Red, a red-haired former Borscht Belt comedian and actor who went back decades with Sinatra, wanted to be on the Sinatra plane but was a slow mover. Part of my job was to manage everyone's movements to ensure the entourage was on time. Rudin was still working with Sinatra at that point and all three of us had boarded. Only Buttons was missing. So I went to his limo and opened the door. He was completely passed out, probably from the fear of the limo driving so fast.

"Red, you better wake up. We're leaving."

He hurried onto the plane and sat in the front. Sinatra, Rudin, and I were seated in the back.

Halfway through the flight, Buttons wandered to the back of the plane. There was an open seat next to Sinatra but I knew Sinatra would be annoyed by his company after he held us up, so I motioned to Buttons to sit on the couch opposite our seat configuration. Red didn't say anything at first. Then Johnny Spots came on the microphone.

"We are flying over Los Angeles and will be in Palm Springs in fifteen minutes."

"What do you mean we're flying over L.A.?" Buttons said. "That's my stop."

This was just not the kind of thing you said in front of Sinatra.

"It's his ball and bat," Rudin said, gesturing to Sinatra. "L.A. is the second stop."

Sinatra said nothing, but made eye contact with me. I knew to follow him off the plane. At the bottom of the stairs he said, "Get rid of him."

I fired Buttons and hired someone else. Buttons immediately called Sinatra and apologized. Sinatra felt bad and told me to hire him back, but Buttons never flew with us again.

You just didn't mess with Sinatra's time. Life was ticking by.

Liza and Sammy had their own plane, which simplified things on the Ultimate Event tour.

Sammy was a brilliant entertainer. I've never seen anyone who could do what Sammy could. He was a graceful and talented dancer, played virtually every instrument in the band, had a distinctive voice, did impersonations, and his crooked smile and jutting jaw made him one of the most impersonated people in show business. His heart was in every note and he was happy to be working with his old pal. You could see his admiration and appreciation for Frank every time he looked at him.

When Liza was "on" she was glorious. Her eyes were hypnotic, her energy unparalleled. Her body flowed with exaggerated movements and it was impossible to watch her and not smile.

Every night we had a "New York, New York" medley. Sinatra would go on to sing that song for years. When he sang it alone he always said "Written by Fred Ebb for Liza and stolen by me."

That was the funny thing about Sinatra. He was tough and unrelenting and at the same time as gracious a performer as anyone I've ever seen. He always gave credit where credit was due.

He was loved, feared, and admired by people who knew him. He was hated by some as well. He was temperamental, unpredictable, generous, loving, passionate, and the best friend anyone could have.

I saw more than one powerful person become weak in the knees around Sinatra. Brilliant, erudite people; politicians, captains of industry, and even celebrities were in awe of him and would suddenly stammer or hem and haw. Oddly, other performers often were the most nervous around Sinatra. For all the years they had known each other, Liza was not completely comfortable around him when they weren't onstage. His persona was that imposing. I don't know if I will ever completely understand it. But I do believe he was truly fearless and knew exactly who he was. He also knew his power, he used it, and it was part of who he was both onstage and off. A large part of his enduring talent was authenticity—in lyrical interpretation and in life.

We toured Japan and then Australia. Convincing him to go to Australia was a big move, but getting him out of Australia was what I was worried about.

The last time he was there was 1974 and the country had held him hostage. He later famously quipped, "A funny thing happened in Australia. I made one mistake. I got off the plane." Although I wasn't yet working with him, from what I heard, the Australian media relentlessly hounded him for interviews, which he declined. The fact that there was virtually no security to escort him into the concert venue meant the media had easy access to him and he was pissed. To make matters worse, a newspaper ran photos of some of Sinatra's female friends and used the headline SINATRA'S MOLLS.

He was frustrated and infuriated and when he took the stage he went into a rant, calling the press "hookers" and "bums."

In particular, the hooker comment offended members of the trade unions, who said the remark was an attack on "Australian womanhood." They demanded an apology and when it didn't happen, airport staff refused to refuel his private plane and the hotel workers refused to serve his party. From Melbourne to Sydney, he was being held hostage.

Australia attacked Sinatra's women friends, Sinatra attacked back, and Australian unions would not let him leave. Finally, it took a meeting with the president of the trade unions to come to a compromise agreement. No apology, but Sinatra expressed regret at the incident. It took three days to sort out the mess.

Now, fifteen years later, the press was going wild with speculation as to whether Sinatra would be a no-show.

I spoke to every promoter involved in his concerts to make sure they individually and collectively knew that there would be no problem as far as we were concerned and that they needed to assure us that there would be no problems on their end.

"I want you to check in with your government and make sure there are no residual hard feelings," I said. "We are coming to do a concert and we expect to be welcomed."

They all assured me we would be, while I made sure we had special security arrangements.

If the Australian press anticipated an international uproar, there was none. Australia loved and welcomed him and the shows went off without a hitch.

The international incident came later, in Scandinavia, thanks to a little dog that made a big impact. Liza traveled everywhere with Lilly, her little terrier, until Sweden deported her—Lilly that is.

The Swedes have quarantine laws regarding new dogs coming into the country. Liza flew in privately and snuck Lilly past the customs officials, but she didn't sneak Lilly past the press. When customs saw the dog in the papers, they sent an officer to investigate. Dressed in plain clothes and flashing a badge, he was looking for Liza and ended up in my suite at the Grand Hotel. We sat down in the living room.

"We must quarantine the dog for thirty days," he said. My stomach dropped. That could not happen.

"Let's not create an international problem," I said. I wanted to avoid involving the Boss. He was a dog lover and I knew this would anger him and he would cancel the show and leave the country.

"We just need a few days. I really don't want to disturb Mr. Sinatra with this. You never know what his reaction might be," I said.

He was polite but held firm as he matter-of-factly explained the law. The negotiation went on for close to an hour. In the end, I had twelve hours to ship the dog out of Sweden. We paid a small fine but the big expense was having one of the planes fly Lilly to Paris, where local law welcomed dogs.

The Swedes considered this little dog such a big threat that a newspaper reported customs agents spent the night in the hallway outside Liza's room to make sure Lilly never left the premises until it was time for one of Liza's friends to take the dog to the airport.

"Do me a favor, Liza. Whatever you do, do not tell the Boss about all this. He'll be furious. Let's not have another headache before we leave Scandinavia."

She was upset by the whole thing but agreed. I thought the matter was over. I was wrong. That night we went to dinner at one of the hotel restaurants. Jilly was with us. Sinatra was drinking martinis, and I was enjoying a vodka on the rocks. When Liza arrived, she sat at the table and the first words out of her mouth, uttered in her most vulnerable voice, were, "Uncle Frank, you can't imagine what they did with my dog today."

I couldn't believe it. I braced myself. She told the story and I felt Sinatra's eyes on me.

"Why didn't you tell me, Eliot?" he demanded.

I played it cool. "It's over," I said. "I took care of it. I didn't think you needed to be bothered."

"I want to know about *all* the problems," he said. "Where's the dog?"

"Having dinner at the Ritz in Paris," I said.

"Waiter, bring me a gin martini, please," Sinatra said.

Oh, no. That was a bad sign. Jack Daniel's, vodka, anything was fine, but not gin. Sinatra couldn't hold his gin at all. In the past, I'd seen it transform him. He grew mean and belligerent and could be very tough on people. He became combative on gin and that was never any fun. Jilly and I looked at each other. Jilly could calm Sinatra down better than anyone, but when he was really agitated, no one could.

After dinner we went to the piano bar in the hotel. The player was singing terribly out of tune. He was grating on everyone. One drink later Sinatra said, "Give the piano player five hundred bucks and tell him to go home."

"Boss, I can't do that. He'll be insulted. You don't want to hurt the guy's feelings."

"He's terrible," Sinatra said, ordering another drink.

Jilly went and quietly told the bartender to switch back to vodka. The combination of the alcohol, medication, and the rigorous travel schedule, though, was too much. Sinatra was less angry than he was disoriented.

At one point he went into the men's room and thought he was in his own suite. Sinatra turned to Jilly, pointing to another man.

"Get this guy out of my bathroom," he said.

Jilly convinced the stranger to wait until Sinatra was finished. The man graciously obliged. Afterward, we took Sinatra to his room and called it a night.

Despite his Rat Pack reputation, it was rare for Sinatra to drink too much. Don't misunderstand, he drank a lot of Jack Daniel's, I just rarely saw him intoxicated.

We did five shows in Scandinavia and our last stop was Finland. Barbara wasn't traveling with us this trip so he asked me to join him alone for drinks. He had a bottle of Jack and a bottle of vodka in his room. He poured some JD for himself and vodka for me.

We sat on the balcony to watch the sunset over Helsinki. It was springtime and the days were growing longer, so it was still fairly light out. I was already a little tipsy as Sinatra poured us another drink.

He was breaking his cardinal rule of one ounce of alcohol per hour. He was very disciplined when he wanted to be, and that's how he usually stayed sober. I wasn't sure whether this was good or bad. It was rare for us to be alone together, without the entourage and without Barbara. There was so much I wanted to say to him, things I needed to get off my chest. What I didn't know was that he felt the same way.

"So whatever happened at the theater?" Sinatra said.

I did not see that coming. It had been thirteen years since Sinatra flashed a smile with mobsters at the Westchester Premier Theatre and I ended up in hot water. I thought he'd forgotten about the photo and everything that happened after. I certainly had tried to. It was a real question that demanded a real answer.

"Where do you want me to start?" I said.

"Anywhere you want."

I told him about how Westchester went terribly wrong with delays and cost overruns and how I should have put it into bankruptcy before it ever opened. We talked briefly about how the feds wanted to bag a famous name and kept asking me about him and Rudin. That was old news to Sinatra.

I knew Sinatra appreciated my not dragging his famous name into an investigation just to make authorities happy and maybe help my case. But I really had no idea if he knew about all the work I had done for him over the years.

"I was always grateful to Mickey for letting me handle your bookings from jail," I said.

"What do you mean, handle my bookings?" he said.

As we spoke, it became clear that he didn't know about all the arrangements I'd been making. Sonny Golden told him I was booking him, back before he and Rudin split a couple of years earlier, but he didn't seem to fully understand. He thought I was just a good road manager.

"You mean to tell me all the paperwork, the bookings and projections, that was all you?"

"Yes, even before I went away. Truthfully, I needed the work. Rudin was good to me. He lent me twenty-five thousand when I needed it."

He was outraged that Mickey never told him my family was in trouble when I went away.

"I paid back every dime, with interest," I said.

I could see his face flush red with anger. "You what? Why didn't you tell me all this?" he said.

"That's not where I come from," I said. "I'm sure Mickey didn't want to drag you into my mess back then."

"Maybe, but what about before and after you went away? I had no idea the work on his letterhead was being done by you," Sinatra said.

"Boss, that was years ago. I tried to keep you and Mickey together. I even offered to go to Palm Springs and help repair the situation. You were a very successful team and I didn't think that should end. He said absolutely not."

I explained that Rudin had told me his professional career would be better without him and it would give Mickey more time to acquire some new, bigger clients. During the course of the conversation, I mentioned how I was never paid for the economically disastrous 1987 Italian tour. He shook his head, picked up the phone, and called Sonny Golden.

"Sonny, I want you to send Eliot a hundred thousand dollars. Work out the details," he said, handing me the phone. He went to the bathroom.

I told Golden, "Forget it, Sonny. Don't waste your time. I won't cash it. It's a privilege for me to be with this man. He pays me enough."

Now that Sinatra knew the whole story, it was all water under the bridge and I was happy to be sailing on Sinatra's ship.

After I hung up the phone, I realized the world had changed in that moment. I had spent so much time wondering about what Sinatra knew and didn't know. It was a tremendous relief to have him finally know the truth about all my efforts. *We separated the shit from the buckwheat.*

I knew Sinatra appreciated that I never went to him complaining. He had a new level of trust and respect for me after that conversation, and he would soon come to prove it in many ways.

TWENTY-FIVE

The top floors of the Waldorf-Astoria are known as the Waldorf Towers. When the Waldorf Towers were your home away from home, New York took on a unique perspective. It was powerful to stand on the parquet floor at the edge of an Aubusson rug, looking through the sky-high windows at a vast and bustling city below. Over the years, the Towers have hosted presidents, royalty, heads of state, Cole Porter, and of course, "the Chairman of the Board," Frank Sinatra.

Sinatra had a regular and very luxurious suite there. At one point he owned an apartment at the Towers. After he sold it, and depending on availability, he booked one of several suites that had similar floor plans. While we were in New York on tour, the Waldorf was our private enclave in the heart of midtown Manhattan. We would take most of the floor in the Towers and have private security stationed in the hallway.

The Waldorf is located on Park Avenue between Forty-Ninth and Fiftieth Streets, but the Towers had more than one private entrance with a white-gloved doorman. A walk out the back door put you on Lexington Avenue right across the street from what at the time was Rocco Maselli's jewelry store. Sinatra used to call it the "candy store."

Rocco was a soft-spoken, distinguished-looking Italian man with gray hair, a round face, and eyes that smiled when he laughed. He was among the most honest and personable people I've known. If we weren't in the hotel suites working, we were probably hanging out having coffee with Rocco.

His jewelry store was a happening in its own right and you never knew whose famous face you might run into there. Everyone from Robert De Niro to Burt Reynolds, Billy Martin, Lauren Bacall, and even former vice president Spiro Agnew shopped there. Sinatra, Liza, Sammy, and I all shopped there as well.

Sammy loved big, diamond-encrusted jewelry. He is the only person I ever knew who could put on the gaudiest necklace, ring, or bracelet and outsparkle it with his personality. Sammy was five feet five with not an ounce of fat on him. He wasn't much bigger than some of the oversize Louis Vuitton trunks he collected, yet he would put on an enormous piece of jewelry and Sammy would still be the first thing you saw. He was that special.

Sinatra stuck to buying jewelry for Barbara, family, and friends. Frank would call Rocco when we were in town if he needed a gift for someone and then send Jilly to pick it up.

Rocco's jewelry store was part of Jilly's New York routine. Of all the people who could have taken advantage of Sinatra financially, Rocco certainly could have done it easily, but it wasn't in his nature. He was a very honest jeweler, and as far as I could tell, charged Sinatra fair market value for the pieces.

Sinatra enjoyed giving jewelry to Barbara almost as much as she loved wearing it. She was a gracious and elegant woman, always beautifully dressed and well put together.

Maria and I were still relative newlyweds when Barbara took Maria under her wing and taught her a few things about shopping Sinatra-style.

One afternoon, Barbara invited Maria, Liza, Sammy's wife, Altovise, and a few other friends to her suite for a jewelry party. Barbara had a box full of Rocco's rocks but she also had a few jewelers of her own in her Rolodex, who were more than happy to set up shop in her suite.

"Go," I said to Maria. "You'll have fun. Barbara has a black belt in shopping."

This was Maria's first real introduction to power shopping. The expertly polished, Chippendale-style dining room table was covered in jewelry; rubies, diamonds, emeralds, sapphires, and pretty much anything else you could imagine. As they perused the jewelry, Barbara examined a few pieces and put them to the side. Later, she handed Maria one of them, a very large cabochon emerald ring, set in heavy yellow gold with diamonds.

"Here, I picked this out for you," Barbara said.

Maria placed the ring on her finger. "Wow," she said. "It's beautiful and heavy." Barbara smiled, then put matching earrings into her other hand.

"Here, go show these to Eliot. They are fabulous," Barbara said.

Maria hurried down the hall, past our security, clutching a bag of jewelry, to our room, but not before Barbara called.

"Eliot, I found something Maria has to have," she said matter-of-factly.

I was still in my pajamas when Maria walked in with the goods.

"Gorgeous. How much?" I said. It sounded reasonable. "Buy it."

Maria was a little surprised but happy. The more she spent time around Barbara, the more that kind of shopping became old hat. She considered herself in training and was having fun with it.

Shopping in Paris and London was always a treat for them. In Paris we were usually based at the Ritz or the Plaza Athénée and in London our home away from home was the Savoy. Tours were tiring. There were so many people, bags, and security steps to go through.

Being exhausted or sick was no excuse to refrain from shopping in a city like Paris, though, and I've been told it can actually cure you. Barbara taught Maria that if you weren't feeling well, all you had to do was lay beneath the damask draping of the Louis XVI bed, with a *French Vogue* and tissue box in hand, and make phone calls. The bellman for our floor would magically appear with bags from famous French labels like Chanel, Dior, Lanvin, and Yves Saint Laurent. It worked in London, too.

Sinatra liked nice things. He was always personally well dressed and he wanted his wife to have the best, and he saw his concerts as the way to fund it all. If Barbara wanted something really big, say a very important piece of jewelry that could cost tens or even hundreds of thousands of dollars, in his mind that was a concert. He didn't think about the taxes to pay or any of the details; he just thought about the cost and the pay he would receive for the concert.

In *Lady Blue Eyes,* Barbara wrote that Sinatra surprised her in Monte Carlo with a jaw-dropping emerald and diamond necklace that had been made for Lady Cartier. It was the talk of Monte Carlo. Maria and I were not there but we both remember that necklace. The first time we saw it, Maria said, "Holy shit." Apparently she wasn't the first or the only one to have that reaction. It became known as the "holy shit" necklace.

I could understand how Rudin thought Barbara had accumulated enough wealth in jewelry and didn't need any of Frank's money. I just didn't think it was a fair distribution of wealth for a woman who was completely devoted to Frank. Which is why I tried to look out for her interests as best I could.

Barbara wasn't the only recipient of Sinatra's generosity. It extended to everyone he cared for. Toward the end of the Ultimate Event tour, for instance, Rocco handed me a red Cartier box.

"It's from Frank," Rocco said. "He wants you to have it."

Sinatra was very thoughtful about gifts, but it wasn't often that he gave gifts in person. He didn't want to wait and watch you open it. He knew I collected watches and lighters. The box was too big to be a lighter. I have to say I was pretty excited. Inside the classic red box with gold scrolling was a yellow gold Cartier Pasha moon phase watch, a feature that allowed the wearer to track time through the phases of the moon.

"So what's with the moon phase?" I said. "If the hands break am I supposed to instruct the orchestra to hit the downbeat by the phase of the moon?"

We laughed.

"Look at the back," Rocco said.

There was an engraving. "Good Job Eliot, Love FAS. 3/88."

I was deeply touched. Later that night we were all meeting for cocktails before dinner.

"Thanks, Boss," I said, showing it to him on my wrist. "The watch is really beautiful. I was really surprised."

"You deserve it," he said. "This wouldn't have happened without you."

It remains the favorite watch in my collection.

TWENTY-SIX

S inatra's beloved Palm Springs compound was originally a single-story, two-bedroom house on the seventeenth fairway of the new Tamarisk Country Club. In the 1950s, Palm Springs was a sleepy desert community that was about to become a hotspot for jet-setters and celebrities, thanks in large part to Sinatra's influence.

The two-and-a-half-acre property gradually expanded into a compound of multiple buildings. As the house grew, so did the roster of A-list celebrity guests. Yul Brynner, Rosalind Russell, Ronald and Nancy Reagan, Liz Taylor, and Richard Burton were just a few of the legendary stars who filled the guest bedrooms and drank champagne poolside, under fringed umbrellas and lavender desert sunsets. Oh, to have been a fly on the wall for those parties in the heydays of Hollywood glamour.

It was in Palm Springs that Sinatra met the neighbor across the seventeenth fairway, Barbara Marx, and formed a blossoming friendship. After she became his fourth wife, they lived together in that house until 1995. It was where Sinatra was most comfortable.

The main house was named after the Sinatra recording "The House I Live In." It was decorated in wood, stone, Sinatra's own paintings, and what he called the "happiest color," orange, combined with beiges and off-whites. It was cozy. He often ate breakfast by himself at the backgammon table.

There was a guesthouse originally designed to be the "Western White House" for his pal President Jack Kennedy. It was equipped with all the electronics necessary to convert it into a place the president could conduct business from, within forty-eight hours. President Kennedy never spent a night in the guesthouse, though he did stay in a guest room on the property, as a young senator.

There were also four bungalows, a movie theater named "Send in the Clowns," an art studio, a helicopter pad that was turned into a flower garden, and a tennis court. The houses were furnished with photographs of Sinatra's famous friends, including portraits of Ronald Reagan and Nat King Cole. He had an extensive and valuable art collection but his own art was often the focal point for his friends.

There was a brown train caboose called "Chicago," which housed a barbershop with orange walls, a massage table, and a sauna. My favorite spot was right next door, the train house. The walls were lined with shelves that held Frank's model train collection and the center of the room had a large table with his working layout and track plan. It included a miniature replica of Hoboken, his hometown.

Sinatra and I shared a passion for train collecting ever since we were kids. I would often find trains for both of us in hobby shops across America as we toured the country. I had my own train room in Florida and we shared numerous discussions about finding the best foliage, blinking lights, and buildings to complement our train layouts.

Palm Springs was also home to the Frank Sinatra Celebrity Invitational golf tournament, supporting the Barbara Sinatra Center for Abused Children. Sinatra did numerous charity benefits and raised millions of dollars for cancer research for Memorial Sloan Kettering Cancer Center. When Barbara started the Barbara Sinatra Center in 1986, it quickly grew into a world-class facility and became

Sinatra loved to decompress during our late-night dinners after the show.

One of the perks of running the theater was meeting the talented and the beautiful, such as Elizabeth Taylor.

Willie Mays, Frank Sinatra, Greg DePalma, and Jilly Rizzo during the heyday of the Westchester Premier Theatre in the mid-1970s. Little did I know that DePalma and his mob connections would bring the business to its knees.

All photos © Eliot Weisman unless noted

Frank Sinatra, Dean _____n, Greg DePalma, and Richie Fusco enjoying an afternoon of golf. Fusco also ha_ _mob connections an_ _uld be indicted along with DePalma when the feds came calling.

The infamous photo that caused an uproar—April 11, 1976. Despite my protests, Sinatra released the photo and it led us down a path that would ultimately put me in prison. At least I had the good sense not to be there that night. From left to right: Paul Castellano, Greg DePalma, Frank Sinatra, Tommy Marson, Carlo Gambino, Aladena Fratianno, Salvatore Spatola, Seated: Joseph Gambino, Richard Fusco.

The heart of the Rat Pack rehearses at Sammy Davis Jr.'s home. It was a great joy to reunite them on tour, though to Sinatra's disappointment Dean's heart was not in it, and they couldn't recapture their old magic.

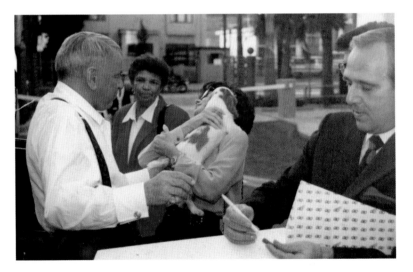

I'm helping Sinatra as he signs autographs. In the red jacket is Sinatra's longtime and indispensable personal assistant, Elvina Joubert, or "Vine." She was my accomplice many times in managing Sinatra over the years. Next to her is Tina Sinatra, holding her father's King Charles Spaniel puppy.

Touring Ireland in 1989 with Sammy and Liza, my wife, Maria, threw me an uproarious birthday party at a local Irish pub. Sinatra wore the green carnation all night long and laughed so hard he cried. "An Irish celebration for Eliot's birthday."

After the unorthodox party, Sinatra gifted me a rather unorthodox card, a signed bodhran.

Rizzo was Sinatra's longtime friend, confidant, and bodyguard. He grew up on the mean streets of the Lower East Side of Manhattan and knew how to take care of himself—and Sinatra. The eagle emblem pendant was his favorite piece of jewelry.

Maria joined Liza in meeting Pope John Paul II with Pier Quinto Cariaggi, the Italian promoter who arranged the visit. I'm not sure if this photo was taken before or after the pope said to Liza, "I heard you have been married many times."

Near the end of the Ultimate Event tour, Sinatra gave me a gift, a Cartier watch with the engraving "Good job Eliot, Love F.A.S. 3/88." Sinatra was always thoughtful and generous with his gifts, though he didn't want to wait and watch you open them.

Lévon Sayan was a major European promoter, who managed Charles Aznavour and whom I worked with over the years with our talent, and he became a good friend.

Ben Vereen, my son David, and me backstage in 2002 at the Booth Theatre in New York City.

On the road with Hank Cattaneo and Jilly. Cattaneo was Sinatra's longtime concert production manager. Sinatra put his faith in him night after night onstage for more than a decade.

Maria and me with Eydie Gormé and Steve Lawrence, with whom we shared the best and the worst of times.

Judy Tannen, who for decades was Steve and Eydie's personal assistant and confidant.

Sinatra was not big on hugs, especially from fans. When my mother-in-law was carried away by the moment and hugged him like a bobbysoxer, I was mortified. Sinatra playfully hugged me later, saying, "See how you like it."

Don Rickles was the greatest disappointment of all my clients, despite all the good work we'd done together.

A tour jacket with a classic Sinatra saying. He was not a patient man while on tour. The clock was always ticking.

Having a drink with Sinatra was a genuine pleasure in life. He could ring-a-ding-ding with the best of them, even in his waning years.

Maria introducing our son, David, to the Boss and Barbara at their Beverly Hills home.

The Boss and me, 1995.

a focus of their philanthropy. Sinatra even posed with Barbara, tugging at a string of pearls, for Revlon's "Most Unforgettable Women in the World" ad campaign. Their friend Dennis Stein arranged it to benefit Barbara's charity.

The Celebrity Invitational was entirely Barbara's doing and Frank was more than willing to help raise funds for the victims of emotional, physical, and sexual abuse. For Frank and Barbara it was clearly a heartfelt and personal cause. For me it was an opportunity to relax over a long weekend in Palm Springs with Maria and play my favorite game with friends. All the Sinatras' closest friends were there. Greg and Veronique Peck, Robert (R.J.) Wagner and Jill St. John, producer George Schlatter and his wife, Jolene, were among the regulars. Every year, celebrities like Clint Eastwood and astronaut Alan Shepard would be invited to play.

The first time we entered the gates of the compound, we knew we were in for a fabulous weekend. It was clear that both Barbara and Frank had put an enormous amount of work into making sure every detail was taken care of. A golf cart met us at the entrance, driven by one of their perfectly dressed staff members, who took us through a pathway of sand, gravel, desert plants, and flowers.

The staff took our luggage to what would have been the "Western White House," though no one ever referred to it that way in front of Frank (more on that later). We knew it as just the guesthouse, and the other cottages were referred to as the bungalows. It had multiple bedrooms, a living room, kitchen, and pool.

"There's bottled water in the refrigerator and at your bedside, along with some chocolates," the butler said. "Breakfast will be served here for you prior to your tee time as well as a bit later, in case Mrs. Weisman would like to sleep in," he said.

"Thank you," Maria said.

"Breakfast will also be served in the main house and all the bungalows. The kitchen is staffed twenty-four hours a day in case there is anything you desire after hours. The chef is always happy to prepare something for our guests. May I unpack your bags?"

There were candles burning throughout the guesthouse. The bathrooms were furnished better than some of the best hotels, with toothbrushes, robes, hair spray, and any toiletry item you could ask for.

"Please just ask, if there is something else you need," the butler said. "We have pretty much everything."

This main guesthouse accommodated multiple couples, and the first time Maria rolled out of the shower in her robe and wet hair and ventured into the living room looking for coffee, she ran into someone waiting for his tee time. His head was buried in the newspaper.

"Do you know where the coffee is?" she said.

"Over there," he pointed. When she heard the voice she realized it was Clint Eastwood.

Friends who stayed at the compound called Sinatra the "Inn Keeper" because *everything* was taken care of.

While the golfers were out on the course, the nongolfers, mostly women, relaxed poolside, walked through the beautiful grounds, or took one of the available cars into town. A manicurist and hairdresser were available, too.

An elaborate and elegant lunch buffet was served on the tennis court.

Eventually, all the guests would meet at the best bar in town— their own.

There were usually fourteen to twenty people staying at the Sinatras' home for the tournament. There were rolling chairs around a low bar, in the den. It looked like a scene out of a 1960s film. The bartender always made the Boss's drink as soon as he arrived, Jack with just the right amount of ice, three or four cubes, depending on the glass. Across from the bar was the cage where Rocky, the crazy green parrot, lived.

Sinatra loved animals. In fact, there were several dogs and cats in residence, some rescued from the local pound. Rocky, though, was the exception. Rocky seemed to feel the same way about Sinatra. Sinatra would walk by the bird cage and say, "Fuck you."

Rocky would respond with a "Fuck you" of his own. When he squawked, Sinatra would say, "I'm going to put cement shoes on you and throw you in the pool."

One day Barbara was walking around with Rocky on her shoulder.

"Here, darling, let me put him on your shoulder for a few minutes."

She gently placed the parrot on Sinatra's shoulder.

"One wrong move and you're dead," Sinatra said to the parrot.

With that, Rocky took a bite out of Sinatra's ear and blood gushed out. Barbara quickly removed the bird. It's amazing Rocky survived all those years.

I'm pretty sure they didn't dare take him out of the cage when guests were around for the tournament. From what I understand, pretty much everyone who didn't stay clear of Rocky was bitten. I stayed clear.

Barbara's dinners were the highlight after a long day on the golf course for those who were staying at the compound. She seated everyone next to someone different every night for a family-style dinner of pot roast, pasta, meatballs, sausage, filet mignon, and veal scaloppini. It was always served by the staff. After the lavish dessert display, Roland the oversize chef emerged with a huge and grateful smile, to a round of applause. There was a black-tie gala at a local hotel and a separate, private after party in a tent, complete with chandeliers, set up on the Sinatras' tennis court. Sinatra was always the last to go to sleep and eventually we would break into small groups and relax.

I can only imagine the many personal things that people told Sinatra in the wee small hours of the morning, on nights like that in the quiet desert, drink in hand. People always seemed to want to tell him things, to confess their souls. It was as if he had a magic wand and telling Sinatra a painful story or one of regret made it all okay. It was a way of building camaraderie, I suppose, and he could be a surprisingly good listener.

One beautifully clear night, he and I sat at a table outside the main house. Astronaut Alan Shepard was there, along with a couple of other guys. There's nothing quite like the sight of the night sky in the desert. It seems so high and vast. The stars were bright and a full moon lit up the compound.

Alan was the first American in space in 1961 when he soloed on the Mercury spacecraft. He was also the commander of the Apollo 14 mission to the moon, with Stuart Roosa and Edgar Mitchell. Roosa stayed in orbit around the moon while Shepard and Mitchell landed. I remember vividly their trip to Fra Mauro on the lunar surface on February 15, 1971. It was the third moon landing. They did two moonwalks, collected rock samples, and Shepard hit two golf balls to show how far they would go in the moon's weaker gravity. I had admired the man most of my life. I will never forget President Kennedy starting it all by saying in 1962, "We choose to go to the moon in this decade and do the other things, not because they are easy, but because they are hard."

So here I was, under this magnificent moonlit sky, in a house that Kennedy slept in, with a man who actually achieved Kennedy's dream.

"So you really got there," Sinatra said to Shepard, pointing to the night sky. "Are those streetlights as bright as they seem to be from here?"

"The stars are brighter," Shepard said.

"How did you adjust after you came back from there?" someone said.

"I never did," Shepard said. "And that's why I turned into an alcoholic."

No one said a word.

Shepard died the same year as Sinatra.

Imagine all the ghosts that wander around Frank Sinatra Drive, in Rancho Mirage, Palm Springs, California.

TWENTY-SEVEN

One by one, the Rat Pack faded away. Their days of hard drinking and partying had taken their toll. Peter Lawford died at the age of sixty-one in 1984 of cardiac arrest complicated by kidney and liver failure, but he was dead to Sinatra two decades earlier. Lawford, a British actor, was a Kennedy brother-in-law, married to JFK's sister, Patricia.

Sinatra had built the opulent guesthouse at his Palm Springs compound for President Kennedy. Sinatra said Jack had told him it would be the Western White House if he were elected. Then Bobby Kennedy became attorney general and said Jack couldn't stay there. The president instead stayed at Bing Crosby's Palm Springs estate when he visited. Officially, it was deemed more secure because of its remote location, but unofficially, it was because Bobby didn't want his brother to be associated with Sinatra's perceived mob connections.

One night as Sinatra and I were having cocktails, the conversation turned to politics, and Sinatra told me how he'd been informed. Lawford, whom he called the "brother-in-Lawford," called him and said Jack wouldn't be coming to the compound.

"Are you listening carefully, Peter?" Sinatra said.

"Yes," Peter said.

Sinatra slammed down the phone.

I believe this was one of the most hurtful episodes of Sinatra's life, and it wasn't one that he spoke about often. When you were Sinatra's friend you were a friend for life, unless you crossed him.

From time to time Sinatra would talk about the guys from the old days—Willie Mays, Joe DiMaggio, Henry Kissinger, even Richard Nixon—but other than that one time, I never heard him speak President Kennedy's name.

Another Rat Pack member, Joey Bishop, was still alive, but they never spoke. I don't know what happened between him and Sinatra, but whatever it was, it must have been significant. When I asked him why he and Bishop didn't speak anymore, he laid those baby blue eyes on me.

"Don't ever ask me that question again," Sinatra said.

I never did.

After Dean left the tour, he and Sinatra never again hung out, to my knowledge, though they did occasionally see each other and speak.

So Sammy was the only member of the Rat Pack core who was still a part of Sinatra's life. Sammy held special meaning for me as a manager, as well. He was the first person I had ever seen perform live.

It was 1958 and Ron Glazer, my old college roommate, took me to the Latin Casino in Philadelphia. I had never been to a nightclub show before. Sammy sang, danced, played instruments, and never stopped moving. I couldn't believe it. He was incredible.

Years later, when Sammy asked me to represent him, I told him the story.

"You were the first live act I ever saw and the best act I ever saw," I said. He was very touched. I've still never seen a better entertainer.

For a while, Sinatra kept Sammy out of his life because Sammy had drug issues. Sinatra had seen a lot of very talented people fall apart because of drugs and he didn't want anyone with that problem near him, though, as I mentioned, he was more than happy to help them when in need. He and Sammy didn't speak for years, but now that Sammy was clean, Sinatra was very happy to be back on the road with his old pal. We had switched out our black satin tour jackets that said FRANK, DEAN & SAMMY in red lettering for the ones that read FRANK LIZA & SAMMY in big gold script, and never missed a beat.

Sammy was working hard to get himself out of debt. He was upbeat and on top of the world. Meanwhile, we were traveling the world, including several dates in Germany.

When I told the Boss, he said, "Only if we go piss on Hitler's grave." I laughed but I have no doubt he would have done it if I had ever taken him there.

Around this time it was clear that Sinatra was on the decline. He was having trouble reading the lyrics off the monitors, despite an increase in the size of the print and there were memory problems. It was very sporadic and I was convinced the antidepressant was contributing to his problems. I didn't know what to do. I watched him slipping, forgetting names and forgetting the lyrics. If you can't remember the lyrics to something you've been singing for forty years, there's a problem.

Once again, a doctor suggested he transition off Elavil and on to something else, but Barbara told me she was afraid of how he would react during the blackout period, so no change was made. I needed to devise some strategies to keep him strong onstage, but I didn't know how to pull a rabbit out of my hat.

Meanwhile, Sammy's personality sparkled onstage and one of the highlights of the night was his rendition of "The Music of the Night." Andrew Lloyd Webber's *Phantom of the Opera* was the hot show on Broadway, and Michael Crawford's rendition of "The Music of the Night" and its soft and building melody made it hugely popular, sung by men and women across the globe.

Sammy sung it with great power and emotion. He was well known for his renditions of "Candy Man," "Mr. Bojangles," and my personal favorite, "Birth of the Blues." "Music of the Night" was stylistically very different but it became his biggest number on the Ultimate Event tour.

The dressing rooms all had speakers in them so the performers could track the show's progress. Sammy was first onstage and "The Music of the Night" was his closing number. Sinatra would sit in his dressing room listening to him sing the elongated words, "slooooowly, soooooooftly," and from the beginning of the tour it was apparent that Sinatra didn't think that number should be in the show. It didn't fit musically with the rest of the program and wasn't a number you would ordinarily expect to hear Sammy do.

"What, does he think he's an opera singer?" Sinatra said one night. "He's a club singer and entertainer. This isn't right."

"Boss, Sammy does it so great." We were in Sinatra's dressing room, and I had to stick up for Sammy. After all, while Sinatra could hear the song, he couldn't see the standing ovation it always received.

Sammy walked offstage and came to me, as was customary.

"How was the show?" Sammy said.

"Great, Sammy," I said.

Then he went to the Boss's dressing room during Liza's performance and intermission.

When Sinatra went onstage to close the show, I saw Sammy in the hallway. Tears streamed down his cheeks. I was immediately concerned.

"What's the matter, Sammy?"

"Frank wants me to cut 'Music of the Night' out of my show," he said. "You know it's a great song. I don't understand it. If he wants me to take it out, I'll take it out."

Well, I had clearly failed at convincing the Boss. "Sammy, you can't take it out. You have to stand your ground."

"I don't want to piss off Frank," Sammy said.

"If you want me on your team, you should keep singing that song," I said, clapping his shoulder. "He might bitch one or two times but then it will be over. Leave it alone."

Sammy performed it for the next show and the one after that. Sinatra never said another word about it.

Toward the end of the European tour, we were in Dublin. The entire front row was filled with people in wheelchairs. As hard-nosed as Sinatra could be when he wanted to, his compassionate side was never far behind. He sang his heart out for that front row and then did something he rarely did: he walked off the stage and went to greet each one of them. It was very touching.

Maria was on the road with me, as was Susan Reynolds. They planned a birthday party for me at a traditional Irish pub, with ornate tin ceilings, and rows of Irish whiskeys. The down-home local food and color was a great change from the opulent hotels we stayed and usually dined in. There was no pasta or Chinese food in town so the pub served corned beef sandwiches and Maria found someone to make pizzas. She hired traditional Irish jig dancers who came out kicking their heels, tapping their toes, and beating tambourines. Sammy, an expert tap-dancer, couldn't resist. He jumped to his feet and joined in. At least he tried.

"Sit down, Sammy!" Sinatra yelled, laughing all the while. "You can't keep up." We all howled as the dancers kicked their legs higher and higher. Sammy didn't know the steps and was way behind. Sammy tapped his way back to his seat.

The real hit of the night was a local comedian by the name of Brendan Grace, whom Maria hired to perform. Brendan was hysterical. He wobbled and stumbled his way through the tables, slurring his words and scratching his beard like a drunken Irishman. Between the drunken act and the heavy brogue, I don't know how we understood him, but we did and we couldn't stop laughing.

Sinatra laughed so hard he cried. (Grace was so good we booked him as an opening act in London about a year later. Unfortunately, Irish humor doesn't translate to the Brits. He bombed.)

At one point Sinatra picked a green carnation out of the small vase on the table and tucked it behind his ear. He wore it all night long. And at the end of the night one of the dancers handed me the tambourine that was used in their performance. It said, "Happy Birthday Eliot." Everyone at the party, starting with Frank, Liza, and Sammy, signed it. A photo of it actually made the local newspaper the next day.

The tour was officially over in May 1989 and everyone went on a short break. Within a month, I was at the Sands in Atlantic City for a series of Sinatra solo shows.

"Hey, Moneybags, get me five thousand," Sinatra said, meaning get him some cash to carry around. Sinatra sometimes called me "Moneybags," because I settled out the box office. I called him Boss, Mr. S., or FS. I never called him Frank while he was alive. It just didn't seem right. Maria went as far as calling him Francis once or twice, which he let very few people do.

Sinatra loved playing smaller, intimate venues, like the Sands in Atlantic City and the Desert Inn in Vegas. When we played cities with large arenas we would change the typical end stage setup, where the performer is always facing the audience, to either a theater in the round or a boxing ring configuration. That maximized the amount of good seats available for the audience and Frank was most comfortable that way. He said it felt more personal.

Bringing him off the stage in an arena could be tricky. He had to walk down the steps and through the crowd. I would walk backward, with my arms extended, and my right foot, which naturally turned out, would shield him from the onslaught of pushing fans grabbing for him. He hated to be touched.

I always kept eye contact with Sinatra. I made sure he didn't miss the steps in the dark while I glanced backward so I wouldn't land on my ass. I also had to keep an eye on the security behind Sinatra to ensure they were doing their job.

Like many celebrities, Sinatra had his share of stalkers and threats, and of course, Frank Jr. had been kidnapped. There were always legitimate concerns about any performer's safety. End stage theaters were easier venues from a security standpoint. There were wings on either side so the performer just walked offstage and back to the dressing room.

I stood backstage during Sinatra's performance at one of the casino venues. I was talking to Merrill Kelem, who headed Sinatra's security whenever we were in Atlantic City. Merrill also cleaned and serviced Sinatra's pistols at least once or twice a year.

"That's a nice pistol he has out there with him tonight," Merrill said.

"What?" I had no idea what he was talking about.

"The gun he's carrying tonight. It's a nice-looking weapon." Merrill seemed very blasé about it.

"He has a weapon onstage?" I said.

"Yeah. He usually keeps it in those custom-made boots he wears. Sometimes in the small of his back, or hip."

I knew Sinatra had a license to carry but I had no idea he carried onstage.

The boots Merrill was referring to were made by Pasquale Di Frabrizio. Zippered and rising to mid-calf, they were always well polished and Sinatra wore them often. The height of the boot allowed his tuxedo pants to fall naturally when he sat or leaned back on the bar stool during a performance. It also provided a place to conceal a weapon. Fortunately he never had to use it.

After Atlantic City, I went home to South Florida. Sammy was in better shape financially, as far as I knew, and had paid off a portion of his debt. He had a new, vibrant step about him and was a pretty happy guy. He had a corporate date in Orlando for General Motors. My son Eric and I took a ride up there to work with him on his schedule. We had parlayed the success of the Ultimate Event into numerous bookings for Sammy. The tour had brought him back and he was in demand.

We went to the hotel he was scheduled to perform at and Eric and I visited him in his suite before the show. His assistant, Shirley Rhodes, was there.

"Sammy, you better rest up," I said. "I have a year and a half worth of bookings here. You start this fall and are booked through all of 1990."

He was so happy. He turned to Shirley and said, "We're not flying DC-10s anymore," referring to a spate of recent commercial plane crashes, though not all of them involved DC-10s. "Now we've got something to live for," he said.

We laughed and hugged and Eric and I went downstairs to the hotel ballroom to watch him perform. We were proud of what we had done and were looking to the future. It could not have happened to a nicer guy. Sammy had seen his share of tough times, and he was finally turning it all around.

Then something inexplicable happened. In the middle of a song, Sammy stopped singing. I don't remember the song; I only remember the shock of seeing him stop. It was something I had never seen him do in the decades of watching him perform.

"Excuse me, ladies and gentlemen. I have to clear my throat," he said.

He stood onstage for what for me was a painful ten or fifteen seconds. I can only imagine what it was for him. Then he looked to the orchestra.

"Let's start up again," he said and then he continued with the show.

I was scared. It was obvious he didn't stop because he had a frog in his throat. He stopped because nothing was coming out. I was hoping he had a cold or a vocal cord problem, but I was worried.

We immediately went to his suite and waited for him to finish the show. Sammy entered with a worried look.

"Are you okay?" I said.

"I don't know," Sammy said.

I knew he was frightened. I didn't want to make him more afraid than he already was, so I tried to be cool. I could see in Shirley's face that she was concerned, too.

Two days later he went to see Dr. Joseph Sugerman and Dr. Ed Kantor in Beverly Hills. They were the top throat specialists and treated many well-known entertainers through the years.

Shirley called me.

"Are you holding on?" she said.

"Yes," I said.

"Sammy has throat cancer." I could hear the emotion in her voice.

I didn't know what to say. "So what's next?"

"I don't know," she said. Then the bad news got worse. "It's inoperable."

At this point, I wasn't worried about him singing or making the dates, I was worried about him living. Sammy was a big smoker and drinker. I called Dr. Kantor, who explained that the mixture of nicotine and alcohol in the throat in large amounts was often a fatal one.

That Labor Day, Sammy was the New York host of the Jerry Lewis Labor Day Telethon. It was shot out of the WWOR studios in Secaucus, New Jersey, where my coauthor, Jennifer, was the nightly news anchor. She made a brief appearance on the telethon and was talking to Sammy in the control room.

"I never thought this would happen to me," he said. "You have to tell everyone you know not to smoke. If only I had understood." He was sad and emotional, confiding his fears to someone he barely knew. It was as if he just needed to tell someone, anyone who would listen.

"You'll be okay, won't you?" she said. "There are all kinds of new treatments now. Hopefully everything will be fine."

"I don't know," he said. "I really don't know." And then he went out onstage and made an emotional plea to help Jerry's kids.

That telethon raised more than $42 million and set a record that year.

It was Sammy Davis Jr.'s last scheduled public performance.

He appeared in public one more time, for the November taping of an all-star salute to his sixtieth anniversary in show business. The three-hour show was produced by George Schlatter, the creator of NBC's groundbreaking *Rowan & Martin's Laugh-In* and one of the finest television producers and directors in the business. It was hosted by Davis's friend the comedian Eddie Murphy. Friends and show business fans came out to pay tribute to a man who blazed trails, broke color barriers, and opened doors to the future.

Michael Jackson, Stevie Wonder, Whitney Houston, Anita Baker, and Ella Fitzgerald all sang, danced, or otherwise paid tribute to the legendary entertainer who started in show business at the age of four and never stopped performing. Sammy was in the first integrated group in the U.S. Army and started doing impressions of white actors like James Cagney. He befriended Sinatra and the Rat Pack and took over Vegas. He did concerts and movies, made records, and performed on Broadway.

"Sixty years, that's a lot of bourbon under the bridge, baby, I'll tell you that," Sinatra said. "Here's to you, Sam, you know I love you. I can't say it any more than that. You're my brother. You're the greatest," he said.

Then he started to sing, "It seems we stood and talked like this before. We looked at each other in the same way then. But I can't remember where or when. . . ."

Dean followed.

"Sammy, I can remember those great times we had at the Sands back in the sixties, you, me, and what's-his-name," he said and then read a few tributes.

We were shown a video of an old interview with Sammy, taped many years earlier, in which he confessed that his greatest fear was to end up down-and-out in his old age, just like Mr. Bojangles, talking about what he used to be. "Don't ever let 'em say, 'Gee, I didn't like the performance,'" he said. "At least they'll be able to say, 'He performed for me, man, he gave his all.'"

He was undergoing treatment and so couldn't speak live that night, only on tape, but at one point dancer Gregory Hines coaxed a somewhat frail Sammy onstage. He helped him put on his tap shoes and together they did one last dance for a standing ovation. As usual, Sammy left his whole heart on the stage.

The show raised half a million dollars for the United Negro College Fund.

After the show, we took a photo with all of the celebrities who performed and everyone signed it. There was Sammy in the middle of this gathering of some of the greatest artists of our time, with Michael Jackson draping his arm around him. I have that photo hanging in my office. From time to time I look at it and wonder, *Will future generations see a group of talent so great, come together to honor a star so bright?*

TWENTY-EIGHT

Donald Trump astounded much of the world when he was elected the forty-fifth president of the United States.

President Trump was vilified as an unstable wild card and admired as a pragmatist who knew how to get things done. My personal experience with Mr. Trump reflects both sides of his mercurial nature.

I did not vote for Trump and was saddened when I heard that Paul Anka was going to sing "My Way" at Trump's inauguration. Anka and several other performers bowed out shortly thereafter amid a firestorm of criticism from the entertainment world. Anka said he was in a bitter custody battle and needed to spend more time with his son. Whatever the reason, I was glad to see him withdraw.

I believe that Sinatra would never have supported Trump. He respected women and would have been appalled by the vulgar references Trump made about women to Billy Bush before an *Access Hollywood* taping, the so-called "locker room" talk. Trump's insinuation that an American federal judge of Mexican heritage might be biased against Trump because the judge was Mexican would have incensed Sinatra. Sinatra would have considered that racist. At the very least, I know that Sinatra did not respect Trump as a businessman or a man of his word.

Long before Donald Trump was president, he was a developer occasionally drawn to seemingly lost causes. Back in 1986, the Wollman ice skating rink in Central Park was a broken-down, over-budget example of inept city bureaucracy. Mayor Ed Koch had closed the rink down for restoration in 1980 with a $4.7 million budget. By 1985 the rink was $12 million over budget and still broken.

Trump could see the rink from his window in Trump Tower and was presumably tired of the eyesore. In the summer Trump said he could have it ready by Christmas.

"I have total confidence that we will be able to do it," he said. "I am going on record as saying that I will not be embarrassed."

He wasn't. It was up and running on November 1—two months ahead of schedule and $775,000 under budget. The profits were donated to charity.

When Resorts International couldn't complete construction on a lavish new Atlantic City casino, Trump bought it. The Trump Taj Mahal casino was his most ambitious project to date. It was scheduled to open in 1990 amid much fanfare.

Sinatra was the king of Vegas, so I wasn't completely surprised when the chief operating officer of the Taj Mahal called me in the late summer of 1989 to book Sinatra for its grand opening. I had known Mark Grossinger Etess since his days at the Golden Nugget casino. I was also well aware of his family. He was the grandson of the owners of Grossinger's, the famed Borscht Belt hotel in the Catskills.

"Eliot, I need all your acts for the grand opening and beyond," Mark said.

"I can't give you all my acts," I said. "You're not even sure when you're going to open."

"Then let's start with Sinatra," he said.

That made sense. The Sands Hotel & Casino in Atlantic City had been trying to book Sinatra but we hadn't yet made a deal.

Mark and I had several calls in the coming days. He was easy to work with and a great promoter of the new hotel. The more we spoke, the more we added to the shows. Eventually Mark booked everything he wanted and we agreed on terms for Frank, Liza, Sammy (who had not yet been diagnosed with cancer), and Steve and Eydie.

The deal memos were drafted. Mark signed them and said he was working on the contracts. I was expecting the final paperwork for signatures within a couple of weeks.

In the meantime, Mark's daughter Rachel was turning thirteen years old and he invited Maria and me to the bat mitzvah. We were happy to fly up for the reception at the Trump Plaza hotel in Atlantic City. We were seated at a round table and I was next to Donald Trump. Everyone was in a celebratory mood and we made small talk about the opening of the casino. Trump seemed very excited about having my acts.

"This is going to be the best gambling venue, period," he said. "I'll put in a Sinatra restaurant. Whatever you want."

I was thrilled he was enthusiastic but mostly I was concerned about the exact timing of the Taj Mahal opening. We did not have firm performance dates in the deal memos, so my clients were in a holding window, awaiting the Taj's completion date. I was expecting that detail to be finalized shortly.

Mark was developing the casino as a gambling, entertainment, and convention center. On October 10, he and two other Trump executives were at a Manhattan news conference to promote a junior welterweight boxing match in February between Hector Camacho and Vinny Pazienza at the Trump Plaza. After the news conference, Mark, Stephen Hyde, chief executive of the Trump casinos, and Jonathan Benanav, executive vice president of the Trump Plaza casino hotel, boarded a helicopter at the Sixtieth Street Heliport on the East River. It was an eight-seat Agusta

109A, part of a shuttle service owned by Paramount Aviation in New Jersey. It was a clear day.

Eight minutes into the seventy-mile flight to Atlantic City, near Forked River, New Jersey, the helicopter plunged into the pine woodlands along the Garden State Parkway. It was thirty-five miles north of the resort.

The federal investigators said the probable cause of the accident was "fatigue failure" and added it was "the result of inadequate quality control." The main overhead four-blade rotor and the tail rotor broke off the body of the craft. Pilot Robert Kent of Ronkonkoma, Long Island, and copilot Lawrence Diener of Westbury, Long Island, were also killed.

"They were three fabulous young men in the prime of their lives," Trump said in a statement issued from his New York office. "No better human beings ever existed. We're deeply saddened by this devastating tragedy. Our hearts go out to their families."

Mark was only thirty-eight years old, with a wife and young children.

The funeral was held at the same temple as his daughter's bat mitzvah. Trump was there and so was Paul Anka. Paul was as astute a businessman as any Hollywood agent. He was also booked at the Taj Mahal. I was standing next to Paul in the temple.

"Have you talked to Trump yet about the Atlantic City gig?" Anka whispered.

"No. I'll call the office when we leave here. Everything is wrapped up. I have all the deal memos."

"Oh yeah? Now you're going to see what the art of the deal is all about," he said, a sarcastic reference to Trump's 1987 book, *The Art of the Deal*. I didn't think much of what Anka said. As far as I was concerned, everything was done. It was just a matter of signing the contracts.

I reached out to Trump's office to find out who I should be in touch with. At first, I wasn't surprised when they didn't have a straight answer. Three critical executives had just been killed. Within days, though, it became clear to me that I was being jerked around.

I was on the west coast, at the Beverly Hills Hotel. I called Trump four times—once a day. When I could not reach him on Thursday I told his assistant I was on my way to New York. "Tell Mr. Trump I will be at his office at nine a.m. tomorrow morning," I said.

I called my son Eric in South Florida and told him to meet me in New York with the deal memos in hand. I boarded the red-eye.

Eric and I met on Fifth Avenue between Fifty-Sixth and Fifty-Seventh Streets, outside Trump Tower, at eight thirty that morning. I was jet-lagged and somewhat agitated but mostly curious about what Trump was going to say.

We sat down in his office, with floor-to-ceiling views of Manhattan and Central Park as his backdrop.

We exchanged hellos and made small talk.

"Hey, Eliot, how are you?" he said.

I didn't want to beat around the bush. "Not so good," I said.

"What's the urgency?"

"You have four of my acts. I need to set the firm dates," I said.

I also needed to find out if he had insurance to cover the dates if the hotel wasn't completed on time. We never made it that far. It was clear from the beginning of the conversation that his intent was to renegotiate. I was shocked. As far as I was concerned, the deal was done; we had only to agree on a few minor points and formalize it all in a contract.

"Well, what are we talking about here?" Trump said. "Let's go over this, starting with Sinatra."

We had an agreement for twelve Sinatra shows, broken down as four shows three times a year.

"The deal is a little rich," he said. He started changing the specifics. I took a deep breath.

By now, the news about Sammy having throat cancer was out.

"What about Sammy?" I said.

"What are you worried about Sammy for, he's going to die anyway."

I was incensed, and that statement convinced me he was negotiating in bad faith. "Maybe so, but the Boss wants him to have a contract to take to his grave," I said. He didn't respond; he just moved on. Liza would do two shows, three times a year.

"Who's Steve and Eydie?" he said, looking me straight in the eye.

At that point I'd had it. As a general rule, I don't take things personally. It was always about my clients and not about me. I prided myself on not letting my ego stand in the way of a deal. This was different. Not only was it about my clients, but I also took this personally. It was a very visceral response. How could this be? Just a few short weeks ago we were talking about how they needed all my acts.

"I have all the deal memos right here, done and complete," I said. Eric pulled the papers out of his briefcase and handed them to me. "They have the president's signature on them."

"You don't sound like you're happy," Trump said. "Hey Eliot, if you don't like what I'm saying, go speak to the dead man in the cemetery."

I still remember vividly the feeling as my body flushed. I was outraged and I lost it. I leaned across the desk and grabbed his tie, but Eric quickly pulled me back. Trump didn't say a word or react. He didn't call security or even throw us out of his office. We packed up our documents and promptly left. It was clear the deal was over, which I'm sure is what he wanted all along as the outcome.

At this point, I didn't know what he was going to do. I thought perhaps he would call the press. If so, I needed to position myself in front of the story. I called Vine from the lobby of the Trump Tower. It was 8 a.m. on the west coast.

"Hey, Vine, I need to talk to the Boss."

"Are you sure you want to do that? He's sleeping."

"Yeah, I've got a problem."

Sinatra came to the phone.

"Who died?" Sinatra said grumpily.

I told him what happened.

"You've got two choices," he said, now fully awake. "Either you go up there and tell him to go fuck himself or give me his number and I'll do it."

"I'll handle it, Boss," I said.

I rode the elevator back up and walked into his outer office. Before his assistant could stop me, I poked my head in through his door. He looked up at me and we made eye contact.

"Sinatra says go fuck yourself." I walked out.

Before I left the building I called Jay Venetianer, who was responsible for booking the Sands. "If you guys want my acts, meet me in Florida tomorrow and bring your checkbook." They did. I signed every act for what turned out to be a very lucrative run for my entire roster.

Trump's Taj Mahal opened in April 1990 as the largest hotel and casino in Atlantic City. Michael Jackson was the guest of honor and Elton John did the opening performance at the 6,000-seat Mark Etess Theatre at the Taj Mahal.

Eventually the Taj was taken over by Carl Icahn's company and closed its doors on October 10, 2016—the twenty-seventh anniversary of the helicopter crash.

I never expected to speak to Donald Trump again. I was taken by surprise when somewhere around 1995 my assistant said, "Donald Trump is on the line for you." I was sure it was someone pulling a prank, but his voice was unmistakable. The conversation went something like this:

"Hello," I said.

"Hey, Eliot. How are you doing?" Trump said, as if nothing had ever transpired between us.

I was abrupt and to the point. "I'm fine. What do you want?"

"The Mar-a-Lago club is opening and I need some talent."

My head spun for a moment. You're kidding? I wanted to hang up but obviously I had an obligation to my clients. "Rickles is available," I said.

"Good. Who else?"

"You can have Steve and Eydie, if you know who they are now." I was having a hard time keeping my temper under control. He must have detected it because he said, "What are you upset about? You know, you should be thanking me."

"Thanking you?" What the hell was he talking about? "For what?"

"If it wasn't for me, you would have never had that great run at the Sands."

I had no response to that. I tacked on a little extra to the performers' normal appearance fees and told him the money had to go into an escrow account and the conversation was over. I saw him once, from a distance after that, at Mar-a-Lago when Steve and Eydie were performing. He was walking toward me and I walked the other way. We haven't spoken since.

TWENTY-NINE

Sinatra was set to play the Garden State Arts Center, which was always a hassle. It was Sinatra's home state, so there were throngs of friends from the old days, friends of friends, friends of friends of friends, and so on. I had to be very diligent to make sure he made it through the concerts without too many distractions.

At the end of the run he would give his usual line about taking a picture, but I knew we would be back next year; the place had sentimental value, and there happened to be a helicopter pad nearby that brought him in from Manhattan quickly, though we always took a limousine home in the dark.

Maria's mother, Antoinette, or Netta as we called her, was one of Sinatra's biggest fans.

She was a small, sweet-looking woman, with short hair, glasses, and a fabulous smile. She was my friend and sports buddy. I was happy to have the opportunity to introduce her and my father-in-law, Joe, to Sinatra, with one caveat: For days I urged Maria to please tell her mother not to touch him.

"Listen, Mom," Maria said. "Mr. Sinatra really doesn't like to be touched, so when you meet him please don't grab at him."

"How many times are you going to tell me that, Maria?" my mother-in-law said. "I know. I will be very polite and just shake his hand."

So, before a show Maria brought her parents past security to Sinatra's backstage dressing room door. Sinatra was putting on his tuxedo jacket when I ducked in and told him he had visitors.

"It's just Maria's mother and father?" he said.

"Yeah, Boss."

"I'm ready to go. Open the door," Sinatra said.

"Mr. S., I want to introduce you to Netta and Joe . . ."

Before I could finish my sentence, Netta lost it.

"Frankie!" she exclaimed, like some teenage bobbysoxer.

She reached out and impulsively wrapped her arms around his waist in a tight embrace.

I looked at Sinatra and he looked at was. I wasn't sure what he was going to say, her arms holding tight. He had a strange look in his eye and I thought maybe for a brief moment he felt like the skinny young Sinatra prepping to play to a club of screaming kids. Then he laughed. Joe smiled and shook hands with Sinatra, not sure if he should be embarrassed or happy, but I could tell that he too had a special glimmer of nostalgia in that moment. Sinatra made them both feel at ease.

They had a brief conversation and Maria escorted her parents to their seats, believing that moment had transported the three senior citizens back to a precious time that only they could fully appreciate.

As I walked to the stage with Sinatra, he grabbed me in a tight bear hug.

"See how you like it," he said, but I knew he wasn't upset.

"What can I say, Boss? The ladies can't keep their hands off you."

He smiled. It didn't matter if they were old or young—women loved Sinatra.

His exploits with women were legendary. Frank was the guy that men wanted to be. Throughout his life he was associated with some of the most beautiful and desirable women in the world. Yet for all his dalliances, real and imagined, Sinatra formed deep and lifelong relationships with the women he loved and he never lost touch with those he truly cared for.

Sinatra was married to Barbara for more years than all of his ex-wives combined and I knew him to be nothing short of completely loyal to her. He had many opportunities to be with other women and there was even talk of him going back to his first wife, Nancy, for a while, but I believe he truly loved Barbara. Still, all these years later, Nancy received regular payments of 10 percent of whatever Sinatra made and he always made sure she never needed anything. He also frequently spoke on the phone with her when he was backstage, usually just to see how she was feeling. She was the mother of his three children and I believe he felt guilty about leaving her, but he couldn't help himself.

He was always very discreet about his past relationships, out of respect for the women and out of respect for Barbara. His marriage to Ava Gardner was the stuff of Hollywood legend. Like Bogart and Bacall, Taylor and Burton, Sinatra and Gardner was a romance to remember. Ava was in many ways his alter ego. She was independent and strong-willed and far ahead of her time, the 1950s. One of Hollywood's greatest beauties, her relationship with Sinatra was widely known as tempestuous, and when Sinatra grieved over their split, Nelson Riddle famously said, "Ava taught him how to sing a torch song. She taught him the hard way."

Sinatra told me his life was never the same after he saw her in that revolving door of the Pierre hotel, as I mentioned earlier. She walked in as he was walking out and one look at her face through the glass and he couldn't leave. He followed her right back around and he was hooked. "Ava was so much like me," Sinatra said. "I found the female version of myself."

For all the pain and joy, through marriage, divorce, numerous attempts at reconciliation, and the long journey into old age, they retained a special bond and his loyalty to her lasted a lifetime. When Ava fell on hard times financially, Sinatra helped her. When she suffered through emphysema, he helped her with her medical care.

When he performed at the Royal Albert Hall in London, where Ava lived, she would frequently attend and sit in a private box, usually on the opposite end of the theater from the one Barbara was sitting in. I don't know if Barbara ever knew she was there. To my knowledge he never saw Ava, though I'm sure they talked.

Sinatra was performing in Florida in January 1990 when we heard Ava was gravely ill. Frank, Barbara, and Jilly were at my house, where we had just finished a home-cooked meal, courtesy of Maria. They were headed out the door to their car when Jilly's phone rang. I wasn't sure what the call was about, but Jilly's face told me it wasn't good news. The three of us stepped outside while Barbara spoke with Maria in the living room.

"Ava is in really bad shape. It won't be long," Jilly said to Sinatra.

He was clearly saddened but didn't say anything. He just went into his quiet, reflective mode.

"Are you okay, Boss?" I said.

He nodded and walked to the car. I knew Jilly would look after him.

A few days later, on January 25, the word came that Ava had passed. She was only sixty-seven years old. I wasn't with him at the time, but I know Jilly said he and the others close to Sinatra were worried about how to tell him, afraid of how he would react. In the end, Sinatra grieved in his pensive, thoughtful way. He did not attend Ava's funeral; he knew that if he had gone, he would have sent the media into endless speculation about how he still carried a torch for her. He would never have subjected Barbara to that. He did, however, pay for Ava's funeral.

He was also occasionally in touch with his other ex-wife, Mia Farrow. When she was going through her breakup from Woody Allen, Sinatra said she called him to ask for advice. I don't know what he told her, but I do know he was furious at the idea that Allen had an affair with their adopted daughter, Soon-Yi. They talked frequently during that period and he had Sonny send her money. At one point, Jilly and I were sitting with Sinatra at his Beverly Hills home. The situation was particularly nasty between her and Allen at this point, so Sinatra told Jilly to relay a message to Allen that he'd better "straighten up and fly right." Things seemed to calm down, so maybe the message was received.

Four months after losing Ava, there was another tragedy. This one had nothing to do with his ex-wives, but rather Sinatra's pal: Sammy succumbed to throat cancer. It was as if some of the best years of Frank's life had dissolved into the ether.

On May 16, I was in Sinatra's suite at the Waldorf. It was early afternoon and I was sitting in the dining room with the Boss and Barbara, having coffee, when my cell phone rang. It was Shirley Rhodes, and I could tell by the sound of her voice that it was the news we were all dreading. My heart sank. Both Sinatra and I had separately visited Sammy in the hospital and we knew he would never walk out of that place. Still, it was a gut-wrenching moment.

"Boss, I just received news from California. Unfortunately Sammy has passed," I said.

"Oh my God," he said. "I lost my best friend." He put his hands to his face and cried. This was one of the few times I personally saw Sinatra come to tears. I sat there quietly for a time and then went to work. He still had four concerts left at Radio City, but there was no way he could do them. We rescheduled them and all left together for Los Angeles.

Sammy was only sixty-four years old, and while he had been so happy about all the new bookings I had secured for him, he never had the chance to play a single one. The service was very emotional for all of us. Many of Sammy's show business friends were there, as well as many who had just performed at his "60th Anniversary Celebration" only months earlier. Frank and Dean were honorary pallbearers, along with Michael Jackson and Bill Cosby. Dean was very sad, but by this time in his life, for whatever reasons, he always seemed to be in his own world.

There was a rabbi, and Rev. Jesse Jackson spoke. "To love Sammy is to love black and white. To love Sammy is to love black and Jew. To love Sammy is to embrace the human family," Jackson said.

Frank and Barbara, Dean and Liza all sat in the front. I sat a little farther back and reflected on the young man who sang and danced so beautifully; his talent, his grace, and his dignity. Sammy Davis Jr. was the first live performance I ever saw and it remains the greatest I have ever seen.

THIRTY

Nothing brings your own mortality into sharp focus like watching your friends die. Some people are prompted to take better care of themselves and schedule complete medical workups. Not Sinatra. He took care of himself, but going to the doctor with him was never an easy experience, and you could forget a complete physical workup. The doctor would be lucky if he gave him enough time to do an EKG. Occasionally I would accompany him for an annual appointment with Dr. Pasquale Piccione.

Sinatra liked and trusted Dr. Piccione; otherwise, needless to say, we wouldn't have been there. But he didn't like the atmosphere of any medical office and he especially didn't like the time it took. He was always impatient. I waited outside the examination room holding Sinatra's clothes, though he kept his watch on to keep track of time.

"You have thirty minutes," Sinatra said to Dr. Piccione. They ran through the usual questions and checks for a physical, and before long I heard Sinatra say, "You've got five more minutes."

Dr. Piccione told him to put his clothes on and meet him in his office.

"Come on, Eliot," Sinatra said.

I followed along.

After we settled, Dr. Piccione told Sinatra he needed to come off Elavil. He even went so far as to suggest that that doctor who was still writing the prescription all these years could potentially get in trouble.

"And one more thing, Francis," Dr. Piccione said. "You have to do me a favor. You have to slow down your drinking. Just a little bit less will help."

"Ya know what, Doc?" Frank said. "I know a lot of old drunks. I don't know a lot of old doctors." The appointment was over.

Dr. Piccione was just one of many doctors who relayed thoughts on Sinatra's memory loss. In the early 1990s the media was buzzing with stories and speculation about Sinatra's difficulties onstage. That led to a slew of faxes and telephone calls from physicians and regular people voicing their opinions, nearly all from people who had never met him. "He has Alzheimer's," they would say.

My father had Alzheimer's disease and I am firmly convinced Sinatra did not. Those who have loved ones suffering from this devastating, brain-consuming illness will understand when I say that people with Alzheimer's don't bounce back. I watched my father slowly deteriorate as his brain cells turned to mush, one by one, until he slowly died from it. That wasn't Sinatra. He did bounce back.

Sinatra had memory loss, confusion, and hearing and vision problems. In my heart of hearts I will always believe it was caused by the long-term use of Elavil. I came to that conclusion not just because of what Dr. Piccione said, but also from speaking with the pioneering heart surgeon Dr. Michael DeBakey, considered by some to be the best heart surgeon ever.

DeBakey had taken care of Sinatra's father, Marty, and over the years they became friends. When we were in Texas, DeBakey would come to the concerts. In fact, DeBakey was the only person, other than President Reagan, for whom I can ever recall Sinatra telling me to make sure no other visitors would be in the dressing room, so that they could spend some time together alone.

I was surprised that at least for the first few minutes when they spoke, DeBakey always seemed nervous. There he was, this man who held the power of life and death for the people he operated on, and he was nervous around a singer. Of course, calling Sinatra a singer is like calling Dr. Martin Luther King Jr. a preacher.

DeBakey operated out of the Methodist Hospital in Houston. He came backstage before a performance one night. Dr. DeBakey was concerned.

"Frank, you have to transition off those Elavil pills. Take some time and come to Houston. I'll make an entire floor available to you if you need it," DeBakey said. He explained that there were risks in coming off long-term antidepressant use and that patients could become severely agitated. "That's why it needs to be done in the hospital, where you can be monitored for any problems.

"We can set up a private area for you and your friends," he added. "You can even go out to dinner for a couple of hours as long as there is no alcohol. I really think coming off the prescription will help with your memory."

Sinatra agreed and we set a date.

The scheduled time for Sinatra to be permanently weaned off Elavil approached and I was excited to move forward, but despite DeBakey's urgings, Barbara expressed stronger and stronger concern about possible unpredictable reactions. She called my office and told me that she was afraid of potentially aggressive behavior and that if his medication was going to be altered, it would be done with his doctors in Palm Springs.

It was true that there was no way he was going to stay in the hospital for a long enough time to make sure he wouldn't turn violent at some point in the months ahead, after a changeover to a new medication. In the end, the date came and went and nothing changed.

Meanwhile, as I said, news was swirling about Sinatra having memory problems. While in the past he had been extremely sensitive to any and all publicity and wanted to respond to every negative story or article that went by, he rarely saw these new stories, and when he did, they didn't seem to bother him. That was quite a change from back in 1986, when Kitty Kelley published her unauthorized biography of Sinatra. I could barely convince him to contain his reactions. Mickey Rudin had filed a lawsuit to keep the book from being published but lost. Sinatra wanted to hold a press conference to respond to every comment he heard on television or read in a newspaper about what Kelley had written. Thankfully he never read the book.

"Call Susan Reynolds. That two-bit sham of a writer isn't going to get away with this," he said.

I had a tough job convincing him to let it go.

"Boss, if you don't say anything, it will go away in a week or ten days and no one will remember this. If you keep talking, you'll sell her books for her," I pleaded.

The *New York Times* book review said, "Yes, we do know that Mr. Sinatra is no cream puff sweetie pie goody-two-shoes." It went on to say, "How is it possible to write about Frank Sinatra in a manner that suggests his music is in some way extrinsic to him?"

Sinatra relented and stayed quiet.

THIRTY-ONE

Sinatra loved the camaraderie of hanging out with his pals. That's one of the reasons he loved touring. He was a late-night guy and wanted people to stay up drinking with him. As I said, in many ways it was his desire to relive younger days that caused both the start and the abrupt end of the Together Again tour. Sinatra wanted to relive old times but Dean was just old.

In the past, some of his opening acts and touring partners, like Pat Henry and Sammy, always stayed out with him, though Liza hung with her own group. For me, it was part of my job, and of course Jilly was always on the scene. Sometimes I'd have to wake up early the next day and Maria would stay up with him while I went to bed. Barbara sometimes stayed but often ended the night before Frank. There's a reason he sang, "It's quarter to three," with such conviction.

On the road, Sinatra and Jilly would sit around, occasionally till the sun came up, and reminisce about the 1960s and the days of Jilly's saloon, on West Fifty-Second Street. Frank would walk in and Jilly would clear a path and treat him like royalty. It became one of the hottest New York celebrity hangouts of the 1960s.

The restaurant specialized in Cantonese food, and its chef, Howie, was known for making the best barbecued pork in town.

There was a plastic tube that ran from the bar to the kitchen in the basement, which the staff used to call down orders. Frank would go right to the tube and yell, "Fuck you, Howie!" That meant to prepare Sinatra's dish.

"Fuck you, Frank!" Howie would yell back. That meant his food was on the way.

Both Frank and Jilly loved to tell those stories. Each time they would add a new twist or a different tidbit from the hundreds of times this must have gone on. Jilly always made Frank laugh.

One of my favorite Jilly moments was when he called me up in 1982.

"Eliot, you're never going to believe this. Pat Henry woke up dead."

Pat was our friend and a great comedian. He would have loved that call.

Jilly always made Frank happy. The two of them would sit at the bar drinking and laughing at favorite spots in hotels across the world, like Sir Harry's Bar at the Waldorf or the bar at the Desert Inn in Las Vegas. Sinatra especially liked the convenience of Vegas, where he could walk off the stage and right into the restaurants and bars.

He was perhaps the most generous tipper of his day with waiters and waitresses, busboys and valets, handing out hundred-dollar bills to anyone who took care of him. Vine would fold hundreds into little squares for him. They were tiny, about the size of a thumbnail. He would take five or six of them a night and put them in the change pocket of his tuxedo to use for tips. He once famously asked a valet, "What's the biggest tip you ever received?" When the man answered, "One hundred dollars," Sinatra gave him two hundred and then asked who had been the donor of that previous generosity. "You, Mr. Sinatra," was the response.

So, when Sonny told me money was tight, I thought this was a natural and easy place to make a cut. I went to Barbara and asked for the go-ahead to tell Vine to fold up twenties instead of hundreds for Frank, figuring he never really looked, so he would never notice. She agreed and for almost a year he didn't.

Then one early morning, as the two of us were drinking at the bar in the Desert Inn, the scantily clad cocktail waitress came to tell us they were closing up the bar. Sinatra reached into his pocket to give her a tip.

The problem was, on this night, as he was handing the waitress a folded-up bill, someone turned the lights up. He looked down and then he looked at me. He went ballistic.

"Hey Eliot, when the fuck did we go broke?"

I held my breath for a moment.

"Don't ever fucking do that to me again." Then he turned and walked to his room. I called Vine the next morning and told her we were back to hundreds.

THIRTY-TWO

The Ultimate Event had proved to all of us that arena performances were the way to go from a financial standpoint, but with Sammy gone, I felt that Sinatra needed other star power to ensure we would sell out the 10,000–20,000 seat venues. It would also take some of the pressure off him.

Sinatra, Liza, and Sammy were a tough act to top. Where do you go from them and still attract people who will pay a decent price for the tickets? To me, there was one obvious choice—well, two, really. I felt that musically, Steve Lawrence and Eydie Gormé would be a great combination with Sinatra, and I didn't even have another choice. Steve was a singer and actor with a terrific sense of humor, and Sinatra admired him as a great entertainer. He was as easygoing as anyone I knew and truly had a gift for making people feel comfortable around him. We had golfed together and frequently socialized for years. Steve, Eydie, and their longtime associate, coordinator, and confidante, Judy Tannen, were all much more than clients. They were part of my family.

As a singer, Steve had a long career, beginning with the number one hit "Go Away Little Girl" in the 1950s. He did numerous television shows, and between him and Eydie, they won multiple Grammys and Emmys as well as a Lifetime Achievement Award from the Songwriters Hall of Fame in New York. For her part, Eydie was among the most musically gifted singers I knew. She was considered by many of her peers to be among the top three female singers, along with Barbra Streisand and Judy Garland. Eydie won her own Grammy for her solo recording "If He Walked into My Life," from the Broadway hit *Mame*. She was fluent in Spanish and very popular in Latin counties and especially popular in South America, even though they never toured there.

That song, though, with its poignant, melancholy lyrics, took on even deeper meaning after the greatest tragedy of their lives. Years earlier, in 1986, I was on the road with Steve and Eydie and Judy Tannen for an engagement at the Fox Theatre in Atlanta. Judy Tannen called my hotel room.

"You'd better come to Steve and Eydie's room," Judy said. "We just received a call that Michael may be dying."

Michael was their twenty-three-year-old son. It seemed impossible. He was a wonderful young man whom I loved spending time with.

It's hard to know what to do first in a situation like that. The parents were obviously devastated. They needed a calm head around them. Judy and I both started looking for planes. I chartered one and then Judy found a friend of Steve and Eydie's who would send a corporate jet. We all flew back to Los Angeles, but he died of natural causes from an irregular heartbeat, before we landed. They never even had a chance to say goodbye.

We arrived at their Beverly Hills home late that night. By morning, close to a hundred friends and family members, including their other son, David, arrived at the house.

I helped with security and organizing the funeral, and for the next two weeks stayed with the family to help in whatever other ways I could. I just wanted to be there for them.

As I flew home to Florida, I stared out the window, looking at the clouds. I was haunted by the inconsolable grief these parents were enduring. It is the parents' job to die before their child. I realized for the first time that the loss of a child is perhaps the greatest suffering a parent can experience. I thought of my own children with renewed gratitude.

I reflected on the lyrics of Eydie's signature song, "If He Walked into My Life." She always sang it with intense emotion. I couldn't imagine she could ever stand on a stage as a mother who had lost a child and once again sing, "At the moment when he needed me, did I ever turn away?" or "There must have been a million things that my heart forgot to say. Would I think of one or two, if he walked into my life today?"

When I returned home, I suggested she take the song out of her show. She refused. That's the difference between a great performer and the rest of us mere mortals. It is through their performance that they fully experience happiness, sorrow, joy, and grief. Performing that song was cathartic for Eydie. There was never a dry eye in the house.

I knew that that kind of power and authentic emotion was a perfect match for Sinatra and would translate into a win for everyone.

When Steve and Eydie's children were young, the couple chose not to travel outside the United States, so they never built up a worldwide base of concert fans. (Their other son, David, by the way, is a successful musical composer.) Now that they were prepared to travel abroad, I was concerned about whether they would be able to sell tickets. That was my only reservation in using them for the tour, but still, it was a big one.

Both Tina Sinatra and Barbara had other concerns. I was alone, reading a newspaper in the television room of the Sinatras' Beverly Hills home when Tina walked in.

"This thing with Steve and Eydie, are you crazy?" Tina said. "You can't put them with my father." She didn't think they were good enough. She thought I was using Sinatra to prop up my other clients, when in reality I was looking to put her father with artists who I knew would support him if anything went wrong, particularly during the closing medley of the show. It was rare at this point that he didn't screw up a lyric, but for the most part, the audience barely noticed, especially when the other artists helped cover for Sinatra. I explained my reasons and said I was confident in the choice, but within a week, when I was back home in Florida, Barbara called me and also expressed similar thoughts. She said, "I'm not sure this is right."

"Why would you say that?" I said.

"It doesn't compare to Liza and Sammy."

"Nothing is going to compare to Liza and Sammy," I said. "Steve and Eydie and Frank will be great together."

I waited till I was backstage with Sinatra at one of his engagements to tell him about their worries. Sinatra loved them as much as I did. He had nicknamed Eydie "Loudie" for her resounding voice. They had a lot of laughs together.

"Why are you listening to everyone?" he said dismissively.

That was all I needed. I looked for a sponsor for the "Diamond Jubilee Tour" and we spoke to a lot of corporations, including the makers of Sinatra's favorite beverage, Jack Daniel's. Jack Daniel's was not in the market for a million-dollar sponsorship at the time. Chivas Regal was, and was anxious to be associated with the Sinatra magic. As we were closing the deal we invited the Chivas executives to a Sinatra performance at the Sands in Atlantic City.

Sinatra often closed his shows with a toast. He would hoist his glass of Jack and say, "May you live to be a hundred and five and may the last voice you hear be mine."

Occasionally he varied, and this night as he raised his glass to toast the audience and the Chivas executives, he said, "Jack Daniel's killed my father but it won't get me." I cringed, but the Chivas executives clearly didn't care because they closed the deal anyway. I asked the Boss to please drop Jack for the tour and stick with Chivas.

The Diamond Jubilee Tour was launched with much fanfare, on Sinatra's seventy-fifth birthday, December 12, 1990. It was at the Brendan Byrne Arena (aka Meadowlands Arena) in East Rutherford, New Jersey, a mere ten miles from his Hoboken birthplace.

Frank Jr. was conducting and stars came from both coasts to mingle backstage and watch the master show everyone just how cool he still was. Sinatra's old friends were there: Liza, Claudette Colbert, Roger Moore, Robert Wagner, Jill St. John, Alan King, Bob Newhart, Don Rickles, and on and on.

When it was time for Sinatra to sing "New York, New York," he asked Liza to stand up and take a bow. "I love you," he said as he brought her up.

"Happy Birthday, Uncle Frank. I love you so much," she said, giving him a big hug.

He called for a microphone for her and they broke into an impromptu version of "New York, New York," so impromptu that Liza had her purse on her shoulder during the entire performance.

There were a few flubs, but it brought the hometown audience to their feet.

The show ended with a medley. Steve and Eydie and the audience yelled "Happy birthday!"

"This is without a doubt the finest birthday celebration I think I've ever had in my life," Sinatra said. "I just simply want to say I love you all dearly and I thank you for taking part in this wonderful night for me, I should never forget as long as I live. God bless you all, and good night."

After the concert, Barbara took over the Grand Ballroom at the Waldorf-Astoria for a private, late-night dinner party for one hundred of Sinatra's closest friends and family. Frank and Barbara sat with the children and grandchildren. Harry Connick Jr., the young singer famous for his Sinatra-esque style, was seated at the table with Maria, Steve, Eydie, Judy, and me. Steve was emceeing the festivities.

Connick walked in, took his jacket off, and hung it on the back of his chair. That's something Sinatra never would have done, and though I doubt he could identify Connick, or even knew who he was, he noticed the jacket hung over the chair.

Halfway through the night I went over to Sinatra's table to see if he needed anything.

"Who's the guy that took off his jacket?" Sinatra said. He was angry.

"He's a hot young singer with a lot of notoriety," I said. I figured it would only agitate him further if I told him some of that notoriety had to do with being compared to him.

"Maybe someone should give him an etiquette lesson," he said.

I never told him who it was. Sinatra was a very formal guy. I never even saw him loosen his tie. Barbara stood up and toasted her husband.

"Darling, all these years you've given the world beautiful, wonderful music, but you have given me the world," Barbara said. Robert Wagner said, "Your real talent is as a friend." Jilly, in his usual wisecracking style, said, "I never thought I would live to see the day." He chuckled. "A lot of other people didn't think so, either."

Then it was Frank's turn.

"It was six thousand to one that I'd get to be fifty years old, but seventy-five? I love it. I've had some fun in the past weeks and a few tears," Sinatra said. New York celebrity gossip columnist Liz Smith, one of the few journalists he grew to like, was there and recorded much of the night in her column.

I think Sinatra turning seventy-five impacted me even more than my own seventy-fifth many years later. I looked at seventy-five as being past the three-quarter mark, since I don't expect to live to be one hundred. But he seemed to take it all in stride and not even give it much thought. For me, watching him age was tough. Some people you just don't expect to ever grow old. To me, Sinatra will always be timeless.

THIRTY-THREE

Sinatra's version of "New York, New York" was played at every New York Yankees game for decades. It started back in the 1980s and served as an unofficial anthem to the city and team. The song was originally written for the 1977 Martin Scorsese film of the same name, starring Liza and Robert De Niro. It was written by John Kander and Fred Ebb, who in addition to being dear friends and confidants of Liza were also great songwriters. The movie didn't make any money, and Liza's recording of the theme song, which had a Broadway feel, never gained the same traction as Sinatra's, who always publicly credited Liza for the song.

The story goes that it was a disc jockey from the Manhattan disco Le Club that first sent George Steinbrenner, the brash and outspoken Yankees owner, the recording of "New York, New York." Apparently Steinbrenner loved the words and decided to play the Sinatra version after every game, starting in the 1980 season. It was an uplifting message during a troubled time in New York City. After a decade of having Frank's version played and not hers, however, it really started to irk Liza.

"Why is Steinbrenner always playing Sinatra's version?" she demanded. "Can't you tell him to play mine at least some of the time?" Liza happened to be performing in Fort Lauderdale when she told me this, and Fort Lauderdale also happened to be home to the Yankees' spring training camp in those days.

As luck would have it, one night Steinbrenner came to the show and we invited him backstage. He walked in, dressed up in a navy blazer, with another guy from the team. Liza wasted no time when she saw him. "How come you don't play my version of 'New York, New York' at Yankee Stadium?" she said in her sweet tone, which I liked to call her pussycat voice.

I suspect Steinbrenner had been asked that question before, since he replied without hesitation, "Because Frank's version is a guy's version and more men are baseball fans."

Liza looked at me and I winked at her, as a sign that I would take it from there at a later point.

Then Steinbrenner asked her to lunch.

She went. The next day her dressing room and apparently her hotel suite were filled with flowers. She called me at home. "Eliot, I have a problem," she said. "Steinbrenner is a little bit nuts. I think he's looking to make a move with me."

Liza had her own group of friends and she had never called me about anything personal like this before. She knew I was somewhat friendly with Steinbrenner, so I guess she thought I should handle it. "What do you want me to do?" I said.

"What should I do?" she said. "He wants to have lunch again. I want you to come along."

I agreed. I showed up at the restaurant and he looked slightly annoyed. It was fairly apparent to me that Steinbrenner was caught off guard and had expected her to come solo. Liza and I had agreed that I would bring up the "New York, New York" matter when the time was right. Steinbrenner spent most of the lunch focused on Liza.

"You know, George," I said, about halfway through, "I represent both Frank and Liza. Is it possible that you could alternate versions of 'New York, New York' at Yankee Stadium?"

He promptly said yes, though he didn't seem any less annoyed that I was there.

According to the *New York Times,* "The team would play the Sinatra recording when the team won, but the Minnelli version after a loss." I don't remember it that way, but I can't say I'm surprised. That would have been a very Steinbrenner thing to do. Eventually the Yankees went back to only playing Frank's version.

It remained a sticking point for Liza for years and probably still is.

THIRTY-FOUR

Sinatra owned the stage he stood on. A point of a finger, a bit of a swagger, and the audience was in the palm of his hand, even with the memory loss and inevitable mess-ups during the medley as he stood between Steve and Eydie during the Diamond Jubilee Tour. The performances received overwhelmingly positive audience reaction wherever we went, and both Barbara and Tina changed their tune about Frank working with Steve and Eydie.

We toured the world in a Boeing 727 we leased from Kirk Kerkorian. There was a master bedroom with a king-size bed toward the front, a sleeping section with two sets of bunk beds and a queen-size bed in the back, and a lounge with a television and tables in between, making this the largest plane we had toured on. The Sinatras, Steve and Eydie, Maria, Vine, Judy Tannen, and I were on board.

Unfortunately, Jilly wasn't with us. He was embroiled in a federal fraud case involving the Flushing Federal Savings and Loan Association. Sinatra and I had quietly pitched in to help pay his legal bills. Jilly was eventually sentenced to one thousand hours of community service. In the meantime, he wasn't allowed to leave the country.

We had Diamond Jubilee Tour jackets and I had sets of luggage tags made for everyone on the tour; we assigned a number to each set. They said "PAS," for "Personal Appearance Services," which was my company, and "AFPOL," which stood for "Another fucking piece of luggage." That way the luggage could be easily sorted and delivered to that person's room.

Throughout my years with Sinatra, I always suspected he never felt fear the way most people do; not that heart-racing, sweaty-palms kind of fear that sends people running for cover. Our trip to Japan confirmed it.

We left Australia and flew right into a rapidly developing series of thunderstorms. I don't know if they ever attained actual typhoon status, but *typhoon* is the only word I can use to describe how it felt. The pilot said the plane wasn't equipped to fly above the storm, but at the current altitude we were being tossed around like a boat in rough seas.

We turned green from the turbulence and everyone tried to find a spot to lie down—everyone except Sinatra. He just sat there, Jack Daniel's in hand, cool as a cucumber. I couldn't believe it. I figured we had already cheated death when we flew with the faulty engine in Italy; this time I was sure we were going to die. We all were sure. He didn't even seem to care. When we landed in Japan, the rest of us were ready to kiss the ground. Sinatra disembarked as if nothing had happened.

It wasn't all smooth sailing when we arrived in Europe later that year, either. We played Il Foro in Milan. Pierro Carriagi, who was running the Italian tour, tipped off the media to the location and time of our arrival.

The Mercedes sedan carrying Sinatra, Vine, and me pulled up to the front entrance of the theater. It was unheard-of to take us to the front entrance. Steve, Eydie, and Judy were in a separate car behind us. There were several motorcycle officers, as well as security, escorting us. Before we knew it, though, we were surrounded by the media and probably a thousand people in total. All our protection was cut off behind us.

We were afraid to get out, but the car was being jostled and it seemed dangerous to stay.

Sinatra said, "We have to get out."

I was very apprehensive, but there was really no choice. We decided I would exit first and Sinatra followed holding on to the back waistband of my pants, with Vine holding him, so we wouldn't be separated.

In the midst of the crowd, a very aggressive photographer was getting in our faces. I didn't know how to manage him, so I kept pushing forward. Suddenly I heard a loud pop. Sinatra still had his left hand on my waistband and with his right hand had swung and hit the guy in the face. The guy's feet left the ground and he went down. Sinatra was tough. He often worked out on a punching bag, but I would never have guessed a seventy-five-year-old man could pack such a wallop.

I looked back to see if our team was okay. There was no way to make it to the backstage entrance. We had to walk in the front door, through the arena floor, and onto the stage to navigate our way to the dressing rooms.

When we saw Carriagi we were all furious.

"Are you trying to get us all killed?" Sinatra yelled. "You've never done things the right way, but this is the wrong way."

Carriagi knew he screwed up and quickly but somewhat incoherently blamed it on security. He said they pulled up to the wrong door, but we all knew he was a media guy and wanted to drum up some drama.

Sinatra could be volatile, and that incident, on top of an earlier one back in the States, had me concerned. We were at the Miami Arena and as I walked backward to bring him down the stairs, a woman reached out, grabbed at him, and kept pulling.

He went berserk.

"Get your hands off me!" he yelled.

I was in front as usual and quickly pushed to move us out of there.

That unnerved me. I had never seen him behave like that before. To make matters worse, I never knew if he was carrying a weapon. That, along with his hearing and vision problems and occasional disorientation, seemed like an increasingly volatile combination.

Meanwhile, as the tour went on, Sinatra developed an upper respiratory infection. Fortunately, it was during a lull between concerts. He had a doctor in France who was checking on him two or three times a day. As you can imagine, with his impatience with doctors, that was driving him nuts. When we arrived in Ireland, though he was still not feeling well, he was fed up with them. Barbara called one anyway. I had a feeling this might not go well. The doctor arrived in his suite in the early afternoon but Sinatra was in no mood.

"I'm fine, you don't have to examine me," Sinatra said.

The doctor persisted in a very professional manner, and when he wouldn't back off, Sinatra became belligerent.

"If you don't get out of here I'll blow your head off!" he yelled.

The doctor left in such a hurry, he didn't even wait for the elevator. He took the fire escape down.

"This the second time we're playing here," Sinatra said. "The first and the last."

While we all laughed about it and didn't consider it a serious threat, I wondered how safe it was for him to continue to have access to weapons.

THIRTY-FIVE

I woke up one morning in the Palm Springs guesthouse and found Sinatra walking around, just outside his living quarters, looking at the vast compound he had built. It was ten o'clock in the morning and he was in his bathrobe. This was not part of his normal routine, so I was a little concerned and went over to see how he was.

"I have a lot of things on my mind," he said.

"Well, let's talk about them," I said.

"Good idea. I'm going to go shower and change and I'll meet you in the movie theater in an hour."

The theater, equipped with a sofa, bar, some comfortable chairs, and a movie screen that dropped from the ceiling, was a perfect spot to entertain friends and watch first-run films, but as we sat down in the chairs with our coffee, I knew this conversation was all about business. It was 1991 and I had come to the desert to discuss, among other things, the recommendations I made to Harvey Silbert, a famed Los Angeles entertainment lawyer with the prestigious Loeb & Loeb law firm, regarding a new will. As we sat there drinking coffee and making small talk, Sinatra looked me in the eyes with all the intensity those baby blues could muster.

"I want you to be the coexecutor to my estate," he said, "along with Harvey Silbert. Make sure my kids are taken care of and my wife doesn't get screwed."

Those are the words that stayed with me for years. "I'll do my best, Boss. I'm honored, but why me?" I said.

"Because you know where everything is buried and no one is going to fuck with you on this. Besides, I know you will do the right thing for Barbara and my kids."

For my part, I was certainly comfortable with the financial side of things, and I knew I was qualified to handle the accounting issues. I was not necessarily comfortable with the role of trying to make Barbara and the Sinatra kids happy. Satisfying both sides was not going to be an easy task. I was worried about the heavyweight championship fight that was about to take place.

Most people assemble their will in private and the recipients don't find out about the final disbursement until the person's death. This had already shaped into an open, sometimes public battle for Sinatra's assets while he was still alive and while he was caught inextricably and uncomfortably in the middle. I was confident, though perhaps naïvely so, that I could work everything out to everyone's satisfaction as long as I had some specific provisions.

"Boss, I'm really flattered and very honored to be asked," I said, "but this could end up being the biggest lawsuit in California history."

Sinatra shook his head. "Your job is to make sure that doesn't happen."

I thought about that. Maybe there was a solution. "Then we need a special clause. One that says if anyone challenges the will and loses, they're out."

Sinatra sipped his coffee. He nodded. "You got it," he said.

Arriving at this point had taken years of due diligence to understand the complicated estate of a superstar like Sinatra. In between the rigorous touring, over time I had familiarized myself with his extensive business interests as well as the significant discord that existed between the family—something that Sinatra continued to at least outwardly ignore.

At the time, I felt it was clear that Barbara needed to have her future better defined. I liked Sonny but he was biased toward the kids and made no effort to be impartial. Bob Finkelstein, a slim, dark-haired lawyer with eyes for Tina, represented the kids. Though I didn't know it at the time, they had a personal relationship. Fortunately, Finkelstein was a smart, levelheaded lawyer. He understood that it served no one's purposes to have this whole process dragged through the courts. Together, we began to map out a strategy to satisfy all parties.

It's difficult to pinpoint exactly what causes extended families to bicker, especially when divorce is involved, but this battle was to control not only the estate of Frank Sinatra but also the man himself. In the latter instance, Barbara seemed firmly in charge.

Sinatra deeply loved and cared for his children, but he also loved Barbara and had a responsibility to her as well. He desperately wanted everyone to be happy. The infighting tore him apart. Tina was tough, the most like Sinatra of all the kids. Barbara was pretty tough, too. They made for formidable foes. I knew it was crazy to take on this new role, but I was confident I could negotiate the differences.

A tomato sauce company called Artanis—that's Sinatra spelled backward—was formed in 1990. An irrevocable trust called Somerset Trust owned a Budweiser beer distributorship that went to the children, and a company called Sheffield owned the rights to his name and likeness, which went to the kids, along with his Capitol royalties and control of the masters of his Reprise recordings.

Sinatra owned houses in Palm Springs and Beverly Hills, and some other property; his personal artifacts, including some valuable art; and a few bank accounts. I estimated that Sinatra needed to earn between $5 million and $10 million a year after taxes to take care of his kids and grandkids and continue to live the lifestyle he and Barbara were accustomed to.

Sinatra had a multimillion-dollar bond account and life insurance that would be dispersed as cash to beneficiaries. Cash would go to his first wife, Nancy, children and grandchildren born in wedlock or lawfully adopted, and Bobby, Jilly, Vine, and Dorothy Uhlemann, his executive assistant.

Upon his death, the kids received the rights to Sinatra's name and likeness as well as most of the rights to his music catalog. The real estate, personal belongings, and anything that was not specifically allocated in his will went to Barbara.

One night I met with Tina, the designated spokesperson for the children, and Finkelstein at Silbert's Beverly Hills home. Silbert was a distinguished-looking lawyer with white hair and bushy dark eyebrows, which he quickly furrowed when Tina said the ownership of the Sinatra name and likeness was not worth as much as the Palm Springs and Beverly Hills houses and everything in them. She wanted more.

I completely disagreed, and put the value of his name and likeness at approximately $20 million. In addition to the Budweiser distributorship, the kids' package was worth at least $30 million, and I considered that to be a low estimate. Eventually, partial ownership in his name and likeness would sell for many millions more. At the time, Tina vigorously fought the valuation. I told her to be grateful and just move forward.

Sinatra's future earnings would not only go to supporting his and Barbara's lifestyle but would build the nest egg that Barbara would look to from here on out. So I focused on finding Sinatra work, which was his safest haven from the family turmoil.

As details were laid out, Sinatra told Silbert to share what was in the will with Barbara so she would feel more comfortable. We were out on the road working and they had started to build a house in Malibu. The new will was created in 1991.

We also started work on a company that featured Sinatra's colorful artwork on a limited edition of neckties, a Sinatra cigar, a credit card from MBNA (the largest MasterCard issuer in North America), and even a limited-edition Korbel champagne bottle.

Sinatra shot a Japanese television commercial for ANA airlines, with the tagline "They do it my way." The company wanted a couple of days to shoot it, but in Sinatra's usual style, we shot it in a couple of hours under the direction of the very talented producer and director George Schlatter.

Tina wrote in her book, "Eliot had become the point man for Dad's management team, at the center of his business affairs—which worried me, since I knew how close he was to Barbara." She also quoted me as saying, "You have to believe that I have the best intentions for the family—the *whole* family. I can make this come out right for all of you."

I believe I did that. As Sinatra continued to build his legacy and his assets, with the control of Sinatra's name and likeness firmly in the hands of the children, Tina would declare, "I am Frank Sinatra."

THIRTY-SIX

Don Rickles had impeccable timing and was a true legend. He would sip one or two vodkas before going onstage and adeptly personalize his standard material to suit individual audience members, to create his unique and famous style. He didn't curse and he didn't tell jokes but he kept his audiences howling. He picked on people. He picked on people, mercilessly. He picked on Italians, Jews, and the Polish. He picked on short people, tall people, skinny people, fat people, black, white, brown, young, old, ugly or beautiful, it didn't matter. He was an equal-opportunity insulter.

Going to a Rickles performance was like going to a scary film. His bald head and acerbic wit elicited fears from his audience and tears of laughter. The audience sat in nervous anticipation of catching his eye. No two shows were ever the same, and you never knew if you would be "it." No one knew what would come from his sharp tongue.

The truth is, Don Rickles was a sweetheart, and a gentleman.

Rickles was not just a client. He and his wife, Barbara, were dear friends and Maria and I considered them part of our family. I had known him since my days at the Westchester Premiere Theatre, and he was a lifelong friend of Sinatra, too. I went out of my way to take on his representation during a difficult time in his career, taking a tremendous risk.

It started with a phone call in the early 1990s from Rickles's manager, my old friend Joe Scandore, whom I also knew from the Westchester theater.

Scandore had owned the Elegante, a nightclub on Ocean Parkway in Brooklyn. With his tough talk, dyed dark hair, and half-unbuttoned bold-print sport shirts, he gave the impression of a midlevel wiseguy, and for that reason, Sinatra disliked him. Sinatra knew his share of mobsters, but the big guys, the important ones, didn't act like they walked off a movie set about thugs. While Scandore was not directly connected to the mob, he had underworld contacts.

The way I understood it, Scandore met Rickles when he performed at the Elegante, and started to represent him as his manager. He helped Rickles hone his act as an "insult comedian." In *Rickles' Book: A Memoir,* Rickles wrote, "Like any savvy promoter who came up in the thirties and forties, Joe had connections outside formal show business. That was the way of the world. Without those connections, you never left the dock; with them, you sailed." After my Westchester experience I was determined to stay as far away from that world as possible.

So, when Scandore asked me to meet to talk about a client, I was apprehensive. I had a lot on my plate and wasn't excited about adding to my client roster. When he said it was Rickles, whom I was always fond of, I agreed. Scandore's wife was living in Brooklyn, but he was living in Los Angeles at the time, where I happened to be on business. So I went to visit.

Scandore was very sick with emphysema and in the hospital. He was having trouble breathing. Still, the first thing he said when I walked in was "I'm dying for a cigarette." I laughed along with him but knew that wasn't a good sign.

"I'm not going to be around much longer," he said, speaking between labored breaths. "I want you to take over for Rickles when I die."

Scandore knew that having me represent Don would put Don closer to Sinatra, which would be good for Don's career.

"Joe, I think Don needs to tell me that," I said. "When you're better, let's arrange a three-way call and we can discuss it." I finished my business in Los Angeles and left a few days later. We had the call soon thereafter and we all agreed that when Scandore died, I would become Rickles's manager.

About a year or so later, toward the end of 1992, someone called to tell me that Joe had passed away. The funeral was in Brooklyn. I did not go, but Rickles was there, and in his book he made fun of the wiseguys who showed up to pay their respects. "As I sat in my front pew, I heard people say, 'Hey, there's Louie Zambatone. When did he get out?'" Rickles wrote. What he left out was what happened next, at the end of the funeral.

I was at my office in South Florida when he called. He was in a panic. I could hear the tension in his voice and the muffled sound of people around him. It sounded like he was calling from the funeral home, but wherever he was, he clearly did not want to be overheard. "These guys are all over me," he said in a low voice. "They're telling me that now that Joe is dead, I get 40 percent of my income and they get 60 percent. What am I going to do?"

I groaned inwardly. What had I gotten myself into? I had never heard Rickles so scared. I took a breath. "Don, do you have a contract with Joe?"

"Yes."

"Go home and I'll meet you there. You need a lawyer, so I'll set up a meeting with Harvey Silbert. Call me from Kennedy Airport when you're on your way and I'll make arrangements to head out."

I met Don and his wife, Barbara, in Silbert's upscale L.A. office. Silbert was well respected and known for his philanthropy as well as his celebrity clients. With the two of us in the room, Don seemed calm and hopeful. We were seated around a small conference table when Barbara pulled the contract out of her bag.

Scandore had some scattered bookings for Rickles, extending out for several months. The way the contract was written, now that Scandore was dead, Rickles didn't have any further financial obligation to him or his heirs. He didn't even have to pay Scandore's family the commission on the future work Scandore had booked.

"It says my commissions to him end at his death," Rickles said. He thought he was done paying, but I thought that was wrong and Silbert agreed. It was our opinion that Scandore's wife needed to be paid for the dates that were already set.

"What kind of deal would the two of you have if Eliot represents you?" Silbert asked.

"I paid Scandore 15 percent. I would pay Eliot the same thing," Rickles said.

I told him that wasn't necessary. "All my clients pay me 10 percent, including Sinatra," I said. "I also have a commitment to travel with Sinatra, so I would not be on the road with you. You can use the extra 5 percent to pay someone to travel with you."

Don liked the sound of that and agreed.

"Paying Scandore's estate the 15 percent for all the dates that were previously booked would have to be a condition of our working together," I said. It was the principle of the thing. To his credit, Don agreed.

There was still the matter of the wiseguys from the funeral.

"If you are willing to pay his family for the dates, Harvey and I will do the best we can to solve your problem," I said. I didn't know if we would be able to accomplish anything, but I figured it was worth a try to get these guys off his back. I had one ace up my sleeve, but was this the moment to use it? I really didn't want to go there.

For a decade I had carried around that small piece of paper that Sinatra gave me, with a name and phone number. "If you ever have a problem with anyone, here's a number. Use it," Sinatra had said back in 1982.

Before I left L.A., I convinced myself that this was the moment I'd been waiting for all these years. I pulled the tattered piece of paper out of my wallet and carefully unfolded it to reveal the name "Matty" and a phone number.

By now, I knew Matty was Matty "the Horse" Ianniello. He had reached out to me once when he was in Florida, curious to meet the man Sinatra trusted enough to share his number. He was a giant of a man, with a thick head of gray hair, who spoke like he had marbles in his mouth. I could barely understand a word he said. I just nodded and said yes to everything, in constant fear that he would ask me a question about something that he had just said and I wouldn't know the answer.

Initiating contact with him was the last thing I wanted to do, yet I knew there was a high probability that a call to Matty would solve Don's problem. I held my breath and made the call. He told me to meet him at a bakery in Little Italy in Manhattan.

I flew directly to New York and took a cab to Ferrara's bakery. I wanted in and out of this meeting as quickly as possible.

It was around three o'clock in the afternoon and Matty was waiting. He was drinking coffee, so I ordered an iced cappuccino.

"I have a problem," I said, keeping my voice low. I explained about Joe Scandore dying and the guys who were hassling Rickles.

"So what's your problem?" Matty said, as if for him this was no big deal.

"What do you mean?" I asked. "We're willing to pay Joe's family the 15 percent on the shows booked, even though the contract says he doesn't have to. But these other guys should not be involved in Don's life. It's not right."

He looked at me closely and took a sip of his coffee. "You're a busy man," he said, "and you look tired," then finally, "Go back to work. You've got no problem. You'll hear in a couple of days." I left as quickly as I could and hopped on a flight back home.

A few days later, one of the men who had approached Rickles called me. *The moment of truth,* I thought. I picked up the phone, not sure what to expect.

The caller was to the point. "You misunderstood us," he said brightly. "We are so happy you are willing to pay his wife for the dates Joe booked, and after that, Don is on his own."

I thanked him, hung up, and called Silbert.

"Hey, Harvey, everything is cool. Please tell Don so he doesn't worry," I said. He knew exactly what I meant.

I called Rickles the next day. "Everything is okay," I said. "Let's meet at Silbert's office when it's convenient."

Don started to speak. I did not want to have this conversation on the phone. "Let me know when it's a good time and I will meet you at Silbert's," I interrupted.

It took a couple of weeks for me to make it back to L.A., but when I did, there were a lot of smiles and a few thank-yous at Silbert's office.

I worked for almost a year for Don without pay, while he paid off commissions on the dates Scandore had previously booked. I really didn't mind and was happy he was free of that burden.

I had my work cut out for me. Don had a long history of television and film work dating back to the 1950s, and was mostly known for his numerous appearances on Johnny Carson's *Tonight Show*. His live performance work was mainly limited to Las Vegas, Atlantic City, or other gambling venues, which was a very narrow market, making $15,000–$20,000 per show. There was no chance to make a good living that way. I knew that if we were going to increase his earning potential, he needed to expand his potential markets and secure gigs at performing arts centers in cities across the country, so that the people who had seen him while on vacation at a gambling venue could see him back home, and vice versa.

I had one other hurdle that I wanted to overcome quickly. I remembered that Scandore always complained about Barbara Rickles butting into his business, so I used a different tactic and made her a part of all conversations and decisions from the get-go.

In my world, the roles of the agent and manager complement each other. It is primarily the agent's job to find the client work, and they are paid a percentage of the work the artist does. The manager's job is to plan, organize, staff, and direct the career and life of a star. The agent finds the work and brings it to the manager, who in turn presents the opportunity to the client.

It is the manager's job to strategize and formulate a plan for the client's success. So I had to figure out how to best direct Rickles's career and make sure he was in demand and stayed in demand. Additionally, the manager looks after the client's financial well-being, including investments and insurance needs. Because of my strong financial background, my main point was to always make sure my client's net worth was higher at the end of our relationship than when we started.

Over time, we built up the number of Rickles's performances and his fees. I moved him from ICM to the William Morris Agency. I wanted to use Kenny DiCamillo, a friend of mine at William Morris in New York, but the brass there said Rickles had to have a California agent, so the job went to Ben Bernstein and then Rob Heller. That was fine by me. Regardless of who it was, it was my job to stay on top of the agent and push for more bookings. I also arranged for bookings for Don myself.

I secured some television commercials for Don, including a Snicker's commercial that helped increase his visibility. At one point I put Don together with another one of my former clients, Joan Rivers, who was perhaps the easiest performer I have ever worked with. We went back a long way, from when she was the opening act for Steve and Eydie in the early days of the Westchester Premiere Theatre. She also happened to grow up just minutes from where I did.

I represented her for a short period of time, shortly before her husband, Edgar Rosenberg, committed suicide. She had very little ego and never had the usual fight with other entertainers about who was the opening act and who was the headliner. She was happy to open, do her show, and go home. Above all that, Joan was smart— she wrote all of her own material—and was funny and irreverent.

I thought her piercing but self-deprecating style would be the yin to Rickles's yang. Sure enough, Rickles and Rivers did some very successful shows together. As the success of her jewelry and apparel business on QVC grew, though, she limited the time she was on tour and we parted ways.

To build a career, you have to keep the act crisp and exciting. So I also put Rickles with Lorna Luft and LaGaylia Frazier in an effort to give the show more life. (Oddly, LaGaylia's father, singer Hal Frazier, also performed with Rickles in the 1970s.) LaGaylia was a beautiful woman with the voice on the level of Whitney Houston and the performing skills of Liza. She grabbed her audience and held them. I took on LaGaylia when she was in her early thirties. We secured a record deal but labels were focusing their promotions on increasingly younger performers, like Mariah Carey and Mary J. Blige, both in their early twenties. Eventually she gave up on her U.S. career and found success in Scandinavia. I'm convinced that if I had had her as a client ten years earlier, she would have become a superstar.

I also connected Rickles to Michael Martocci. He worked by day at a travel agency that packaged entertainment experiences, and moonlighted as a Sinatra-esque singer. As a performer, he sold out gambling venues on his own, so when I put him as Rickles's opening act, they were a hit in Vegas and Atlantic City.

In addition to Sinatra-esque performers, I also put Don with the genuine article. One night, as we were reviewing Sinatra's schedule at his home in Palm Springs, I asked Sinatra what he thought about Rickles being his opening act for a short stint at the Desert Inn.

"Great idea," Sinatra said. It had been a while since they worked together, and with Scandore gone, and me as his manager, there were no complications.

A few months later, I was backstage with Sinatra listening on the speakers when Rickles started singing early in the show, which was part of his routine.

Sinatra made a face. "Since when did he become a crooner?" he said. "Tell him to tell jokes."

"Boss, he's always had a few songs in his act," I said, but that didn't matter to Sinatra.

"People come to hear him tell jokes, not sing."

When Don finished his act, I went to his dressing room to explain. It was difficult to tell him, but I had to be blunt. Don wasn't happy, and I didn't blame him. This was his act. Nonetheless, he made a small change to his singing time. Yet it wasn't enough.

Sinatra became so irritated by his singing that he cut Don's time down from a half hour to seventeen minutes. It's never fun to make your client unhappy, but I had to be the bearer of bad news. The tension was becoming too much and I couldn't wait for that gig to be over.

Rickles was in a much better place with a top agent and a new strategy in place. With the exception of standard agent/management fees, all the proceeds went to him. He used a father-and-son team of Jerry and Bill Braunstein as his accountants to help sort out all the numbers. When Rickles sat down with them to figure out his net worth, the answers made him nervous. He called me, blaming the Braunsteins for a lack of financial security and saying he wanted to fire them. I told him to slow down and not to make any impulsive changes. After all, he had a big beach house and a beautiful house in Beverly Hills.

"Downsize your homes, Don, and get your liquid net worth to where you are comfortable," I told him. He did, and that, along with the fact that we raised his fees gradually to $50,000–$75,000 per show, made for a more comfortable life. Even when his health began to deteriorate, and it was difficult for him to navigate airports, I worked to make sure he wouldn't see a dip in income. We hired private jets for nearby bookings like Vegas, and both I and his agent Heller threw in a portion of our commission to make sure he could travel in comfort.

We had significantly increased both his fees and the number of bookings he received and had more than doubled his live performance income. He was working corporate events and special events in addition to performing arts centers.

Despite all the good things happening, Rickles asked me and Heller to cut our commissions by a percentage point. He said his son-in-law had a financial setback and that he needed to figure out how to come up with some extra money for his family without changing his and Barbara's lifestyle. I agreed, although I didn't think it was right to be asked.

When he asked me a second time to reduce my commission by another percentage point, again to help out his family, I reluctantly agreed once more. I understood he needed to take care of his family, but that had no bearing on our professional relationship. It wasn't appropriate. Honestly, he was making more money than ever and asking me, who formulated the plan for his success, to take less money. At the same time, as his health continued to deteriorate Barbara was taking more and more control over his life—what he ate, how he dressed, how he ran his business affairs.

Don't get me wrong. Rickles and I were friendly and spoke several times a month. I wanted him to succeed, and for our arrangement to work. Then his publicist booked a date at the Apollo Theater in Harlem. My office sent the standard bill for the date on the calendar and Rickles sent back half of what we billed. It was very disappointing. I called him and he said he didn't want to pay my full commission on the gig, because I hadn't booked it. I told him that was wrong.

There were plenty of dates I booked that William Morris had nothing to do with, but they still received their commission. So I was annoyed. By now, 2014, the older Braunstein and Silbert had passed away. So all the guys who were part of our original agreement were gone. Now it was just me, Heller, and Don and suddenly it seemed our arrangement had changed. Bill Braunstein, the son, called me to say Rickles wanted to pay me 5 percent to do nothing, but only if I agreed to never speak publicly about our relationship and all the things that had occurred over the years. He wanted editorial control over what I could say about him.

It seemed crazy and downright insulting. Even Sinatra never asked me for that. Like with all my clients, I had no contract with Rickles. It was all based on trust, and when that was gone, what was the point?

So, in the summer of 2014, after twenty-two years together, Don Rickles and I parted ways. When he terminated our agreement in a single-paragraph letter, I was dumbfounded, deeply hurt, and felt completely wronged. He was eighty-eight years old, facing his own mortality, and he was still working when he was ninety.

I suppose you can consider me an "old-timer," but it just wasn't the way we did business. The Don Rickles I knew was a loyal, stand-up guy who paid his dues and his debts. He was a great talent and I was sorry he was no longer a good friend. He did the one thing Sinatra never did: He forgot where he came from.

THIRTY-SEVEN

I started my business with a client roster filled with top entertainers from genres that I understood. As my clients grew older, my son Roy, unbeknownst to me, was looking to find the next generation of artists. I was in Tokyo on tour with Sinatra and Steve and Eydie at the end of 1991 when I called my office in Florida looking for Roy. I was surprised to learn from my assistant that he was in upstate New York.

"What are you doing in Yorkville?" I asked when we connected.

"Dad, you can't believe it," he said. "I was watching *Real Life with Jane Pauley* and I saw a kid playing the guitar. He was amazing. I had to come up to see him." He sounded genuinely excited.

"Are you crazy? Since when are you a talent scout?" This was well beyond Roy's job description, but he was so enthusiastic I figured I would give him a shot at spreading his wings.

"This kid is phenomenal," he continued. "He is the best guitar player I have ever seen and he's only thirteen."

I was intrigued. "Can he sing?"

"No," he said.

"You have no idea what he's going to sound like later, anyway," I said. No one can predict how someone's voice will change after puberty.

"His parents want to meet you," Roy said.

I thought my kid had really lost it this time. He knew nothing about signing a new client, and here we had a child who could play guitar and not sing and Roy had already set up a meeting? The whole thing sounded crazy.

I was planning to be in New York for one of Liza's Radio City dates when I arrived back to the States, so I told him we could all meet then.

We met at the Rihga Royal Hotel, on West Fifty-Sixth Street. The child prodigy whom Roy was so excited about was Joe Bonamassa. His parents were lovely people; his mom was a schoolteacher and his father owned a guitar store. Joe himself was a pudgy little kid with a tiger in his eye, meaning I thought he had the drive to be a winner. He handled himself extremely well for a thirteen-year-old boy. Maybe he had what it took.

Roy was completely sold on Joe, and the parents understood we had the connections to possibly make things happen.

"Your son is very talented," I said. "Roy believes in him wholeheartedly. I have never taken on a new artist before, but I know a lot of people in the business. I have all the confidence in the world that Roy will push as hard as he can to figure out a game plan for Joe's future."

The parents were on board, so we signed the young prodigy and Roy went about putting together a strategy for his career. We brought in Willie Perez, a well-known vocal coach who had worked with Gloria Estefan, among others, to give Joe singing lessons. Short term, it might help him land a record deal.

Joe was developing a voice, but it was a long, slow process for a teenager, so Roy came up with an interesting idea. He pulled together a band composed of the children of musicians, added Joe, and called it "Bloodline."

He took on Erin Davis, Miles Davis's son; Waylon Krieger, the son of Doors guitarist Robby Krieger; Barry Oakley Jr., son of the late Barry Oakley, one of the founding members of the Allman Brothers Band; and veteran keyboard player Lou Segreti.

Joe was the youngest of the group, under sixteen at this time, and they called him "Smokin' Joe Bonamassa."

The kids rehearsed for close to a year with Barry Jr. as the lead singer. Sure enough, after about a year, Roy signed them with EMI Records and they released an album.

Not long after, the group decided that they wanted to go forward without Joe. Roy came to me with the news.

"I have a lot of money in this deal," I said. "Joey is the only one I'm interested in. If the others want out, I'll take my losses. Joe is going to be a superstar."

Roy agreed, so I advised him to let the other kids go and keep Joe; we would continue to support him. Joe was seventeen. Bloodline would dissolve fairly soon thereafter.

Roy had a family and two kids to support at this point. He was feeling a lot of pressure and beginning to second-guess his own judgment. There were bright spots but it was a tough road. They traveled across the country in a small van. They played every little gig that would take them. I don't know how they did it, or how Roy pushed on. There's nothing worse than managing an act that's not making money.

At one point, looking to be a better provider to his family, Roy thought about moving to New York and taking a job at a big company. I did what I could, which was to give him 100 percent of my support and encouragement and suggest that he not give up.

About six or seven years in, Roy was at a low point, but I was noticing that every time they went back to a town, the audiences grew larger.

"Listen, Roy," I said, "I thought you were crazy when you flew to New York to meet this kid. It made no sense to me at all. Now I think you're crazy if you don't stick with him. He's going to be a superstar."

Pretty soon their persistence paid off. Today Joe Bonamassa is considered one of the best blues rock guitarists in the world. He's graced the cover of virtually every guitar magazine multiple times and has sixteen *Billboard* No. 1 blues albums. He tours the world and has played everywhere from Radio City to the Royal Albert Hall in London. He's also a big Sinatra fan and starts all his concerts at 8 p.m. sharp in tribute.

Roy learned how to market on the Internet and use social media not only to acquire hundreds of thousands of followers, but also to convert that audience into ticket buyers, which in turn allowed them to sell out concerts faster than usual. He parlayed Joe's popularity into a growing souvenir business surrounding the tours, selling hats, T-shirts, jackets, artwork, and guitar picks. There's even a highly successful annual "Blues Cruise" for die-hard Joey fans.

They have shared in the wealth by creating a nonprofit organization that works to keep the blues and its long tradition in American history alive in our schools. Roy and Joe are partners now.

Maria and I recently had dinner with Joe's parents in Fort Lauderdale. Lenny, his father, said, "Thanks for making my son a millionaire." I did my part but the real credit goes to Roy.

Roy took an outstanding musician and marketed his talent using the same tried-and-true strategies I taught him. Then he took it to another level with his promotional expertise. He capitalized on something I couldn't teach him, using the latest technology to widen Joe's visibility and create a highly successful brand.

And that is exactly what a manager is supposed to do.

THIRTY-EIGHT

Sinatra hated conflict. That's one of the reasons he loved being on tour. The stage was a place of peace and comfort for him. There were no conflicts when he stepped up to the microphone, only his performance. Offstage, there was no one he was more at peace or more comfortable with than Jilly. As I've said, Jilly was his steadfast companion when we traveled, with the exception of the overseas portion of the Diamond Jubilee Tour. Not having him there had been a disappointment for Frank, but now at least there was his birthday to look forward to.

May 6 was Jilly's birthday, just a few days after mine, May 2. When we were on tour, it became a multiday celebration. We both loved horse racing, and since the Kentucky Derby was the first Saturday in May, watching the race was part of our annual birthday tradition. We celebrated for at least two weeks, and every night at dinner there was a belated happy birthday dessert.

Unfortunately in 1992, we weren't on the road for Jilly's seventy-fifth birthday. For that, Jilly was planning an old-fashioned backyard party at his house in Palm Springs. Jilly spent much of the day before cooking and preparing things. Shortly after midnight that night, he left his house, right across the golf course from Sinatra's, headed for his girlfriend's place.

It had been raining that night and a twenty-eight-year-old alcoholic plowed his Mercedes right into Jilly's car, a white Jaguar with dual gas tanks. It exploded into flames. Jilly struggled to escape the car but the door locks were jammed. He was trapped.

The driver, who had a long list of DUIs, fled the Mercedes on foot. He left Jilly to burn to death just minutes after turning seventy-five. Jilly's body was identified by Tony Oppedisano, Jilly's bearded, red-haired pal, whom we called Tony O. Tony said his body was too badly burned to recognize, so he identified him by his jewelry. The driver who smashed into Jilly's car was eventually arrested, convicted, and sentenced to life in prison.

Jilly's death was a shock to the many of us who knew and loved the rough and tough but privately sensitive guy known not only for Jilly's Saloon, but also for appearances as himself on *Laugh-In,* and who mostly became famous as Sinatra's friend, confidant, and right-hand man.

When Jilly's youngest son, Willy, called me early in the morning at my Coral Springs, Florida, home to tell me the news, I was speechless.

"My father was killed in an automobile accident," he said. He wasn't crying and seemed to be stunned, as I was. It took me a full twenty seconds to even collect my thoughts enough to speak. "What happened?" I said.

I was mortified as I listened to the details of the tragedy. "I'll be on the next plane," I said. "Let me know if there is anything I can do." I hung up the phone and tried to focus my thoughts.

It was too early to call Frank in the desert; besides, Jilly had a lot of friends there who I was sure would reach out to Vine and Barbara to convey the horrible news. My assistant called Vine and told her I was on my way to the compound.

When I arrived, I saw Frank and we gave each other a hug. We were standing in the living room.

"I can't believe this," he said. "This is really tough on me."

"I know, Boss. Jilly always seemed so"—I paused to search for the word—"indestructible."

We were both lost in our grief.

Jilly was not polished and he did not have a formal education. Nonetheless, I didn't know anyone in the Hollywood set who didn't love him. The bigger they were, the more they loved him.

People came from all over the country for Jilly's funeral. The vast majority were celebrities. Sinatra was a pallbearer. Jilly was buried in Palm Springs with a simple tombstone, engraved with a picture of a soaring eagle and JILLY RIZZO, 1917–1992 "HE WAS THE BEST" Those closest to Jilly went back to the Sinatras' house. I was pretty broken up. There were few times in my life I remember feeling that bad. On top of losing a dear friend, I had lost my number one confidant and certainly Frank had lost his. Jilly was also Frank's best friend and protector. As I said, Jilly was officially in charge of Frank's security detail and he was with Sinatra all the time to smooth things out if they went awry. Replacing Jilly would be impossible.

A year earlier, Sinatra's road manager, Nifty Victorson, was fired. With Jilly on the road and others picking up the slack, I had never replaced him. Now I needed a permanent road manager, someone that Frank could feel comfortable with to take care of his personal needs while on tour.

I was sitting with Judy Tannen in the family room at the Sinatras' house after the service at the cemetery.

"What the hell am I going to do now?" I said. I didn't want to think about this, but I had to. We had some local California dates at the end of the month, and while I had already made other arrangements for our upcoming trip to London, Spain, and Greece, we had a full roster of Vegas dates in June that I had been counting on Jilly for.

"What do you mean?" Judy said.

"Who's going to go on the road with Sinatra? I need someone who's close to him and can be the liaison between myself and the Boss when he needs things. I need a really good road manager."

"Maybe consider Tony O.," Judy said. Tony was considerably smaller than Jilly, but since this was not a security position, size didn't matter. Tony O. had been trying to make it as an actor and producer in Hollywood. Because of his friendship with Jilly, Tony had been around Sinatra long enough that Sinatra knew who he was, though not necessarily by name.

A few days later I spoke to Barbara, who said she had no problem with the idea of Tony O. going on the road with Sinatra. When I asked the Boss, he agreed and so Tony O. became the point man for anything Sinatra needed of a personal nature on the road.

Jilly was irreplaceable, and losing him left a hole in all our hearts. He spoke his own unique and colorful language, a hybrid of the hard-knock streets he grew up on and the opulent world he navigated with Sinatra. I will always remember his wit, loyalty, enduring dedication, and of course, the deep and rare bond of one of the greatest friendships I have ever witnessed.

THIRTY-NINE

S hirley MacLaine sang, danced, acted, and even wrote her way into the public's heart dating back to the early 1950s. Before she was known for her New Age spirituality and reincarnation beliefs, she was part of the female Rat Pack. She once shared a house with Sinatra and Martin while making the 1958 film *Some Came Running,* directed by none other than Liza's father, Vincente Minnelli. To Sinatra, she was a great girl, a high-energy entertainer whose talent he admired.

With Liza and Steve and Eydie having moved on, I again found myself looking for someone who could help sell tickets and support Sinatra if anything went wrong onstage. Shirley was Mort Viner's client and her performance charisma combined with her long history with Sinatra and popularity in New York made her the perfect fit to join him for several performances at Radio City in November 1992.

On closing night, Barbara Sinatra threw a party at New York's grande dame of chic eateries, the "21" Club. In Barbara's usual style, the private upstairs dining room was softly lit and filled with a who's-who of Hollywood elite and New York power brokers, all seated according to rank at a long banquet table, drinking martinis and sipping champagne.

I was seated directly across from Charles Koppelman, the CEO of EMI, which owned Capitol Records. Sinatra had recorded at Capitol from 1953 to 1961, producing many memorable tunes memorialized in a recording called *The Capitol Years.*

Koppelman was the ultimate image of a high-powered business-man, with a medium build, glasses, and impeccable clothes. He had a happy demeanor and an easygoing personality, which belied the power he wielded in the music business. My interest in Koppelman was in talking about the band my son Roy was representing. EMI had already produced Bloodline's first album and I wanted to pitch him on another one. Koppelman had another agenda, though.

"Why can't I have Sinatra's next album?" he said.

First of all, everyone knew Sinatra worked with Mo Ostin and Warner Bros. Records. It was also common knowledge that he didn't have a contract there, but Sinatra and Ostin were friends since at least the 1960s. Ostin was also close to Mickey Rudin. Koppelman knew that nothing significant had been produced with Warner since *L.A. Is My Lady,* back in 1984. That was eight and a half years ago.

We had all been drinking a bit. Everyone at the table was engaged in their own private conversations and Koppelman kept telling me why I needed to make another Sinatra record happen for EMI. I was not excited by the prospect. The idea of Sinatra prepping to sing original material at this stage of the game was incomprehensible. Finally I said, "Charles, how do you expect me to get him to remember the lyrics to twelve new songs?"

"That's your problem," he said, shrugging. "Figure something out."

"It's not going to happen," I said. "I'm not going into a studio and watch him learn new material." Sure, Sinatra could learn a couple of new songs, but his memory wasn't strong enough to learn new lyrics for an entire album and his eyesight wasn't sharp enough to read new lyrics out of a book. Besides, I would never want to put him through that kind of pressure. He was a perfectionist and this could only go badly.

I have always believed that money was secondary to the long-term interests of my client, but at his age, Sinatra's long-term interests were now. Sinatra was a legendary spender and I had to provide the income for his outgo. A recording, if successful, was by far the easiest way to shore up his finances, but every time the topic of a recording came up, Sinatra said no. He was not about to commit a lesser voice to history.

"What are you going to do to make it worth our while?" I said to Koppelman.

He leaned in. "You'll get the best record deal there ever was," Koppelman said. He was a man of great confidence.

A few days later, Don Rubin, who worked for Koppelman and was in charge of Bloodline, called me.

"Koppelman really wants Sinatra," he said.

I didn't have any answers, though. There was just no way it was a good idea to have Sinatra waltz into a studio and make a new album. For days I would knock my head against the wall, but inspiration came unexpectedly.

I woke up in the middle of the night from a dead sleep and sat bolt upright in bed. I was thinking about what Jilly had told me several years earlier, that Mo Ostin bugged Sinatra to record new material, and though Frank would go into the studio for a couple of days, nothing would come out of it. He would learn a song or two and then not go back.

"They're wasting their time," Jilly said. "He's not going to remember new lyrics. I told all the morons at the record label to get big stars to sing their favorite Sinatra songs with Frank."

Jilly died six months before my conversation with Koppelman. Now his words were haunting me, echoing in my mind.

I woke up Maria.

"I got it," I said.

She turned over and went back to sleep.

I called Koppelman the next day. He picked up right away.

"I have an idea," I said.

"What took you so long?" he said.

I explained.

"Is it realistic?" I said.

"Not only is it realistic, it's a super idea. We can get this done."

I was very excited. I hung up the phone and a few minutes later I called Koppelman back. I had forgotten a couple of things.

"You'll have to assume all the risk," I said.

"That's fine. The record company takes risks all the time."

I had another question. "How will this work with the singing partners?" I said.

"They will split the commissions and royalties fifty-fifty," he said.

"No way. I'm not going to let people come in and take his royalties."

He was taken aback. "Well, what do you propose?" Koppelman said.

I went for it. "Why can't Sinatra get 100 percent from the original album? Eighteen months later we will give each artist the produced song and they can put it on any album or do anything they want with it on a one-time use."

Koppelman laughed. I could tell he thought the idea of asking the duet partners to do it for free and take no royalties on the original was crazy, despite the fact they would have the right to use the cut on their albums. "If you can get away with that, it's brilliant, but I don't think it will fly."

That was the beginning of the *Duets* album phenomenon. It was as if Jilly had reached out from the grave. I laughed at the irony that the whole thing started after Sinatra's concerts with Shirley MacLaine, perhaps the only person who would think Jilly actually *did* reach out from the grave.

FORTY

The idea of a new Sinatra album was a deal teetering on extinction from the beginning, but I knew if we could pull it off, we would make music history—and history always comes with a price.

Frank Sinatra had long occupied the rarified space of superstar, but perhaps even more telling than the veneration he had from his loyal fans was the respect and admiration he garnered from fellow artists. Koppelman underestimated Sinatra's influence, which may have been greatest among his peers. After all, who better to understand the skill and difficulty of being all that Frank Sinatra was, than other singers? So, while I believed I could convince the best artists to perform with Sinatra on our terms, first there was the little detail of convincing the man himself to agree to the project.

I waited until we were together on a gig. It was January and we were at the Desert Inn in Vegas when I went to his dressing room backstage. Sinatra was sitting on the sofa with a cup of tea on a cocktail table. We talked over some business and had a very relaxed conversation. Before he went to vocalize and put on his tux, the mood seemed right, so I broached the subject.

"Boss," I said, "Koppelman is very excited to do a project with you. We think we can get the top talent out there to sing their favorite Sinatra songs with you."

He matched my enthusiasm with a lack of it.

He took a sip of his tea, put the cup down, and looked me straight in the eyes. "If they want duets, go back and take the original cuts."

"It doesn't work that way," I said.

"I'm not going to rehearse with a bunch of singers," he said.

"You won't have to. You'll record on your own and we will marry the voices electronically." He looked at me deadpan. The conversation was over.

I didn't expect him to jump for joy but I had been hoping for a little encouragement.

I waited a couple of days and then I called Barbara. I figured that if I could explain the importance of the project, she would engage him from her end and together we would have a chance. "This is a fantastic opportunity to put a fabulous album out there," I said, "and if I can pull off what I think I can, it's going to be a big moneymaker. But I'm going to need your help."

Barbara agreed to privately encourage him, then she put her finger on what she thought was the biggest challenge. "Maybe he's scared," Barbara said. That honestly had not occurred to me. Sinatra was seventy-seven years old and firmly entrenched as a legend. He was also a senior citizen with a lavish lifestyle and legendary generosity. Many of those around him acted like he was immortal, and his attitude reflected that: "If I need more money," he would say, "I'll go out and earn it."

I was focused on the opportunity, so I didn't anticipate the many reasons for his reluctance. He still had his commanding style, but his voice had changed; it had deteriorated. No one is in their prime in their seventies. And he hadn't recorded for almost a decade. A lot can change in ten years in the music industry. If I could help him overcome those doubts, I thought, we could make something special happen. So I pressed on.

Over the course of the coming weeks, we had several conversations, mostly before shows in his dressing room, whenever the time felt right.

"Listen, Boss, if you're afraid of what your voice is going to sound like, Koppelman has assured me that if you don't like what you hear, it won't be released. He's assuming all the risk."

He was unmoved.

Sinatra trusted the opinion of his longtime concert production manager, Hank Cattaneo. A bearded guy with bushy eyebrows and gentle eyes, Cattaneo was someone Sinatra put his faith in night after night onstage for more than a decade. I asked Cattaneo, who was certainly up on all the latest technical advancements, to help put him at ease.

"You don't have to worry," Hank said, one night in his dressing room. "If a note is a little off and doesn't sound right, we can fix it. There's a lot we can do now with technology."

Cattaneo was part of what became more than a month of discussions, cajoling, urging, and encouragement to talk Sinatra into signing on. When he finally said yes, it was without conviction. Sinatra was a man of his word, but that didn't mean he didn't frequently change his mind, so I knew this recording deal could fall apart at any time. When faced with this over the years, I had learned that the best course of action was just to keep moving. If he wasn't strongly against something, he might become used to it in time, as long as you didn't wave it in his face. So, after he agreed, I didn't have a long conversation with him about it. I just put my head down and forged ahead.

Barbra Streisand was my number one pick for a duet partner. She was as close as there was to a female equal of Sinatra. Though she was younger than he was, like Sinatra she had a talent that took her effortlessly from records to film. I considered her the greatest female singer of her generation. She had the voice, longevity, popularity, and star power to be the perfect partner. She was also a huge influencer, so if I could bring her on board, others would fall into place.

I was friendly with her manager, Marty Erlichman, who is best known for having discovered her but also had a business bottling and labeling wines for celebrities. I had helped him find talent for his wine business some years before, so we were on good terms. Marty happily explained the premise to Barbra, and within a few days I had an answer. Streisand was in. The project was a go—as long as I could keep Sinatra on track.

Once Streisand was firmly committed to the *Duets* project, I worked with Cattaneo and producer Phil Ramone to come up with a list of artists we thought would complement Sinatra's voice and style.

Natalie Cole, Aretha Franklin, Gloria Estefan, and Luther Vandross were all in. We wanted a variety of popular singers, so Phil Ramone suggested U2's Bono, and though Bono's voice didn't seem on the surface to match with Sinatra's, we knew his style and attitude did. A known Sinatra fan, Bono would also draw a younger audience to the album. Barbara turned us on to Julio Iglesias, who came on board, too (and became a client as a result).

In fact, almost everyone we approached for *Duets* said yes, and after a while everyone kept referring to the project as "Duets" and the name stuck.

By early summer 1993, less than a year after that dinner with Koppelman, everything was set. Sinatra and I were on tour in Germany. Shortly after returning to the United States we would head to the studio to record, which meant we had to nail down the details and avoid any potential problems that might cause the Boss to back out.

Word was out that Sinatra was going back into the studio to record and it was a hot property. I heard through the grapevine that Mo Ostin, with all his history with Sinatra, was furious, though I never heard from him directly. Since *Duets* was really about Koppelman pushing me, I didn't feel it was fair to pit one company against the other, so I never approached Mo or any other studio. Sony's chairman at the time, Tommy Mottola, was much more aggressive.

On June 4, the day before Mottola's marriage to Mariah Carey in the fairy-tale "wedding of the year," he called me in Germany.

"If Frank is leaving Mo Ostin, how the hell can you go to Koppelman?" he asked. "I'm getting married tomorrow, but I'll send the plane for you or I'll come see you myself. You can have whatever you want but I want Sinatra."

"If Koppelman doesn't want to do the deal, you can have it," I said, but at that point the train had left the station. I told Mottola to enjoy his wedding and that if anything changed I would let him know.

We didn't actually have a signed agreement with Koppelman; in fact, we didn't sign a piece of paper until the whole deal was over. As with my client agreements, we lived our lives on handshakes and promises.

Before I left Germany, Liza called to express her disappointment that I would miss her opening at Carnegie Hall with Charles Aznavour. I didn't understand the purpose of the call, as she knew I traveled with Sinatra.

Aznavour, or "Le Petit Charles," as the French called him for his diminutive five-three frame, made up in voice and talent what he lacked in physical stature. His manager and my friend Lévon, a man of similar stature, whose house Maria and I were married in, knew Liza well. He would also be there. There was no obvious reason for her to need me. I had missed many of her dates when I was on tour with Sinatra. I told her I would catch up with her in Washington.

When Sinatra's German tour was over, we flew to London to pick up the Concorde, the ultraluxury, supersonic jet with only one class—first. As we boarded the droop-nose jetliner, I knew this was likely my last opportunity to cement the idea of going into the recording studio. London to New York would take roughly three and a half hours (as opposed to eight hours for a subsonic flight), so I didn't have much time.

The Concorde was a narrow plane with two seats on each side of the aisle and a digital monitor that indicated when the plane hit Mach 1 and 2, which is faster than the speed of sound and twice the speed of traditional aircraft. Sinatra sat in the window seat, so he wouldn't be bothered by the other hundred or so passengers, and I sat on the aisle. We were about an hour into the flight, having cocktails and staring out the window at the edge of space. We were flying so high I could see the curvature of the earth below. It was breathtaking.

He had a look in his eye that made me think he was contemplating his legacy. With that view, you couldn't help it.

"I'm excited to go into the studio with you at the end of the month," I said, raising my vodka rocks in salute. "The guys are all looking forward to the recording session."

Nursing his glass of Jack Daniel's, Sinatra glanced at me and said, with all seriousness, "What recording?"

He knew that those closest to him were concerned about his memory loss, and as I've said, at times he used that to his advantage. I believe he remembered our recording session—we had just talked about it at the hotel in Germany—but he wasn't going to make it easy on me. I decided then and there that pressing the issue would only make things worse. I felt that familiar knot in my stomach, but I changed the subject. I would have to wait for another time.

Over the course of the next several days, I made it to Washington in time to see Liza and Aznavour at the Warner Theater. Aznavour wrote more than one thousand songs in his career, including some for Liza, and his passion, power, and fluidity made for beautiful and memorable medleys with the two. It was a great show, and I went backstage to tell her so, but Liza gave me the cold shoulder. Clearly she was angry that I didn't see her opening at Carnegie Hall.

A few days later, I called her from my office. I thought a good way to break the frost would be to discuss *Duets*.

"We're recording at the end of the month," I said. "Of course, I have you singing 'New York, New York.'"

"I'm not doing that," she said abruptly.

"Are you crazy?" I said. "How can you not? It's the franchise."

She insisted no. I asked her to pick another song.

I knew she was annoyed with me, though I still didn't entirely understand why. In any case, Liza wasn't thinking clearly about the opportunity and was steadfast in her refusal. I made it clear that if she didn't sing it, someone else would. Stars often live isolated lives. They lose perspective and they believe whoever is surrounding them at the time. And someone was advising her she would lose the franchise if she sang "New York, New York" with Sinatra. I *knew* who was advising her. It was my old boss, Mickey Rudin. He was still licking his wounds from his split with Sinatra all those years ago and angry that not only had I taken over Sinatra's career, but I was about to take it to another level.

So I wasn't all that surprised a week or so later, the day before I was set to leave for Los Angeles to begin recording, when Liza called me.

"Darling, all good things have to come to an end," she said cavalierly. After sixteen years together, Liza terminated our relationship with a simple sentence. She continued with Mickey Rudin as her lawyer.

I hung up the phone. I was furious at the ingratitude. I had built up her personal appearance career, hooked her up with Sinatra, and taken her from a net worth of zero in 1978 when I became involved in her career, to more than $15 million.

I didn't have much time to mourn her departure, though. The time for recording *Duets* had arrived.

FORTY-ONE

When the recording day came, I felt the weight of the world on my shoulders. Koppelman had put up a couple hundred thousand dollars for the band and I had arranged for all of the duet partners, as if it were one hundred percent going to happen. But with Sinatra, who knew? Again I warned Koppelman that I couldn't guarantee Frank would follow through with this. He didn't care. "The recording company takes risks all the time, just do your best," he said. That was reassuring, but it didn't lighten any of the pressure.

Sinatra only recorded at night. As we made our way down Sunset Boulevard that evening in the back of the limo, on our way to the Capitol Records Building in Hollywood, I remember thinking it was all up to me. Sinatra had been in a good mood, riding the wave of another successful world tour filled with endless admiration by fans of several generations. He was a master showman and he knew how the excitement of a live venue, the acoustics, and a great band could together cover a multitude of sins on a concert tour. A recording studio, though, is an entirely different animal and can produce a permanent record that will live on for generations.

In the more than twenty years I knew Frank Sinatra, I never saw him flinch—until we were ready to record. I had watched him laugh at scenes that made others cower, and at times had questioned his very capacity for fear when we were on those scary flights. Fear had no place in his public persona and even less in his ego, but it was a formidable foe when it reared its head, and at the most inopportune time. I suppose fear of death and fear of losing his image were two completely different motivators. Death didn't seem to faze him. Death of his iconic status did.

Everyone followed Sinatra's lead. In the back of the limo, there was none of the usual chitchat, no talk of news or sports. I sat next to him. Vine and Cattaneo were facing us, looking out the back window. We all sat silently, waiting for a cue. Sinatra was glancing at his fingernails, as he sometimes did. "So, what are we doing here, Eliot?"

My heart was in my throat. "We're on our way to record the album, Boss."

He looked up at me. "What album?" Deadpan.

I looked at him closely, waiting to see if he was indeed serious.

"This is bullshit," he said, as he turned to look out the window. "Just take some old tracks."

Now I was really nervous. "We can't use old tracks," I said, trying to keep my voice calm. "What, do you want to be Milli Vanilli?" alluding to the singing duo that was stripped of their Grammy in 1990 when it was discovered they didn't actually sing their award-winning song. Sinatra obviously had no respect for fake artists.

As we approached the building at Hollywood and Vine, I certainly wasn't thinking about all the history that had been made at Capitol Records. I was thinking about survival. But there it was— an unmistakable landmark, the world's first round office building, so unique and yet so completely tied to its past that it resembled a stack of records topped by a stylus. Maybe that's how Sinatra felt, like an old record in a world that had made the transition to iridescent compact discs.

It had been thirty years since he strode in the entrance of the Capitol Records Building in his prime. Sinatra understood the sense of history better than most. Sinatra, the Beatles, Nat King Cole, Bing Crosby—they'd all had a hand in creating the ambience. Photographs of those glory days still decorated the halls, but he never stopped to glance and look the past square in the face. As an entertainer, Sinatra was the ultimate competitor onstage. Now he was forced to face the ultimate competition—himself in better days.

There is comfort in familiarity, so I had Studio A filled with all his favorite things—a pack of Camels, Tootsie Rolls, Life Savers, and Jack Daniel's. But the technology would be totally foreign to him.

I held my breath as he walked into the large, paneled studio where the band was set up. This was the same room he had recorded his Capitol hits in, almost forty years earlier. Only this time, in the middle of the studio was a soundproof booth for the singer, essentially a large box that had a microphone, headsets, and a music stand inside. Stage left was a window, behind which were the soundboards, producers, and engineers.

"What is this, a rocket ship?" Sinatra asked, pointing to the booth. "I don't record in a booth," he said. "I record live with the orchestra."

Making the change for that to happen meant a different setup, which required time, but I understood. He was a creature of habit; still, I knew he was apprehensive. I told someone to get Barbara on the phone. If it's true that beside every good man is a good woman, then beside every great man is a woman who encourages, motivates, inspires, and sometimes pushes and challenges him to a higher level.

"He's nervous, Barbara," I said.

"Well, what do you want me to do, Eliot? Do you want to put him on the phone?" I didn't think that would work. I knew we needed to stick with our routine and head to a late-night dinner.

"Can you meet us at La Dolce Vita? We have to make some changes in the studio." I figured being at one of our regular hangouts might take the edge off.

"I can be there in an hour," she said.

Dinner was uneventful, but Sinatra always liked to go out to dinner when we were working to discuss necessary business. We talked about the changes that would be made to the studio and all seemed on track for the next night.

In the meantime, I instructed the crew to tear down the walls of the recording booth and erect a platform so Sinatra could sing with the band.

The next night I drove us all to the studio. Sinatra sat in the front and Vine and Cattaneo sat in the back. It seemed less formal than a limo, like we were just going for a ride to the studio, no big deal.

"You know what, Eliot? This whole idea sucks," Sinatra said.

I kept my eyes on the road. "Come on, Boss, it's going to be great. You've done this a thousand times."

"It's a dumb idea," he said.

No one said a word the rest of the way.

Everything had been fixed in the studio by the time we arrived. There was a small stage facing the band. Patrick Williams, the multiple Grammy- and Emmy-winning musical director and conductor, was in clear sight. There was a microphone hanging from the ceiling. A pair of headsets was draped over the top of the music stand and the teleprompter was off to the side. It was a perfect setup.

I escaped upstairs to a lounge, hoping that if Sinatra had no one to complain to, he would just sing. High stress sometimes led me to smoke, a habit I had not yet completely kicked. I sat down and lit up a cigarette. I was alone, waiting for an all-clear from Vine to go into the studio. That never came. Within fifteen minutes the Boss was looking for me.

When I returned to the studio I could see he was nervous. Worst of all, he could find no more excuses, or so I thought. Sinatra pointed to his throat.

"It's bothering me," he whispered. "I can't sing."

You learn a lot about a man when you spend as much time with him as I did with Sinatra. You couldn't be within a hundred yards of Sinatra and not know he was there. He took control of every situation he was ever in. His mannerisms, his gait, his jokes, his sarcasm, the way he stood, the way he pointed a finger, everything said "I'm the Boss."

The Sinatra who made powerful men weak in the knees, though, wasn't there that day. I saw it in his eyes. In a way, I couldn't blame him; I wouldn't want to compete with myself as a young man, either, much less compete with Sinatra as a young man. Still, I knew this could work, particularly with his unique style of singing.

Though many tried, no one could imitate him or replicate his breath control. In the early days of his career, Sinatra picked up his unique breathing technique by watching Tommy Dorsey play the trombone. Dorsey would suck in air from the side of his mouth while simultaneously blowing out. Sinatra perfected the difficult technique for his voice, which enabled him to create phrasing that was almost impossible to duplicate. Even if the voice had changed, the phrasing was still there.

"Give me a little bit of time to explain to the band what's going on and we'll go to dinner," I said.

I went to the phone and called Barbara again.

"I don't know what we are going to do, Barbara. He's not singing. We're going to head to La Dolce Vita again."

"What?" she said. I could hear the anger in her voice. "I'll be there as soon as I can."

Sinatra and I arrived first and ordered a round, a martini for him and a vodka rocks for me.

Sinatra barely said a word, and I had run out of things to say. About the time we were ordering our second round, Barbara walked in.

"Are you a washed-up singer?" she said. "Have you lost your balls?"

I could see his face flush red with anger. "My throat is bad," Sinatra said.

"Bullshit. You must be afraid of something," she said.

It was late and the people around us were just finishing their dinner. Barbara was furious, and although she wasn't loud, the looks from the surrounding patrons made it clear they were aware there was a disagreement going on.

It was a fight that, for a time, I didn't think they would survive. It made up in passion what it lacked in volume. Barbara spoke to her husband like no one spoke to Sinatra. She did everything—she pushed him, she challenged him, she used every trick she could think of.

"Maybe you don't think you can do this?" Barbara said. "Everyone else thinks you can do this, but maybe you don't?"

"Don't tell me how to sing," Sinatra said. He grew quiet and took another sip of his martini.

"Maybe you might as well just quit," Barbara said. "If you're not up to it, that's what you should do."

He continued sipping the martini without responding. A few moments later he turned to Barbara. Then he looked at me, and back at Barbara. He had come to some decision.

"Screw you both. I'll do it tomorrow."

Now I had my hopes up. There was a slight problem, though. "Tomorrow is the band's night off," I said.

He was livid and said, "Go find them. Give 'em a different night off. I want to sing tomorrow."

Barbara had pushed all the right buttons. There is no doubt in my mind that without her, *Duets* would never have happened.

I immediately started making calls from the restaurant but it was too late to reach all the players to make a change.

My second call was to Koppelman. It's okay to lose if you get a run for your money, but now I was calling him to say I couldn't even bring Sinatra to the post that night. I was embarrassed and he could hear it in my voice. It was one thing to have Sinatra sing and then decide not to release. It was an entirely different matter to be unable to deliver my artist. "Charles, I don't know how to tell you this. I feel horrible," I said.

"Stop with the shit, Eliot. I'm a big boy. I've lost before and I will lose in the future. If anyone can get this done, you can. Just keep going." Koppelman wanted to complete this album not just as the head of EMI, but as a Sinatra fan.

The band took the day off and after two sleepless nights, by the time we arrived at the studio, I was completely wiped out. No one said a word during the twenty-minute car ride from Sinatra's home on Foothill Road in Beverly Hills.

I could feel the tension as we walked down the halls, quiet, but palpable nonetheless. We were all on edge.

As we walked into the bustling studio, a hush came over the band. Everyone waited to see what would happen next as Sinatra, looking distinguished as usual in his collared shirt and Members Only windbreaker, lit a cigarette. He put on his glasses. He looked pretty hip for an old man. Meanwhile, I was in agony. We were so close.

He wasn't that skinny kid with the Brylcreemed hair who made the young girls faint, or even that middle-aged guy with the hat cocked off to one side and the self-assured smile that curled up on the same corner the hat tipped down. He was rounder now, a toupee replacing those thick dark waves, but there was still a twinkle in those old blue eyes, and he could still make the women swoon and the men wish they were in his shoes.

At least that was the Sinatra I saw. I hoped that was the Sinatra he felt like.

I was still plagued by doubts. Maybe I had been wrong about this whole thing. Maybe I shouldn't have forged ahead with little encouragement from Sinatra. Maybe I should have taken his cues more seriously.

I wasn't the only one praying for Sinatra to sing. Everyone there was pulling for the Boss to come through. The band, the crew, they were all paid whether Sinatra sang or not, but this was their shot at making magic with Sinatra, too. Everyone wanted to own a piece of this moment.

Phil Ramone was producing and Cattaneo was coproducer. The history, Cattaneo's familiar face, along with Sinatra's respect for his work, meant all the world. Ramone himself was a music prodigy who had played violin for Queen Elizabeth II at age ten and went on to become a mixing and engineering genius. He was new to Sinatra, but he had worked on albums for Streisand, Paul McCartney, Bob Dylan, and Billy Joel. Cattaneo and Ramone, each with his graying beard, gentle demeanor, and oversize talent, were designed as a catalyst for Sinatra's rebirth and success.

As he approached the microphone, I knew I needed to move out of eyesight. There could be no more excuses. I told the crew that if he asked, "Tell him I had to go out."

Upstairs, the lounges had speakers. I was too exhausted to pace. I just sat there on the couch preparing myself for the reality that this might not happen. The piano started to play. I listened to every hit of the piano key in slow motion like a child playing chopsticks. Then, right on cue, I heard his voice.

"It's quarter to three. There's no one in the place, 'cept you and me. So set 'em up, Joe. I got a little story, I think you oughta know."

It was one perfect, sultry note after another—the pauses, the phrasing, the melancholy. It was pure Sinatra, the Saloon Singer.

You could hear the confidence build. It was the best of Joe DiMaggio, Secretariat, and the seventh game of the World Series.

"We're drinking, my friend, to the end of a brief episode. So make it one for my baby, and one more for the road."

Frank Sinatra had found his balls. He *had* changed on the long, long road. His voice had matured. He was flawless. And once he was rolling, I knew there was no turning back.

Sinatra didn't know exactly where I was, but he was sure I was in earshot. When he was finished, I heard him say, "If you don't like this, Eliot, you don't like vanilla ice cream."

I sprang to my feet. The crew broke into applause. Some yelled out in spontaneous release. There wasn't a dry eye in the house. Hallelujah!

It was the only take he did of that song. It is cut thirteen, just the way he sang it for the very first time that night, "One for My Baby (and One More for the Road)." It is the last cut on the album and the only cut that isn't a vocal duet. No one could sing that with Sinatra. Kenny G played saxophone and it later became "All the Way/One for My Baby (and One More for the Road)."

Maybe you can hear it, the mastery that never left him, the electricity, the feeling that gripped his audiences, the emotion he *lived* when he sang. Nothing could take "the Voice" out of Frank Sinatra. It was the way he introduced a song, the intensity, the sureness. It was his unique way of being him. Age couldn't keep him from being who he was.

Sometimes when I listen to that song, I can imagine him sitting there on a bar stool, popping back a shot of Jack as the bartender closes up. Sinatra turns to look at me. He gives me a wink and smile, and heads out the back door.

He treated the recording session like a live performance, and while I was confident this was going to happen, I was still nervous. He had hit a home run but the game wasn't over. My fears were unfounded, however. He didn't believe in multiple takes, and he rarely did more than two. He never picked up a track in the middle of a song. He would go back to the top and do it all over again, if he had to. We cut eight tracks that night, all in one or two takes, which is unheard-of with most artists today. I remained in the lounge by myself and listened to one take after another, afraid that if I went into the studio I would break the spell.

When we wrapped for the night, the band was ecstatic. Ramone, Cattaneo, and Williams were all smiles. Sinatra was feeling good and I could tell he was proud of what he had done. We were all certainly proud of him. Everyone talked about how great the night was. July Fourth weekend was almost upon us, but it felt like New Year's Eve.

La Dolce Vita stayed open late for us that night. Barbara joined us and Sinatra brought along some of the crew, including Cattaneo, Ramone, and Don Rubin from Capitol. We spent the night discussing how wonderful the session had gone. We were all jubilant and Sinatra had his persona back. The atmosphere was night and day from where we left the previous dinner.

We were set to go back in the studio the next day. If all went as well as it did Thursday, it would be a wrap. Then Vine called me the next morning.

"Eliot, I think you have a problem."

"What now, my love?" I said.

"He says it's a holiday weekend and he's not singing," she said.

I drove from the Peninsula hotel to his house. Vine answered the door and gave me a look of patient resignation, which only confirmed that there was little I could do.

Barbara was off somewhere and Sinatra was still in his robe, having breakfast. He completely ignored me, knowing why I was there. Having been in this situation before, I sat down at the dining room table and waited.

Finally, he looked up.

"It takes somebody two months to do eight cuts. I'm going to the beach for the Fourth of July, Eliot. You're either coming or you're not," Sinatra said.

I knew the times I could argue, and this wasn't one of them. Maria and I spent the weekend at their beach house in Malibu, where they threw a big party on the Fourth.

Despite not recording over the holiday weekend, we were on a high. Everything was going extraordinarily well. I tried to tell him how amazing he was, but the truth was that Sinatra became embarrassed when people talked too glowingly of his abilities. He wouldn't keep that kind of conversation going, but I believe he was starting to believe in his own greatness again. I was feeling a little better. How could he quit after that fabulous session? But I knew we weren't out of the woods yet, and my stomach was still in knots. We ate, drank, and talked about how great everything was going. We talked about his voice and who of the other artists should sing what songs, though ultimately those decisions were left to Ramone and Cattaneo.

On Tuesday night, we went back to the studio and he sang eight more songs. This time I sat in another room upstairs that had a speaker on the wall. I couldn't see him, but I could feel the easy sway of his body as he wrapped up the album, one cut after another, all in his trademark one or two takes. In all we cut fifteen tracks. We only needed twelve, which meant to me that we were three tracks into another album.

Sinatra was impeccable as always. He never criticized the band if someone made a mistake, but he always knew it was there. He had great respect for the musicians and their contribution to his songs. It was clear he had recaptured his mojo and was feeling good.

It was only after we wrapped the sessions that someone pointed out the pictures of him that lined the halls, taken during a time when

Sinatra had produced one of the greatest bodies of work in popular music. Sinatra paused, looked at the photos and smiled.

For a minute, the pressure was off, but a new phase was just beginning. I still had thirteen egos and their managers to deal with.

FORTY-TWO

We always knew there was no way Sinatra was going to rehearse with singers who had their own styles and weren't used to his one-take philosophy. From the beginning, the duets were an electronic puzzle, using all new technology at the time. Ramone and Cattaneo assigned a song to each singer according to their preference and what they thought would work best, having heard Sinatra's takes. Each artist recorded in a studio most convenient to them—Aznavour recorded in Paris, Bono laid his tracks in London, and most everyone else came to Capitol studios with their own crew.

While I was only present for Sinatra's recording, I did need to know who was recording, where, and when, so I was furious when Cattaneo called to say Liza was set to record at a different recording studio in Los Angeles. I didn't even know what song she was going to record. After she had fired me, she and Mickey kept me completely out of the loop. I don't know if it was meant as a final slap or that she simply couldn't face me, but Cattaneo told me Liza didn't even want me in the studio while she was recording. This was my project and I wasn't about to let it take place without me.

I went to Sinatra's house and explained what happened. He was already annoyed that Liza didn't want to sing "New York, New York" and he had agreed that we could figure out another song.

"If she has an attitude, just forget her," Sinatra said.

"I'm in a difficult position, now that she fired me," I said. "I don't want to part ways on bad terms."

"You tell her I want you in the studio. If you don't go, the project is over," Sinatra said.

I went, with my wife, Maria. She had never joined me for a recording session, but she wanted to be supportive. She's always been there, personally and professionally, for me in so many ways, but I hadn't paid much attention to the pressure that was on her through the whole *Duets* saga. In addition, Maria had lived through the years of tension with Rudin and the years of loyalty and dedication to Liza, so she knew how much I wanted this project and needed it to be a success.

Maria always had a good relationship with Liza, and we both hoped having her at the studio would help ease the strain. We were wrong. The pressure was apparent to everyone. Cattaneo came to me first. As I stood in the greenroom waiting for her arrival, I was insistent on staying calm.

"Eliot, you have to leave," Cattaneo said nervously. "She's not going to sing with you here."

He was trying to appease everyone, that is, everyone but me. I had introduced Cattaneo to Liza and Sinatra. He wouldn't have been there if it weren't for me.

"You forget where you came from, Hank," I told him. It was the only disagreement I had with the guy before or since in thirty years of knowing him, but I wasn't going anywhere.

I could smell Rudin's cigar before he ever walked into the room and I heard him yelling at someone with his gravelly, intimidating voice. Then I saw Rudin's large body in his usual disheveled suit and tie, sucking on that cigar, with his briefcase in one hand and Liza's dog, that Maria always called Toto, for obvious reasons, in the other.

I was sitting on the sofa and could see Liza through the glass as she swept into the studio. Rudin marched over and towered over me. I didn't bother standing.

"You really should leave, Eliot. Liza's not comfortable. She's gonna have a problem recording," he said.

"I'm not going to bother her," I said evenly. "I won't even speak to her."

"I'm gonna call Frank," he said.

"Go ahead," I said, as Maria walked into the room. When she laid eyes on him, something inspired a jolt of unfiltered anger in my normally nonconfrontational wife. There she was on tiptoes, all five feet five inches of her, nose-to-nose with Rudin like Billy Martin to an umpire.

"How dare you tell my husband to leave," she said, finger wagging. "Liza isn't asking him to leave. You're asking him to leave. You're the one who should leave. Just back off and let my husband handle it."

He backed off, about twenty feet, to the wall, with the yapping Toto still in hand. Maria said it better than I ever could. I had never seen that look on Rudin's face before and never would again. I can only describe it as flustered. He paused a beat, then turned and walked out of the room and into Liza's dressing room. He and Liza chatted briefly, and then they left. At this point, I didn't care if she never made it onto the album. If she turned something in, that would be fine, and if she didn't, it would be her loss. We had plenty of other artists to choose from. When I explained to Sinatra what happened, he didn't care, either, and said, "No big deal."

Vandross turned in the first cut. Three other artists then completed their recordings before Liza finally laid down her track for "I've Got the World on a String," in South America of all places. As for "New York, New York," Sinatra's close friend Tony Bennett stepped up to perform it. Did we take a great song and do it justice? Not in my opinion. Nonetheless, the Sinatra-Bennett version enjoyed wide play.

Barbra Streisand decided just before the final cut that she wanted to personalize "I've Got a Crush on You." She called Sinatra "Francis" in the song and she wanted Sinatra to call her "Barbra." Cattaneo and I went to Sinatra's dressing room at the Sands in Atlantic City, tape recorder in hand. We had our piano player hit a key and asked Sinatra to say, "My Barbra." He said it twice, and that's how it stands. It was a winner.

While Sinatra and Streisand had mutual respect and admiration, when I told him Bono would be recording "I've Got You Under My Skin," he said, "Who the fuck is that?" All the traditional Sinatra people thought it was crazy, it didn't fit. Ramone had talked about Bono's great love for Sinatra and the Sinatra style. When I explained that Bono was the lead singer of U2, one of the most popular rock groups of the day, and that Bono himself was considered a man of style and attitude, I think the Boss understood. If not, at least he trusted me.

Gloria Estefan was a delight. In my opinion she found a whole new voice when she sang "Come Rain or Come Shine." Sinatra later met her for dinner one night in Fort Lauderdale, and I told her husband and manager, Emilio, that she should record an entire album in that smooth, sexy style. It's one of my favorite cuts on the album and among my favorite pieces of her work.

Sinatra and partners had made their magic separately. Luther sang "Lady Is a Tramp," Aretha "What Now My Love," Julio "Summerwind," Natalie Cole "They Can't Take That Away from Me," Charles Aznavour "You Make Me Feel So Young," Carly Simon "Guess I'll Hang My Tears Out to Dry," and Anita Baker sang "Witchcraft."

There was one song that was a glaring omission from *Duets*. I wanted the Chairman of the Board/the Boss to sing the anthem of every self-made man of a certain generation—"My Way." If I had to pick one thing that made Frank Sinatra who he was, it's that he truly was up and down or over and out, but he always made it back and did it his way. In a way, he was "everyman," or at least the way every man wanted to be. So was Bruce Springsteen. It was a natural—two guys from New Jersey who exceeded everyone's expectations, except their own, and never lost touch with the average Joe.

Springsteen turned us down, though. He said he had a prior engagement. There were some other notable rejections, like Elton John and Billy Joel, but Springsteen especially smarted for me.

Anyway, now it was Ramone and Cattaneo's turn to work their magic and marry the voices. The first thing was to sweeten all the voices and fix any notes that were off. Then Ramone would have to figure out how and where he wanted to weave in the other voices with Sinatra's cuts. Whether the artist sang to Sinatra's track or sang it solo, they basically took Sinatra out where they put them in or mixed the voices together. The whole process took several months.

When the final CD finally arrived, my anxiety level shot up again. We were at the Sands in Atlantic City, where Sinatra was performing. I needed to hear it alone, so I kicked everyone out of my suite, sat down on the sofa, put on headphones, and listened. When the last track played, I was thrilled and said out loud to the empty room, "This is a hit. But what if the Boss doesn't like it?"

I knew Sinatra also needed to hear it alone, without distractions. He and Barbara were staying at a rented beach house in Atlantic City, overlooking the water. I sent the cut home with Barbara for him to listen to after his show. I told her to call me no matter what happened and what time of the night it was. I was on pins and needles.

I expected to hear from them the next day. Instead, she called me at three in the morning. I was wide awake.

"Well, Eliot, there's good news and bad news," she said. "The good news is he loved it. The bad news is, he said, 'If you knew what the fuck you were doing, you would have done it a long time ago.'"

FORTY-THREE

Frank Sinatra didn't care for rock and roll. He didn't like music that didn't have a story he could understand. Popular music just wasn't his thing and I didn't know a single pop star he admired. His collaboration with Bono on "I've Got You Under My Skin" took Sinatra's classic song through a time tunnel. It turned out to be among the most memorable cuts on *Duets* and put Sinatra in front of a whole new generation. In fact, at least one pop station deejay introduced the song by saying, "Many of you may not have heard of Frank Sinatra, but here's Bono's new recording."

Bono, perhaps more than any other artist on *Duets,* was stretched to a completely foreign level. He actually had the guts to call Sinatra an "old fool" on the recording, and remarkably, Sinatra thought that was cool. While on the surface it might seem like they wouldn't have much in common, both men liked to drink and hang out. Both were painters and they bonded as artists and singers. For all these reasons and more, Sinatra became very fond of Bono.

Sinatra sang on film and tape countless times, but modern music videos were new to him. He was seventy-six years old and still experiencing things for the first time. Bono went to Palm Springs to shoot the music video for "I've Got You Under My Skin." We shot them meeting in a bar and riding in the back of a limo. At one point,

Sinatra told Bono, "I don't usually like guys who wear earrings." I think Bono thought that was cool.

Eventually we produced a memorable, cross-generational video for the time.

"Don't you know Blue Eyes, you're never gonna win?" was delivered with a combination of attitude and admiration that Bono later expressed in his introduction to Sinatra at the 1994 Grammy Awards in New York City.

Sinatra, who already had a Lifetime Achievement Award and a Trustees Award, was about to receive the Grammy Legend Award, making him the first and only artist to receive all three "Special Merit Awards" from the Recording Academy. I had no idea when I walked into Radio City Music Hall that night that Sinatra would become the biggest newsmaker of the evening.

Sting performed. So did Whitney Houston, who won Record of the Year for "I Will Always Love You." *The Bodyguard* soundtrack took Album of the Year, Toni Braxton won Best New Artist, and Natalie Cole sang a tribute to Curtis Mayfield. Then came the moment Barbara, Susan Reynolds, Hank Cattaneo, and I had been waiting for: Comedian Gary Shandling introduced Bono to present Sinatra's award.

Bono had just lobbed an f-bomb while accepting his own Grammy for Best Alternative Music Album for U2's *Zooropa,* saying, "I think I'd like to give a message to the young people of America— and that is we shall continue to abuse our position and fuck up the mainstream. God bless you."

What most didn't know was that before Bono introduced Sinatra, the two had met backstage in the greenroom, which had a fully stocked bar. Bono started pouring for both of them. What happened next was likely a combination of the young rock star trying to keep up with what he perceived of the legendary Rat

Packer and the aging legend not wanting to be outdone by the brash new star.

Whatever it was, Bono was throwing 'em back at a pretty good clip and Sinatra was keeping up. Remember, Sinatra was the guy who believed in one ounce of alcohol per hour. In all my years with him, I never saw him take more than a sip or two of alcohol before going onstage. It wasn't his way. That night I saw him take three or four shots. Seeing him break his own rules before a major acceptance speech had me concerned.

Bono went onstage smoking a cigarillo. He unfolded a piece of paper, swayed a bit, and barely looked up as he proceeded to read one of the most poetic and accurate tributes to Sinatra that anyone could have hoped for.

"Rock and roll people love Frank Sinatra because Frank Sinatra's got what we want: swagger and attitude," he said. "Rock and roll plays at being tough, but this guy well, he's the Boss of Bosses, the Man, the Big Bang of Pop. I'm not gonna mess with him, are you?" He pointed to the audience.

"You know his story because it's your story. Frank walks like America—cocksure," he said, looking up from his script.

"To sing like that you've gotta have lost a couple of fights. To know tenderness and romance, you've gotta have had your heart broken . . . This is the conundrum of Frank Sinatra . . . Troubleshooter and troublemaker. The champ who would rather show you his scars than his medals."

Bono broke into a smile and continued.

"Ladies and gentlemen, are you ready to welcome a man heavier than the Empire State, more connected than the Twin Towers [*laughter from the audience*], as recognizable as the Statue of Liberty and living proof that God is a Catholic."

Sinatra walked out to a standing ovation that lasted more than a minute, with "Young at Heart" playing in the background. He walked to the microphone and took a bow. Bono handed Sinatra a crystal award. Holding it close to his chest, Sinatra said, "That's the best welcome I ever had." It was obvious he was deeply touched.

The audience was still standing and the applause resumed.

I was standing backstage with Cattaneo. He was overseeing the sound and lighting for the show and communicating with the control room via headset. I studied the expression on Sinatra's face in the monitors, worried that the drinking would have an adverse effect.

"This is like being in baseball. The bases are loaded and you're at bat and you don't know what you're going to do," he said. There was so much emotion in his voice, and every sentence brought more applause.

"Isn't that pretty," he said, holding up the award. He really didn't seem to know what to say, and at one point he took a deep breath and looked disoriented. For a minute I thought he didn't know why he was there.

"This is more applause than Dean heard in his whole career," he said. There was laughter, which seemed to encourage him. He was rambling now and I was growing more nervous with each word. He talked about drinking and then he looked for Barbara.

"Where's my girl? There she is. Say hello to Barbara, everybody please."

She stood and blew him a kiss.

"I love you. Do you love me?"

The audience again laughed. "I don't quite know what to say to you. You know, there was no discussions about singing a couple of songs; otherwise if we had there would be an orchestra here with me. But apparently that's not what they wanted tonight and I'm angry."

More laughter. He shrugged his shoulders. "I'm hurt."

He was becoming increasingly sentimental. When Sinatra became sentimental you never knew what was coming next. He might start talking about Ava or Nancy. I didn't know what he would say, but I couldn't stand by and let him melt down on live television.

"Tell them to go to commercial," I said to Cattaneo.

He looked at me with wide eyes.

"Sinatra's manager said we should go to a commercial," he said into the headset he was wearing.

"I'm just happy to be here in the Apple," Sinatra said. "I love coming back all the time. It's the best city in the world."

The director cut to a wide shot of the audience and the announcer came on as CBS cut to commercial.

Sinatra looked bewildered.

"You got a big pair of balls," Cattaneo said, but I think he knew I did the right thing.

Susan Reynolds was backstage. She was one of the select few who knew what happened, and worked to handle the publicity fallout.

After the commercial break, Shandling apologized for the "mistake," as he called it. When Billy Joel was onstage performing "River of Dreams," he stopped midway and looked at his watch. "Valuable advertising time going by," he said. There was a lengthy pause. "Dollars, dollars, dollars," he added before resuming with the lyrics, "In the middle of the night."

At the postshow EMI party, Barbara pulled me aside.

"What happened?" she asked, referring to him being cut off, not the impending meltdown.

"I have no idea," I said. I didn't have the heart to tell her the truth. Ultimately, the official word was that the production people made a mistake and cut to commercial by accident.

Sinatra never asked what happened, thankfully, and I was grateful to Susan for taking the heat and having to explain the situation to the New York media. The next morning, I hopped on a plane to Florida.

I didn't answer my phone for a week, though I kept track of the news and television coverage. "Weekend Update" on *Saturday Night Live* did a skit about it, which tells you what a story it had become. And rocker Neil Young later commented in his memoir that he wanted more Sinatra and less of an introduction. Many people shared the same sentiment, wanting to give Sinatra his moment.

Maybe he would have been fine. Who knows? All I know is that I could never have lived with myself if he had truly become the "old fool."

FORTY-FOUR

Duets went triple platinum and became the biggest-selling album of Sinatra's career, which is saying something. For all the critics' complaints that the album wasn't technically a duet, because the singers all sang separately, the audience loved it and Sinatra's fan base increased.

It also gave Barbara a piece of the Sinatra recording legacy to call her own. We kept him singing during *Duets* so we had extra songs, which meant we were potentially already a quarter of the way to *Duets II*. Koppelman didn't need much convincing. He loved the idea. The artist LeRoy Neiman, an old friend of mine, whose brightly colored, energetic style suited Sinatra, designed the cover for *Duets* and agreed to do *Duets II* as well.

As for Sinatra, he was acting like his old self—confident, or as Bono would say, cocksure. It was easier getting him into the studio now. He walked into a place he had been a million times and he knew what to do. Unlike the start to the first *Duets,* you could clearly see it was in his bones again.

We all knew this would prove to be the final curtain of his recording career and were all determined to have him go out with a bang. He was on, his voice cleaner and crisper than the first time around. That's what the renewed confidence did for him.

I didn't think I'd ever say this, but I personally preferred the power, the passion, and the struggle of *Duets*.

Nonetheless, *Duets II* is a great album. There were still a number of artists who wanted to be on the first album and hadn't made it, so we had plenty of vocalists to choose from the second time around. It created a strong lineup: Gladys Knight and Stevie Wonder, Luis Miguel, Patti LaBelle, Jon Secada, Linda Ronstadt, Antonio Carlos Jobim, Chrissie Hynde, Willie Nelson, Steve Lawrence and Eydie Gormé, Lena Horne, Jimmy Buffett, Lorrie Morgan, Frank Sinatra Jr., and Neil Diamond.

Sinatra was as smooth and elegant as ever. A lot of people can sing his songs but the lyrics don't have the same strength of meaning as they had for Sinatra. The lyrics were about his life, and when he sang them you understood that. He brought passion and believability to a song. I wanted to make this last hurrah truly worthy of a man who had done so much, and meant so much to so many.

Above all, to me *Duets II* was all about "My Way." I personally felt that song more deeply than any other that Sinatra sang. I considered it an anthem, a song that I had yet to hear anyone else sing and not been disappointed. We hadn't been able to secure Springsteen for "My Way" on *Duets* but I was determined to find the perfect partner for Sinatra on *Duets II*.

We started with Willie Nelson, who took a shot at it. When I heard it I knew immediately that it was all wrong. We asked him to sing "A Foggy Day" instead. We also asked opera singer Luciano Pavarotti, but he had a tight schedule and couldn't complete it in time to make the record. So again we went without "My Way."

My personal favorite on *Duets II* was Steve and Eydie's rendition of "Where or When." I also loved what Gladys Knight and Stevie Wonder did with "For Once in My Life." Sinatra and Lena Horne had sung medleys together back in the days of black-and-white television, so I loved reuniting those old friends on "Embraceable You." There were few people other than Lena who could have believably responded to Sinatra with "Come to mama, come to mama do, my sweet embraceable you."

In all, the album was the last dance of his recording career. I'd like to say I reflected on the significance of him standing there, his body moving to the music like a much younger man, but the truth is, I was always thinking about survival, not just for him but for me. There was a lot of money at stake. I was there to do a job. I wasn't sitting there as a spectator, thinking sentimentally about how this was the last time Sinatra would record.

For years my son Roy had come to my office and said, "Don't you owe it to Sinatra fans to get one more record done?"

Nope. I feel very lucky to have done two.

FORTY-FIVE

These are the stories that are rarely told about icons. They are the stories that millions of families face every day with parents, grandparents, friends, and loved ones. They are the stories of decline.

When the person is larger than life, when he or she is the strongest person you know, when you owe them so many things— these days can become unbearable. Yet Sinatra, for his part, handled them with the same dignity, grace, and strength as he did his life. No one wants to face encroaching mortality. The days when Sinatra was forced to face his own were the hardest, not just for him but for all of us who loved him.

The New York tabloids were increasingly rough with speculation that he had Alzheimer's. While that speculation was wrong, I was always so busy trying to keep things together that at the time I rarely reflected on the importance of some of the occurrences. Except for one that frightened me.

We were in Atlantic City and Vine knocked on my door to say I needed to come across the hall. She had a look of disbelief on her face. "He's at the dressing table. Go over and take a look," she said.

I immediately walked over. I didn't know what to expect. I walked in the outer dressing area of the hotel bathroom and saw

Sinatra standing there holding his toupee in his hand. He was trimming it with a small pair of cuticle scissors.

"You can't believe how fast it's growing," he said.

I wasn't prepared. I didn't think, I just blurted out.

"Are you fucking crazy?" I said. "That's you're toupee. Do you know how much that costs? Stop and maybe I can have it fixed."

I saw the look on his face and immediately felt horrible. He looked so crushed and vulnerable. In that moment, he wasn't a megastar, but an elderly man. I wished I had kept my mouth shut. He had a couple of toupees, so what did it matter? I was just shocked.

Sinatra was quiet and sullen for the rest of the day. It was as if my comment had lifted him out of the prescription-drug-induced fog he was in and brought him swiftly back to the disconcerting reality that his thinking was not right. So, here was this icon who lived to perform in front of thousands of people, trying to hold it together day by day, sometimes in the most basic of ways. Barbara and the kids were always worried about him being embarrassed onstage, but Junior and I both believed that if he stopped working he would die.

I was concerned, however, that with his advanced age and medical problems he might still occasionally carry a weapon. Although he was permitted, I didn't think that was safe for him or anyone else. As Tony O. grew close to him, one night backstage I asked him to make sure there weren't any bullets in his gun. "He'll notice if I take the bullets out," Tony said, "but I can file down the firing pin and that will completely disable the gun." That was the end of that.

It was a constant battle to see him through the performances. More and more, he was forgetting the lyrics, and his eyesight was so bad he was having difficulty reading the teleprompters. One day Junior came up with the idea of giving him an earpiece that would feed him the song lyrics. He put together the equipment with his trusted friend George Schlatter and we tested it out at the Malibu house with Sinatra.

He put the device in his ear for maybe ten seconds. "Fuck you," he said. "If you think that's what I need, we're done."

I'm sure the awareness of his decline was more painful for him than for any of us. Even the tiniest things were painful to witness. Sinatra was an avid reader and one morning I founding him reading the newspaper as usual, only he was reading it upside down. I didn't have the heart to say anything.

In March 1994, while doing a show in Richmond, Virginia, the heat became too intense for him and he collapsed onstage. It was one of two concerts I missed, in all the years I was his manager. He was flying in and out of Richmond, heading home to California the same night, so I had taken a flight back to Florida. He ended up in the hospital. Fortunately, he was released that same night and went directly home. It turned out it wasn't a major health problem, but the air-conditioning hadn't been working in the theater and he was dehydrated.

At one point, in August 1994, Dr. Piccione came on the road with us. Sinatra had a particularly bad show in Baltimore, where he forgot more lyrics than usual. He was able to cover it up onstage for the most part, but he knew what had happened and he was sullen and unhappy when he walked offstage. Later, Dr. Piccione, Tony O., Vine, and I were with Sinatra in his suite at the Harbor Court Hotel. I can still see him sitting at the head of the dining room table, his back to the window, with Baltimore Harbor in full view.

It felt like an intervention, but he wasn't angry. He knew we were all trying to help him.

"Boss," I said, "the medications you're on are beginning to affect your performance."

As Dr. Piccione spoke with him about the problems with the medication, Sinatra offered no resistance and agreed that he needed to make a switch.

He started to weep. My heart broke yet again.

After Baltimore, we had three more shows, in Massachusetts and Ohio. Dr. Piccione made an adjustment to Sinatra's Elavil dosage and the shows began to improve.

Barbara was not on this trip, and when she found out we had again tried to talk him into coming off Elavil, I heard through the grapevine she was not happy. To me the proof was in the pudding—we took a few weeks off and when we met up for some concerts in Texas in September and October, he was back on the regular dose.

Then we had two back-to-back arena openings in major cities: the Kiel Center in St. Louis and the United Center in Chicago. These were big events and I didn't want him to be embarrassed. I went to Sinatra and suggested he cut back his medication for the two days. He did and he had two flawless performances.

Despite all of his sad decline, *Duets II* was released to much fanfare. *Duets* had sold 7 million copies; *Duets II* would sell close to 3 million. Impressive numbers for an artist in the final years of a six-decade career. A career that I was afraid was coming to a close. Still, I held on, hoping for one more gig, and then another.

We ended the year in Japan, with two concerts at the Fukuoka Dome. He was back on Elavil and the shows became increasingly sloppy. Little did any of us realize that these would be his last professional appearances. In retrospect, though, it is clear we had come to the end of the road.

Japan was never an easy trip, because of the distance, even on Kirk Kerkorian's luxurious plane. Natalie Cole, Sinatra's opening act, had flown out separately. We arrived late, the day before the first performance, Japanese time. Sinatra had only one night to sleep and rest up, which is a lot to ask of any performer, especially someone who is nearly eighty years old. It was clear by the following afternoon that he had not adjusted to the clock. He seemed lethargic and unexcited about the show.

Natalie, a tremendous talent whose career had been sidelined by drug addiction and depression, had won a Grammy for *Unforgettable* two years earlier. It was a posthumous duet album with her father, the great Nat King Cole, whom she sometimes called the "Black Frank Sinatra." Sinatra loved her father, and while he didn't know Natalie well, he respected her as a performer. Natalie would go on to garner twenty-one Grammy nominations and nine Grammys in her lifetime. Her duet with Sinatra, the Gershwin hit "They Can't Take That Away from Me," had been well received.

By the night of the first performance, Sinatra seemed lost and discombobulated. He was spacey. I'm not entirely sure he knew we were in Japan. He always reacted to the audiences and loved the feedback loop. The more they gave, the more excited they were, the more excited he was, and the more he brought to the performance.

Japanese audiences were very reserved. They didn't react with the same enthusiasm as American audiences. I'm not sure if that impacted the shows, but Sinatra had two very poor nights. That's the only way I can describe them.

The teleprompters were operating but he still struggled with the lyrics. While he had forgotten lyrics in the past, usually a few words here and there, this night he forgot entire chunks. They were difficult shows to watch. I believe he knew the shows were poor, too, but he seemed helpless to do anything about it.

Natalie asked if she could join our flight home, which of course was fine. She was dressed casually, and when she boarded, Sinatra didn't recognize her. She hadn't been on the plane on the way out and it confused him that she was traveling back with us.

"Who's that black girl?" he said. I explained it was Natalie Cole and he nodded. He didn't ask about her again. He was quiet and out of it for the rest of the flight and dozed off a few times.

As I sat on the plane feeling depressed about what was happening, I tallied up the shows. It was hard to believe, but he did close to seventy shows in his final year of performing. That's an impressive schedule for a man who had just turned seventy-nine and it is a testament to how much he loved performing. The stage was where he wanted to be.

When we landed in the States, we all went our separate ways. A few months later, in February 1995, he was set to perform for the Barbara Sinatra golf tournament. I was playing in the tournament and staying at the Sinatras'. I was happy to see the Boss.

He looked like himself again. He was well rested and looked forward to singing that night. He had his regular musical staff there, and he was cheerful. Sure enough, he took the stage and did what he had been doing his whole life—knocking audiences dead with his heart, soul, and voice.

He was truly flawless, and that night he raised almost a million dollars for the Barbara Sinatra Children's Clinic.

I went home to Florida and wondered if maybe this wasn't really the end. But I was just fooling myself. Neither Barbara nor the Sinatra kids wanted him performing in public again. It was one of the few things they actually agreed on. We never discussed it. There were no more calls, no more complaints about open dates on the calendar, no more "Hey, Eliot, what are we, retired?" comments.

Barbara and Frank sold the Palm Springs house not long after that concert. He loved Palm Springs. It was everything to him, but Barbara wanted to move to Beverly Hills, where they had not only their friends but also the best medical treatment.

Meanwhile, life continued. Maria gave birth to our son David on August 18, 1995. A few months later, I was in California on business and took Maria and David along. I wanted Sinatra to meet my son and I wanted my son to meet the man who had meant so much to my life. We went to see the Sinatras at their Beverly Hills home.

It's a bittersweet memory for me. I passed my infant to the Boss and was so happy to see the huge smile on his face. With David in his arms I could see all the warmth and tenderness that he expressed so brilliantly in his music. He was such a mass of contradictions: tough guy, soulful humanitarian—legend. Barbara was there, too. They looked like proud grandparents and both seemed very content and in a good place together. I took a photo of that moment, knowing that someday it would be very important for David. To this day I remind David that Frank Sinatra was one of the first people other than his parents and grandparents to hold him in his arms. David, like many of today's young people, is a Sinatra fan.

FORTY-SIX

Nineteen ninety-five, Sinatra's eightieth year, was a very good one, if you measure it by exposure.

In November, Reprise released a twenty-CD set of Sinatra's 1960–88 studio recordings. Columbia released *The Best of the Columbia Years.* Capitol had *Sinatra 80th: All the Best,* which included 1953 to 1961. *Sinatra 80th: Live in Concert* was the recording I was involved in.

There were also new books—Will Friedwald's musical appreciation, *Sinatra! The Song Is You,* and Nancy Sinatra's scrapbook, *Frank Sinatra: An American Legend*—along with a syndicated eight-hour radio retrospective.

During the 1990s we had released several products in an effort to increase his income. There were neckties with Sinatra's geometric paintings, the idea inspired by the success of the Grateful Dead's Jerry Garcia and his artwork-turned-necktie collection. We also did a high-end cigar deal, selling cigars in cedar boxes emblazoned with Sinatra's face and name. The black lacquer humidors with Sinatra's signature immediately sold out but the rest of the business didn't fare as well and both the cigar and the tie ventures were short-lived. A couple of years later, we would also have a 1997 limited-edition Korbel champagne that featured Sinatra artwork on the bottle, and a Sinatra MasterCard to purchase it with.

Dan Deluca of the *Philadelphia Inquirer* wrote, "The intensity of the explosion of Sinatra product on this anniversary can be traced to one word: 'Duets.' And the 'Duets' albums built upon a groundswell in interest in Sinatra as he has become more accepted among a new generation of cocktail-swilling rock fans."

Frank's eightieth birthday turned into a public celebration that he was in little shape to participate in, though the press speculated that he would do a farewell concert or a short tour. We had proposals come in from all over, but it was never going to happen, either live or in studio. When bookers would call asking for dates, I would say he was on hiatus, or Susan Reynolds would say, "He's accumulated a lot of well-deserved vacation time and he's taking it now." I never bothered to test the waters with Sinatra or the family and we never officially stopped touring.

After his stellar golf tournament performance, with no dates on the books and no tour to look forward to, his decline was steady. When I was visiting him in Beverly Hills, I saw him forget how to even tie his tie. That seemed unbelievable to me, but not entirely unexpected at this point.

We put together the *80th Live* album as a compilation of earlier recorded concerts. My favorite part was the bonus track—we could finally address my obsession with getting "My Way" recorded as a duet. As I said, we had asked Luciano Pavarotti to record it for *Duets II* but he could not finish it in time. When Pavarotti finally delivered, I loved it, and I'd been waiting for a way to include it on an album. So it became a bonus track on *80th Live*. It remains my favorite of all the duets.

Pavarotti brought life and emotion to the song. Sinatra was a big fan of Pavarotti and marveled at his control and power.

Listening to Sinatra sing, "And now the end is near and so I face that final curtain," at this point in his life took on a melancholy cast that I hadn't anticipated during all the hard work of putting it together. To me, it was the most important song Sinatra ever sang. "I did what I had to do, I saw it through without exemption." That was his life. It was mine, too. When he sang, "I did it my way," I could hear his voice falter with emotion.

To hear the power of Pavarotti singing it still gives me goose bumps. He held his own in a song with Frank that no one could top.

That song was a culmination of all I had tried to achieve with both *Duets* albums.

At the same time, Barbara and George Schlatter were planning a two-hour eightieth-birthday special on ABC. It was called *Frank Sinatra: 80 Years My Way* and it was taped on November 19 at the Shrine Auditorium in Los Angeles.

The Sinatra kids didn't want their father paraded out as a public spectacle. At least that's what we heard from Tina and Nancy. Junior, as usual, stayed out of the fray.

On the other hand, it was something for Sinatra to look forward to, and there was the charity aspect. I had nothing to do with this special but I know that in his mind, the celebration would be less about him and more about a fund-raiser for AIDS Project Los Angeles and the Barbara Sinatra Children's Center. Fund-raising had always been important for him; George Schlatter once estimated that during his lifetime, Sinatra raised more than $1 billion for charity.

In the end, the show went on and the kids were there supporting their dad.

It proved to be a wonderful salute.

Frank and Barbara were seated at the front of stage right, at a round, club-style table so they could watch the parade of artists and tributes. Steve Lawrence and Eydie Gormé performed, along with Natalie Cole, Hootie & the Blowfish, Bob Dylan, Tony Bennett, Little Richard. Then Bruce Springsteen, whom I had wanted so much to do "My Way" for *Duets,* introduced Sinatra. Sinatra walked out onstage, took a few bows, and went to his seat.

Springsteen, another Italian Jersey boy, called Sinatra the Patron Saint of New Jersey. "On behalf of all New Jersey, Frank, Hail Brother, you sang out our soul. Happy Birthday." He sang "Angel Eyes," an obscure, saloon song for Ol' Blue Eyes. Dylan sang one of his own, older songs, the melancholy "Restless Farewell." It ends with the line, "So I'll make my stand and remain as I am and I'll bid farewell and not give a damn."

Gregory Peck, Don Rickles, Arnold Schwarzenegger, and Vic Damone all paid tribute. Sinatra's new pal Bono performed via satellite from London. Hootie donned a fedora and sang "Lady Is a Tramp" while Frank smiled and snapped his fingers.

Robert Wagner introduced Patti LaBelle, who sang a song close to Frank's heart, "The House I Live In." It was from a 1945 short film he had done designed to defuse racial tension. It was about the beauty of this country and living in peace and harmony, with the lyric "All races and religions, that's America to me." LaBelle's performance blew everyone away and you could see Sinatra light up watching her. He was so moved that he stood for her, the only standing ovation he gave that night.

Wagner mentioned that Frank had received a special Oscar for *The House I Live In* that meant more to him than the one he was awarded for *From Here to Eternity*. He also named his house in Palm Springs after it. For all he had done to fight against bigotry, to be all that Frank Sinatra was in his life and talent, and to be remembered for this song he had performed fifty years earlier, was an incredible gift to him. When LaBelle approached him after the song, he kissed her hand.

Springsteen introduced a video of Sinatra singing "New York, New York" that was interspersed with police officers, firefighters, cabdrivers, and regular folks chiming in with the lyrics. The entire star-studded cast, some of the biggest stars of the day, assembled onstage for the finale, which also included Patrick Swayze,

Tom Selleck, Rosie O'Donnell, Danny Aiello, and Tony Danza. Springsteen and Bennett brought Sinatra onstage, where he briefly sang with the group. He extended and held what would be the final professional note of his career, then received a standing ovation.

On December 1, before Frank's December 12 birthday, Barbara auctioned off art and memorabilia from the Palm Springs compound at Christie's, much to the chagrin of the kids, who had no part or say in it. They didn't think she should be auctioning off their father's property around his birthday. The whole thing struck them as an exploitation of their father toward the end of his life.

With the spat over the special, and then the auction, what happened next shouldn't have been all that surprising. Maria and I were visiting at Sinatra's house. Over the years, the kids had spent almost every birthday with their father. On Frank's actual eightieth birthday, George and Jolene Schlatter were planning to throw a dinner party for him. The kids were not invited. Barbara made arrangements for the kids to be with him the following day, on December 13. When she told Tina her plans, Tina was furious. Making matters worse, Maria and I were invited to the Schlatters', too. I believed that was wrong.

I tried to calm Tina down, but she would have none of it. She went and told her father what had happened. I could see how torn he was, once again in the middle of a tug-of-war between his children and his wife.

Sinatra protested to Barbara but in the end he went to the Schlatters' without the children. That widened the already deep divide between Barbara and the kids.

Tony O. told me Frank spoke to Dean Martin on Christmas Eve.

On Christmas Day, Martin died.

Barbara called to tell me.

I didn't know Dean all that well, but he was part of a generation of artists that was disappearing before my eyes. Watching them perform had given me countless hours of joy. Their talent had inspired my dream to be in show business and knowing them had been among the greatest joys of my life. Fortunately, Sinatra was still with us.

Frank spent the next two years passing the time with Barbara and a few close friends. The kids and grandkids would visit, as would Maria and I. Sinatra wasn't the type to talk socially on the phone. If I wanted to talk about something other than business, I went to see him at Foothill. During one such trip, we were watching television. I had long ago learned to stay out of his way when he was sullen and possibly depressed, as opposed to just tired. He was quiet and he seemed to be all those things that day. At some point he turned to me and said, "Dying is corny."

I was in shock to hear that come out of Sinatra's mouth. Was he reaching out? Did he need to talk? What should I say? I didn't know. Like all relationships, mine with Sinatra had a pattern, a history that kept things stable and comfortable. There was no pattern, no history of conversations that provided me with a response to his statement. I regained my composure.

"Do you want me to see if I can find a baseball game?" is all I could think to say.

He ignored my comment, as I had ignored his.

I last saw him two weeks before he died. It seemed to me that he had lost his purpose and his desire to fight. Sinatra was known to say, "You've got to love living, 'cause dying is a pain in the ass." There is no doubt that for someone who lived an extraordinary existence, this wasn't living. He was in bed, weak, frail, and clearly very ill. Still, when I left him I was sure I would see him again. I thought maybe he would rebound. I didn't expect it to happen so fast.

FORTY-SEVEN

I don't sing and I don't dance. Entertainers have egos—big ones. So I stayed in the background and kept my ego in check. I didn't horn in on their conversations and I didn't make their successes about me. That was the secret to my longevity with my clients. I didn't impose myself on their lives, yet they were all so much a part of mine. Sinatra undeniably had the biggest piece of my heart.

When the phone rang in the middle of the night in Florida and Maria handed it to me, I took one look at the expression on her face and time stopped for a moment.

"Eliot, this is the call you never wanted to get," the voice on the other end said. It was Bob Finkelstein, the lawyer for the Sinatra children, and it felt like a knife to my stomach.

"When did he die?" I said.

"Earlier tonight," he said.

"I'll be there by the afternoon." I hung up the phone and stayed in bed, going over the details of our lives together in my head until it was time to get dressed.

He died of heart failure. I wished I had been there.

By the time I arrived at Foothill, the house was surrounded by members of the media and fans. Barbara was sitting at the bar speaking with one of her lawyers. I hugged her and then went to pay my respects to the kids, who were outside by the pool.

I was grieving, for sure, but I knew that I was also there to work and make sure everything went smoothly. As coexecutors to the Sinatra estate, Harvey Silbert and I had put a lot of effort into making sure everything was in order before the Boss died. There were many years of animosity between Barbara and the children that we wanted to head off. Despite all that effort, though, little went according to plan.

By the time I arrived, Harvey had already sent over a copy of the will. Barbara was furious when she saw it. I was horrified. It was the wrong will.

The will he sent over was dated days before the final version. We had had one of Sinatra's doctors present to testify he was of sound mind and body and we videotaped the entire process. Then, four days later, Sinatra made a material change to his will. But that will, the correct version, wasn't delivered to all parties until later that day.

Harvey and I gave the corrected will to Finkelstein. This one was dated September 3, 1991. It gave Barbara an additional several million dollars, provided enough funds remained in the estate after debts were paid and everything else was distributed. It also included a 1993 amendment that transferred some cash intended for Jilly to Vine, after Jilly died.

Barbara had felt she was not receiving her fair share, and she and her lawyer, Arthur Crowley, came up with the dollar amount. I strongly believed in my heart that the value of Sinatra's recordings that had already been gifted to the children in the 1990s, along with the value of his name and likeness, were worth much more than the value of the real estate and art that Barbara would receive. So I felt this addition was reasonable. I also knew that it was likely that when all was said and done, there would not be such a large amount in the estate to give Barbara.

Nonetheless, Barbara was happy to see the updated will. Tina was incredulous. I knew everyone would be upset about something, but I honestly believed that this will was a victory for Sinatra and his family. I knew how important it was for him to take care of all of his family. Without it the lawyers would have ended up with a lot more and his family a lot less.

There were a lot of people going in and out of the Sinatra house. At one point when I saw Tina, I told her not to worry. I repeated what I had been telling her for years, that she and her siblings would not be screwed. But this provision was more fuel to the fury over the fact that the children had not been called to the hospital to see their father before he died. I couldn't fault them for that.

Why it happened was anyone's guess.

May 14, 1998 was the night of the last episode of *Seinfeld,* Tony O. remembered. He said Barbara was out for the evening and Vine called him to tell him that Sinatra was upset. He told her to call the doctor, but a few minutes later she called him back to say that Sinatra was being taken to Cedars-Sinai Medical Center, on Beverly Boulevard.

Tony said he arrived at the hospital shortly after Barbara. Several of Frank's doctors and Susan Reynolds were there. Barbara said in her book, *Lady Blue Eyes,* that there was no time to call anyone.

At Sinatra's bedside, both Barbara and Tony said they told Frank to fight. "I'm losing," he answered. They said they were both holding his hand when he flatlined.

Tina said in her book, *My Father's Daughter,* that she didn't receive the call until 11:10 p.m., after her father had already passed. She and Nancy rushed to the hospital.

Tina should have been called. I was surprised that Tony O. didn't at least do it, or that Barbara didn't instruct someone to do so. This created a family wound that would not heal.

On my second day in Beverly Hills, Tina, Bobby Marx, Finkelstein, and I went to the funeral home to see Frank's body. When the casket was opened and I saw him lying there, it hit me like a ton of bricks. He was really gone. I don't think I was the same for at least twenty-four hours.

Nancy convinced President Bill Clinton to authorize a full military honor guard for the funeral, with an American flag to be draped over the coffin. Barbara said no, though. Frank hadn't served in the armed services, because of an eardrum injury, and she felt that would be an embarrassment. We were at the house and Tina was crying. I told her I would try to work it out.

"Free at last, free at last," I reminded Tina, as she seemed to be counting the days until she would no longer have to engage with Barbara.

It was Susan Reynolds who came to the rescue. She negotiated the details between Barbara and the White House. There would be a small military honor guard at the cemetery and the flag would not be draped over his coffin. However, a folded flag would be presented to Barbara.

In the end, I believe Barbara was correct, and that having full military honors would have been criticized, since Sinatra never served. On the other hand, in his lifetime Sinatra received both the Medal of Freedom and a Congressional Gold Medal, so it was appropriate for there to be some military honor. You could argue that they were both right and Susan did an expert job of navigating the crocodiles.

The funeral was at the Church of the Good Shepherd in Beverly Hills. It was filled with fragrant flowers. The casket was draped in a blanket of gardenias. People came from all over the world for the funeral, including both of Frank's living ex-wives: his first wife, Nancy, and Mia Farrow.

Several friends and family members shared stories. Frank Jr. spoke poignantly and from the heart. Bobby spoke along with Kirk Douglas, Gregory Peck, George Schlatter, and Robert Wagner.

When Tony O. was asked to take wine to the altar for communion, he quipped, "The old man's gone and I'm still bringing him booze."

There wasn't a dry eye in the house when the sound of Frank's voice singing, "Put your dreams away for another day and I will take their place in your heart," filled the church.

I was a pallbearer. As the service was coming to an end, I looked out the front door to make sure the police were waiting and the pallbearers were all set to go. Tony O. and I, then Rickles and Bobby Marx, were on one side. Steve Lawrence, Sonny Golden, and comedian Tom Dreesen were on the other.

The casket was extremely heavy. We were halfway down the stairs when I felt a tremendous strain on my shoulder. Rickles, who was behind me, had suddenly let go. After the casket was inside the hearse, I turned around and said, "You're kidding me. Why did you let go?"

"Jews don't do this kind of work," he said.

I didn't find it at all funny.

I couldn't help but think of Sinatra singing "Come Fly with Me" as the family took Kerkorian's plane to the desert for the burial. As I understood it, the military portion of the ceremony took place and the flag was handed to Barbara "on behalf of a grateful nation." Barbara gave the flag to Frank Jr.

Sinatra was buried with his favorite things. His love for Jack Daniel's and Camel cigarettes lit by a Zippo lighter was well known. In earlier days, he liked to keep a roll of dimes in his pocket in case he needed to make a phone call. We kept Wild Cherry Life Savers and Tootsie Rolls in his dressing rooms. All of these things—including a dog biscuit and a few stuffed animals from his grandchildren—were placed in the casket.

Sinatra is buried with his mother and father, near his best pal, Jilly.

There is a simple granite grave marker, "FRANCIS ALBERT SINATRA, 1915–1998, BELOVED HUSBAND AND FATHER." Along the top, "THE BEST IS YET TO COME."

FORTY-EIGHT

People in the entertainment industry had thought I was crazy for taking on the executorship. It was suggested to me that resolving this will to the satisfaction of everyone would involve numerous lawsuits and would tie up the next ten to fifteen years of our lives. So the fact that we wrapped it up just short of five years after his death, with no lawsuits, I considered a big accomplishment.

I made a promise to Sinatra that I would make sure his children and his wife were taken care of and that no one was shafted. I was determined to follow through on that commitment come hell or high water, knowing that both sides would be angry with me at one time or another.

Sinatra's death marked the culmination of years of power struggles and hard feelings between Barbara and the Sinatra kids. To my knowledge, after his death, there was little to no direct communication between Barbara and Bobby on the one side and Tina, Nancy, and Frank Jr. on the other side. The communication was done mostly through the lawyers and me.

While all three of the Sinatra children had achieved some success as singers and musicians, it was Tina who represented the children's business interests where their father was concerned. She was like her father in many ways. When she became angry, she was like him on his worst days.

I always told Barbara that I had specific instructions from Frank and that she shouldn't worry about her future. "It will take some time, but it will all work out," I said. I always believed that deep down Barbara trusted me, and I appreciated that.

I said the same thing to Tina, but I never felt that she trusted me.

The lawyers at Loeb & Loeb liquidated assets and paid bills according to the directions of the will. As I've mentioned, much of the Sinatra kids' inheritance had already been distributed prior to their father's death in the form of the musical rights gifted to them in the early 1990s.

The will dealt with the distribution of the remaining property. Barbara was to keep the Beverly Hills and Malibu homes as well as a house near Palm Springs. The contents of all the houses, which included silver, furniture, and a significant amount of art, were hers.

One work alone, *Two Clowns Taking a Bow,* by Edward Hopper, one of the most important realist painters of the twentieth century, was valued at $4 million. Barbara also kept Sinatra's awards, including a copy of the Special Award for *The House I Live In,* a National Trustees Award, a Grammy for *Duets II,* a Kennedy Center Honors Award, Grammy Legend Award, and numerous leather-bound presentation scripts for his films, including *From Here to Eternity, Young at Heart, Guys and Dolls,* and *High Society.*

Barbara kept several film posters, including one for *The Manchurian Candidate,* the platinum albums for *Duets* and *Duets II,* and gold albums for *Frank Sinatra Trilogy* and *Ol' Blue Eyes Is Back.*

Tina, Nancy, and Junior and Sinatra's first wife, Nancy, all received cash, as did Bobby. An additional $1 million was added to the trust funds of his two granddaughters, Nancy Jr.'s children.

Sinatra also left money to Vine and to his personal assistant, Dorothy Uhlemann.

Whatever was left would go to Barbara, up to several million, after paying final closing expenses, commissions, and approved fees. There were film rights for films made after his marriage to Barbara in 1976, an oil and gas lease, and various accounts.

Before we could close, we needed a judge's final approval.

It seemed like everything had been moving according to plan over the years. There were no lawsuits, and everyone in the family was aware that any suit, with a loss, would remove their right to inheritance.

So, whenever anyone became angry about a particular issue and started to debate the legality, I told them, "Take your best shot." They would have been foolish to do so. No official challenge was ever raised. I was confident I had negotiated every land mine and we were on our way to a conclusion as amicable as could be expected considering the family history of infighting.

There's an old saying: "Just when you think you got something nailed, you find out you've been screwed."

That's exactly what I felt like in May 2001, when I opened a letter from a woman calling herself Julie Sinatra. In the letter, she referred to Sinatra as "dad." She said she needed help with a book and her own original songs.

My mouth hit the floor. From time to time people had appeared claiming to be a child or sibling of Sinatra's. I stayed out of it. I assumed this was another unfounded claim. I forwarded the letter to Harvey Silbert as fast as I could and forgot about it. I never heard another word—at least not right away.

Then, on September 28, 2002, Silbert passed away.

There was a hearing two days later. Everything was in order. The estate was ready to be closed. The only thing that remained was for the judge to put his rubber stamp on the noncontested will and then the final payouts would be made. I didn't even bother to book a trip to California. Everything was resolved and attorney Jeffrey Loeb said it wasn't necessary.

After the hearing, Loeb called me. Julie Sinatra was in court without a lawyer and representing herself. She claimed to be Sinatra's daughter. The judge gave her an October date to file the necessary documents to object to the settlement of the will and request genetic testing. "How bad is it?" I asked.

"When you see the photos you won't be happy," Loeb said.

Loeb added that the judge had authorized me to conclude the estate as sole executor. The fact that there was no media in that California court to hear Julie's claim, for what should have been the final disbursement of the will of Frank Sinatra, was surprising and comforting. The photos were not. When I received the fax of the photos of Julie, I nearly fell over. The facial resemblance to Frank was astonishing.

As I began to learn, Julie, who originally went by the name Julie Alex-Rider, her maiden name, and then Julie Speelman, her married name, legally changed her name to Julie Sinatra on June 1, 2000, in the Superior Court of Arizona after presenting a case to a judge. She said she learned of what she now believed was the true identity of her father in 1996, when she was fifty-three years old. She had contacted Tina, Junior, and Barbara while Frank was still alive. This was the first I had ever heard of it, which as executor was almost as surprising as finding out about her existence in the first place.

In various written documents, Julie said her mother, a married former actress, met Sinatra in 1940, had an affair, then broke it off when she became pregnant. Worried an illegitimate child would ruin her career, she never told Sinatra. Julie was born on February 10, 1943. Dorothy eventually told her daughter in 1996, "Frank was her birth father and where she got her music ability and blue eyes."

But Julie said no lawyer would take her case and that she wanted genetic testing. At one point when she contacted the family she was told to cease and desist; at another she said she was told that the shock of her existence could cause Sinatra to have a heart attack.

My first reaction was, *How fast can I make this disappear?* She was not a woman of great financial means, so I offered her some money to go away. She quickly turned it down. She said she didn't want money, she wanted to be acknowledged as a Sinatra. Sinatra's will, like many wills, had a provision defining children as only those born in wedlock. It's a standard provision that doesn't carry much legal weight.

She said that if the family would not agree to submit to a DNA test, she wanted to have Sinatra's body exhumed. That thought really sent me into a tailspin. I told the lawyers to tell her, "She'll have to roll over my body with a tractor to dig up his grave." Everything went quiet for a couple of weeks.

Then, in a letter to me dated August 14, 2002, Julie said she was having a change of heart after speaking with Junior: "I am willing to seal my lips forever regarding the story behind my identity as Julie Sinatra, if that is what the family wants me to do about these issues. I need financial assistance in order to move on with my new life. . . ."

Through the lawyers, I doubled the offer to Julie and said we needed a confidentiality agreement. I never spoke to her directly. She accepted. Now that the deal was made, I had to figure out how to split this cost between the beneficiaries. I called Barbara. She wanted nothing to do with the whole situation and said that if it had happened, it was long before she was in the picture. She said it was Tina, Nancy, and Junior's problem.

I called Tina and Bob Finkelstein. Tina must have yelled at both of us, mostly me, for at least five to ten minutes. She called me every name in the book. "You did something my father would never have done. You let someone take advantage of us. He would never let anyone take advantage of us like this," she said. I listened quietly.

"If your father was alive he would have given her a lot more money to get rid of her a lot quicker," I said. "It doesn't serve anyone's best interests to have this out there in the public domain. I'm making the settlement and if you don't like it, take your best shot." I believe that was the last conversation I ever had with Tina.

The six-figure amount was a modest sum for Julie's silence. If Sinatra had been alive, I'm confident the negotiation would have started much higher. I charged half to Barbara and half to the kids. Legal fees in a court challenge could have easily amounted to more than the entire amount. The settlement was supposed to be confidential and the story of Julie Sinatra went unreported and disappeared, at least for the time being.

Regarding the will, on January 21, 2003, the order of final distribution was made and the checks were written and disbursed. Barbara was additionally awarded the remaining cash, after paying final closing expenses and fees, though it wasn't anywhere near the multimillion-dollar limit.

Finalizing Sinatra's will was personal to me. I wanted to prove that all the people who had told me this would take a decade of lawsuits to resolve were wrong. I couldn't have done it without Bobby Marx bringing his mother back to reality from time to time and Bob Finkelstein keeping Tina's anger in check. I did what I promised the Boss, at least as far as his wife and the children he knew about were concerned.

Then, in 2011, Julie published a book, *Under My Skin: My Father, Frank Sinatra,* putting the whole story of her life and belief that she was Sinatra's daughter out there in the public domain.

Without DNA, no one will ever know for sure, but I do know that sometimes the system works to keep the truth out.

FORTY-NINE

December 12, 2015, marked one hundred years since the birth of Frank Sinatra. There were celebrations and commemorations large and small around the globe. The one officially sanctioned by the Sinatra family was "Sinatra: An American Icon," a touring exhibition of his music, photos, mementos, correspondence, artwork, and personal items.

When the exhibit went to Miami in the spring of 2016, officials at the HistoryMiami Museum asked if I would participate in a dinner and question-and-answer session about Sinatra.

Sinatra always had a fondness for Miami. He filmed some of his movies in the Magic City and performed hundreds of times at the Fontainebleau Hotel in Miami Beach in the 1950s, '60s, and '70s.

I reluctantly agreed.

I was prepared for questions about alleged mob connections. People don't realize how prevalent the mob was in the entertainment business in those days. Questions about him womanizing: It didn't happen on my watch, to my knowledge. Temper flare-ups? Perhaps there was a different Sinatra in the 1950s—the wild Rat Pack Sinatra who was fighting his way through life.

What I was most afraid of was a quiet, bored audience. Sure, there's always a group of people willing to spend a hundred-plus dollars a head on dinner to see an exhibit and help out a museum, but what would they really want to hear from me? I reflected for days on what Sinatra meant to his friends, fans, the entertainment world, and to me personally.

Sinatra was many, often contradictory, things. He was a one-take, do it right the first time, and don't make me wait kind of guy, but as impatient as he was, if you were in need, he was there. He was the bravest guy I knew, a champion of the underdog, unafraid to stand up for what he believed in, and one who always put his money where his mouth was, through public and private acts of charity. He was a tough guy with a soft heart for all those he loved, especially his family.

The traits that I admired most in him—loyalty, honesty, and integrity—were especially meaningful because they are so very rare in Hollywood. Frank was a man's man and a ladies' man. In my opinion, Sinatra was the greatest entertainer of the twentieth century and the world is still looking to fill the void he left behind.

I too was looking to fill a void.

My life had changed dramatically. I had run at double speed for more than twenty years. I stepped off the roller coaster and reached a new equilibrium. I still had my other clients, Steve and Eydie, and Rickles and I hadn't yet parted ways. I was working with Engelbert Humperdinck and fielding calls from new and aspiring talent. I took on the management of Aaron Carter, whom I considered a very talented young singer with a lot of promise. He had found some success in solo albums touring with his brother Nick's band, the Backstreet Boys, and guest appearances on Nickelodeon. He was popular with teens and preteens. I had him touring with a steady income stream but there were too many problems and we parted ways within a year.

For a time, I even went back to my entertainment roots and ventured into the theater business again. When the 2004–05 NHL lockout shut down the season, I met with Michael Yormark, then the chief operating officer of Sunrise Sports and Entertainment, the company that owned the Florida Panthers. We sat in one of the boxes overlooking the empty floor of the BankAtlantic Center.

"We've got a lot of empty time here," Yormark said. "Can you bring some major acts here?"

"There's not enough time to fill this large a space with big acts in the next few months," I said.

The big arena acts booked up to a year in advance and left plenty of empty arena days in between. "We can increase your revenue if we fill in the dark nights," I said. "You close off one end of the arena and build a portable stage that can be put up and taken down. If you drape it off the right way we can make it look like a theater. That way, you can do the big acts and the rest of the time, fill in with smaller theater acts."

We eventually worked out a deal to do twelve to fifteen shows a year starting the following year. When Yormark wanted to call it the Sinatra Theater I went to Finkelstein and he agreed, but he refused to put it in writing.

At the time, there was tremendous competition for big acts at the venues in South Florida. I started selling the BankAtlantic Center as the prime real estate of the region, with easy access to patrons in Dade, Broward, and Palm Beach Counties.

Streisand was on tour but had no plans to go south of Atlanta.

I called Erlichman. "Marty, I need Barbra to come down here. I know we can sell out two shows and work out a good deal."

The American Airlines Arena was also trying to book her for at least one show, so Marty and I went back and forth.

Eventually, my old friend came through and we did two sold-out Streisand shows in October 2006. At the time, they were the only shows Streisand had ever played in Florida.

Soon thereafter, I found myself contemplating my own mortality. What I thought was indigestion turned out to be a bad heart valve.

A dislike for doctors is one of the many things Frank and I shared. As I made the rounds looking for additional opinions, every surgeon had his or her way of telling me what the mortality rate was. I didn't like any of their attitudes or the pictures they were trying to draw for me.

I found a great surgeon in Dr. Marc Gillinov, and before long I had a new valve in my heart. Around this time, my ex-wife Micky died in New York. Other deaths followed. Eydie passed away in August 2013, in Las Vegas, after a brief illness. I still represent Steve. He's still selling out shows in his eighties, and both he and Judy are among my dearest friends.

In 2014, Don Rickles and I parted ways. As I mentioned, that may have been the single biggest disappointment of my career. Not only was he a very dear friend, but also I believe I did the best job of my career in helping Rickles establish a fresh start when he was at the bottom, and achieve a whole new level of success.

I was saddened that after twenty-two years together, after all we had accomplished, and our deep personal connection as families, that we ended our relationship over a couple of percentage points on commission.

Neither Maria nor I ever heard from the Rickleses personally, and he passed away on April 6, 2017.

I haven't spoken to Barbara Sinatra or Nancy and Tina since the will was settled. On July 25, 2017, Barbara passed away at the age of 90. I was always grateful for her trust and support, and happy to have been able to help ensure she and the children were all well taken care of. I did, however, keep in touch with Frank Jr.

On March 11, 2016, Junior called me. He was doing a short tour in Florida and wanted me to come see him when he performed in Miami. Now that his dad was gone, he had finally added some of Sinatra's music to his repertoire, something I could never convince him to do while Frank was alive.

"You'll be happy," he said.

I couldn't make his Miami date but we talked about meeting for one of his other Florida concerts. It had been about a year since I last spoke with him. We reminisced and he joked about how we were both getting on in years.

"You are, I'm not," I said. "How old are you?"

"Seventy-two."

"I'm older than you. You're not out of the gate yet," I said. "How are your sisters?"

"We don't speak much," Junior said.

"Your mom?"

"She's all right and I'm doing okay," he said. "We should get together more."

I agreed. It was great to speak with him.

Then, five days later, on March 16, Merle, Junior's head of security called.

"Frankie died."

"What are you talking about? I just spoke to him," I said.

"We're in Daytona. He had a heart attack."

I had always been fond of Junior and considered myself in his corner. I was happy to have been able to work out a deal for him to be musical director for his father and felt somewhat responsible for helping father and son to heal some of the wounds between them.

As I walked into the MiamiHistory Museum dinner with my own family, I was thinking about how much Maria, Eric, Carol, Roy, and David all meant to me. Maria and I have been married for thirty years and I am so very proud that all my children have followed in my footsteps in either business, entertainment, or both. My oldest, Eric, is a strategic business consultant; Carol has her own marketing firm, CLC Enterprises; Roy is partners with Joey Bonamassa in J&R Adventures; and my youngest, David, whom Eydie used to call the little manager, spent much of his childhood hanging backstage with celebrities from Ben Vereen to Engelbert Humperdinck and many more. He'll be graduating from college soon, and who knows, maybe he'll use his business degree like I used mine. As I thought about how fortunate I was, I scanned the audience filled with people, young and old.

Frank would have loved it—to see young people there, still wanting to know about his life, still thinking he was cool. The audience wanted to know his habits, his likes and dislikes, what kind of man he was and my thoughts about his performances.

One person asked, "How long did Sinatra work with you for?"

"You mean how long did I work with the Boss?" I responded.

Everyone laughed.

No one ever asked about the mob, bar fights, or the women in his life, other than his wives. Perhaps some of the stories were true; others I can't imagine could possibly be. Stories that had dogged him for much of his career now vanished in the remembering of a man who sang songs about life and lived his life with the same authenticity.

I was lucky, too. I took a man who was well past his prime and allowed him to live up to the potential that wouldn't go away. In the process he allowed me to become more than I ever dreamed.

I always thought he would die onstage with a microphone in his hand, backstage after a fabulous concert, or in the car on the way home with a glass of Jack in his hand. I wanted to give him that, but in the end his body just couldn't do it anymore.

Years after Sinatra passed away, Shirley MacLaine told Larry King that Sinatra reached out to her during one of her channeling sessions.

She said he's in heaven with bodyguards and his buddies.

That wouldn't surprise me.

I looked out at the audience, and watched the smiles on their faces. I'm almost eighty years old now. Carol said I "got my sparkle back" that night. Listening to the sound of the applause, I could hear the Boss in the background.

"Hey, Eliot, you got a camera?"

"Sure, Boss. What do you need?"

"Take a picture of this place, 'cause we ain't never coming back here."

"I know, Boss, but I sure wish we could."

We'll meet again, don't know where, don't know when,

But I know we'll meet again some sunny day.

—FRANCIS ALBERT SINATRA
"We'll Meet Again," *Songs From Great Britain* (1962),
Composer Ross Parker, Lyricist Hughie Charles

AFTERWORD

BY JENNIFER VALOPPI

When Eliot Weisman arrived at my Miami Beach home in the fall of 2016, my teenage son was sitting at the living room piano with his laptop mounted where the sheet music should be, banging out *Bohemian Rhapsody* by Queen as it played along softly on the computer. I told Julian that a friend I hadn't seen in years, Frank Sinatra's manager, was coming over. I wasn't sure if he knew who Sinatra was but as I opened the door to greet Eliot and his daughter Carol, I suddenly heard Julian's voice from the other room; "Someday, when I'm awfully low, when the world is cold, I will feel a glow just thinking of you," he sang as he plunked away on the keys of our out-of-tune baby grand. "And the way you look tonight."

The piano, with its worn-out ivories, belonged to my mother, who entertained the troops for the USO during the era that Frank Sinatra got his start. I was surprised at my son's repertoire, needless to say, and was immediately struck by the look of joy on Eliot's face. He slowly made his way across the living room. Eliot had heard those lyrics perhaps a million times, but this day, we all heard the echo of his boss of over 20 years; a man I consider myself fortunate to have known, and the struggles both public and private, that resonated so profoundly in every word that Frank Sinatra sang.

"Hi," Julian said, rising to his feet and extending his hand as a lock of unusually long brown hair flopped over his left eye. "My mom said you knew Frank Sinatra?" There was more than a hint of excitement in his voice.

Eliot laughed. "Yeah, I guess you could say that. I was his manager," he said. "I remember that song well." The truth is there is not a song Sinatra sang that Eliot doesn't remember well—not a cadence, an intonation, or a phrase.

Sinatra was dead before my son was born. Yet there he was, a teenager in bare feet, shorts, and a tee shirt, looking more rock 'n' roller than Rat Packer, singing the music of a man who rarely sang without a tux, like it was the trending release on iTunes. My other son, Jordan, went on to tell how he and his high school friends had just spent an afternoon lounging in someone's hot tub, listening to Sinatra tunes and singing along. I couldn't help but giggle. Sinatra would have loved that image. Eliot and I marveled at how these young men, including his own son David, who was just a few years older than my kids and had actually met Sinatra as an infant, loved the iconic crooner. And it's not just a boy-thing. Carol's young daughters, Sophie and Sam, are also Sinatra fans, and Sophie has been so inspired by Sinatra's music that she intends to follow in Eliot's footsteps.

People Eliot's age who lived through the Sinatra years, expected his enduring quality. People my age—I was barely out of my twenties when I met Sinatra, who was already in his seventies—at least knew he was a legend even if we didn't fully understand the history that made him one. But today's teenagers? That seemed very odd to me.

Then I reflected on the first time my friend Dennis Stein took me to dinner with Frank and Barbara at Chasen's, the elegant eatery of Hollywood's old guard. I was a television journalist in New York and aware that Sinatra had publicly feuded with a few of my kind, so I was a little uncertain as to what kind of reception I would receive. Within moments I was charmed and I walked out of the restaurant thinking—yes, I know it sounds cliché—that I had just met the coolest man on the planet.

As Eliot, Carol, and I sat on the sofa sipping Pellegrino, he got right to the point. "I want you to write my book." I was honored and juggled in my mind how I would rearrange my schedule to accommodate the dedication this endeavor deserved. Some of the work had been done a dozen years earlier. Eliot, Maria, my husband Christian, and I laughed over dinner in south Florida one night as Eliot told stories and reminisced about the King of Cool. "You really should write a book, Eliot," I said. And so the journey through Eliot's life began, usually in the mornings before the evening newscast I anchored. I would visit him, pen and pad in hand and take down stories; the highs, lows, and all those very good years. Then, for a variety of reasons we put it away. Now, as I tried to remember where I put all those old notes, the timing felt right, so we dusted off his memories.

Eliot is a comeback story about a businessman who found a second shot by working to ensure that one of the greatest entertainers of our time (who had made a few comebacks of his own) would not fade from sight.

To rule the world and stay relevant into old age is a gift. To stay relevant beyond the grave *is* the stuff of legend. The Voice, Ol' Blue Eyes was a muse to generations who fell in love, married, and had their hearts broken. They suffered the pitfalls of life with him reminding them to "Pick yourself up and get back in the race." They lamented over lost loves as the Saloon Singer prodded "Set 'em up, Joe," and of course, in unison they crowed, "I did it my way."

How can some kids, a bunch of teenagers, possibly know what a rare talent he was? Is it all those Sinatra videos on YouTube? Maybe. Watching Sinatra bob and sway, snapping his fingers with confidence and flashing a smile while belting out the words to any one of a number of songs with his famous breath control and attitude, has been among my favorite parts of writing this book.

The Sinatra I knew wasn't the skinny young kid, or sleek middle-aged Rat Packer, he was more mature, slightly rounder, but every bit the Chairman of the Board. Thank you, Eliot, for keeping him onstage all those years, so I would have an opportunity to see a doyen perform, and thank you, too, for pairing him with younger singers in both *Duets* so another generation could be brought into the Sinatra fold. Roughly a hundred books have been written about Sinatra and his music. He never wrote his own book. If he had, what would he have said? Surely it would have been brave and honest; gritty and heartfelt. That's what Eliot and I tried to do.

Frank would have told it, the way it was.

SPECIAL THANKS

The authors would like to thank Mauro DiPreta and the team at Hachette Book Group for their expert guidance, support, and commitment to telling this story. Carol Chenkin, thank you for your numerous efforts to research, market, and bring this book to fruition. It was a pleasure spending the many long days working together. Maria Weisman, thank you for your many insights. Many thanks to Christian de Berdouaré, Willy Rizzo, Fred J. Montilla Jr., Merrill Kellem, Joey Rizzo, Nancy Ciocio, Elaine Etess, Micki Cohen, Steve Schwachter, Artem Polovikiv, Dr. Nick Ramilick, Don and Maria Browne, Lorna Amador, Carol Iacovelli, Marisa Toccin, Suzy Buckley, Michael Horowitz, Julian and Jordan de Berdouaré, and Mikhael and Annalee de Berdouaré Porter.

INDEX

Ackerman, Nick, 36–37, 43–46
The Act, 63
Agnew, Spiro, 147
Agress, David, 64
Agress, Roni, 64
Aiello, Danny, 276
"All of Me," 2
Allen, Woody, 181
Alswang, Ralph, 22
Alzheimer's rumor, 184, 265
"Angel Eyes," 275
Anka, Paul, 65, 69, 74–75, 169, 172
Apollo Theater, 219
Armstrong, Louis, 99
Arnaz, Desi, Jr., 126
Artanis company, 206
Arthur, 132
asset transfer, 101–105, 205, 284
audiences, 6, 8, 56, 71, 73, 247, 269
Australia, 139
authenticity, 73, 138, 294
awards
    Congressional Gold Medal, 281
    Grammy Legend Award, 257–261
    Jean Hersholt Humanitarian Award,
      114
    Lifetime Achievement Award, 190–191,
      257
    Medal of Freedom, 281
    Sinatra, B., possessing, 284
Aznavour, Charles, 70, 95, 236, 237, 251, 254

Bacall, Lauren, 147
Backstreet Boys, 290
Baker, Anita, 167, 254
Bassey, Shirley, 20, 65
Beatles, 99, 241
Benanav, Jonathan, 171–172
Bennett, Tony, 253–254, 274, 276
Bernstein, Ben, 215
Bernstein, Leonard, 99
The Best of the Columbia Years album, 272
"Birth of the Blues," 161

Bishop, Joey, 123, 159
Blige, Mary J., 216
Bloodline, 221–222, 229–230
body language, 8, 70
bodyguards, 26, 294
The Bodyguard, 257
Bonamassa, Joe, 221–223, 293
Bonamassa, Lenny, 223
Bono, 235, 251, 254, 256–258, 262, 275
Braunstein, Bill, 217, 219
Braunstein, Jerry, 217, 219
Braxton, Toni, 257
breathing technique, 243, 300
Brynner, Yul, 151
Buffet, Jimmy, 263
Burson-Marsteller, 117
Burton, Richard, 151, 179
Bush, Billy, 169
Bush, George W., 40
Buttons, Red, 136–137

Cabaret, 63, 132
Cabot, Tony, 19
Cagney, James, 167
Cahn, Sammy, 72
Callas, Maria, 99
Camacho, Hector, 171
"Candy Man," 161
Capitol Records
    holdings, 272
    owners of, 228–229
    photos at, 2, 9
    recording at, 2, 105, 228–229, 239–241
    royalties from, 105–106, 206
Carey, Mariah, 216, 236
Carnegie Hall concert, 59–62, 98–100
Carriagi, Pierro, 108–110, 201–202
Carson, Johnny, 102, 214
Carter, Aaron, 70, 290
casinos
    Desert Inn, Las Vegas, 163, 188–189,
      217, 232
    as favored venue, 8–9

casinos (*cont.*)
  Sands Hotel & Casino, Atlantic City,
    163, 168, 170–171, 175–176, 193, 255
  Taj Mahal casino, 170–173, 175
Castellano, Paul, 30
Cattaneo, Hank
  calls to, 122
  at Grammy awards, 257, 259–260
  on music charts, 118
  as producer, 3, 234–235, 240, 246, 251,
    254–255
  warning from, 252
Celebrity Invitational Golf Tournament,
  152–155, 270
Chagall, Marc, 13
charisma, 71
charity benefits, 152–153
Chenkin, Carol, 17, 117–118, 293, 297–299
Cher, 25, 65
Chiarella, Antoinette, 177–178
Chiarella, Joe, 177–178
civil rights causes, 79, 113
Clark, Dick, 34
Colbert, Claudette, 194
Cole, Nat King, 2, 152, 241, 269
Cole, Natalie, 235, 254, 257, 268–269, 274
collapse on stage, 267
Colombo, Joe, 25
"Come Fly with Me," 71, 282
"Come Rain or Come Shine," 254
"Comme d'Habitude," 74
Congressional Gold Medal, 281
Connick, Harry, Jr., 195
conviction, 113, 187
Corporate Entertainment Productions
  (CEP), 117
Cosby, Bill, 182
Costa, Don, 72
Crawford, Michael, 160
Creative Artists Agency (CAA), 52
Crosby, Bing, 158, 241
cross relic, 111–112
Crowley, Arthur, 102, 279

Damone, Vic, 131, 275
dance music, 2
Danza, Tony, 276

Davis, Erin, 222
Davis, Sammy, Jr.
  bookings, 7, 25, 165, 182
  as core act, 69
  death of, 181–182
  final performance of, 167
  jewelry of, 147
  Las Vegas performance, 125
  live performance of, 159, 182
  love for, 20
  in Rat Pack, 123, 159, 167
  Sinatra influencing, 7
  throat cancer diagnosis, 7, 165–167, 174
  tours with, 124–133, 160–162
  tribute to, 167–168
  Ultimate Event and, 134, 137–142,
    160–163, 190
De Niro, Robert, 147, 197
Dearstine, Jean, 42–43, 47–48, 54
death, 1, 277–280
DeBakey, Michael, 184–185
DePalma, Greg
  deals with, 17–25
  death of, 40
  dinners with, 27
  imprisonment, 40
  indictment of, 34
  on mob picture, 30–31
  plea of, 38–40
  on tapes, 11, 43
  temper of, 36
  trial of, 36
depression, 114, 277
Desert Inn, Las Vegas, 163, 188, 217, 232
Diamond, Neil, 263
Diamond Jubilee Tour, 194–195, 200–203
DiCamillo, Kenny, 215
Dickens, Charles, 114
Dickinson, Angie, 123
Diener, Lawrence, 172
DiMaggio, Joe, 159
Dion, Celine, 73
Dorsey, Tommy, 243
Dreesen, Tom, 282
Duets album
  achievements of, 274
  artists for, 234–235

planning of, 232–234
platinum album, 284
production of, 3–4, 251–257, 300
recording of, 9, 239–250
sales of, 262, 268
Duets II album
platinum album, 284
production and recording of, 262–264
sales of, 268
Dylan, Bob, 246, 274

Earpiece, 266–267
Eastwood, Clint, 153, 154
Ebb, Fred, 64, 120, 131, 138, 197
eightieth birthday, 273–274
80th Live album, 272, 273
"Embraceable You," 264
Erlichman, Marty, 235, 291
Estefan, Gloria, 221, 235, 254
Etess, Mark Grossinger, 170–172

Farrow, Mia, 181, 281
FBI investigation, 10–12, 31–35, 45
fearlessness, 138
Finkelstein, Bob, 206–207, 278–280,
    287–288, 291
Fitzgerald, Ella, 167
Fleetwood Mac, 106
"Fly Me to the Moon," 71
"A Foggy Day," 263
Foothill home, 245, 277–278
"For Once in My Life," 263
Fox Theatre, Atlanta, 191
Fox Theatre, Detroit, 135
François, Claude, 74
Frank Sinatra: 80 Years My Way television
    special, 274–275
Frank Sinatra: An American Legend (Sinatra,
    N.), 272
Frank Sinatra Trilogy album, 284
Franklin, Aretha, 235, 254
Fratianno, Aladena ("Jimmy the Weasel"),
    31, 38–39
Frazier, Hal, 216
Frazier, LaGaylia, 70, 216
Friedwald, Will, 272
From Here to Eternity, 275, 284

funeral, 281–282
Fusco, Richie, 20, 31, 34, 38

Gambino, Carlo, 30–31
Gambino, Joseph, 31
Garcia, Jerry, 272
Garden State Arts Center, 177–178
Gardner, Ava, 58–59, 60, 61, 75, 179–181, 260
Garland, Judy, 63, 64, 99, 109, 123, 132, 191
generosity, 138, 149–150, 188–189, 233
Gillinov, Marc, 292
Giuliani, Rudy, 40, 45–46
Gleason, Jackie, 47
"Go Away Little Girl," 190
Golden, Sonny, 101–102, 105, 113, 143–144,
    282
Gormé, Eydie
bookings and, 7, 174, 176, 192
death of, 292
death of son, 191–192
Diamond Jubilee Tour and, 194–195,
    200–203
Duets II and, 263
eightieth birthday show and, 274
management of, 52–53
Sinatra, T., on, 192–193, 200
talent of, 190–191
tours of, 220
Grace, Brendan, 162–163
Grammy Legend Award, 257–261
Grateful Dead, 272
grave site, 282
"Guess I'll Hang My Tears Out to Dry," 254
Guthrie, Arlo, 106
Guys and Dolls, 284

Hamlisch, Marvin, 63, 69
Hart, David, 58–59
health
checkups, 183–184
effects of Elavil, 115, 184–185
hearing loss, 107, 184, 203
memory loss, 115, 187, 200, 237
vision loss, 107, 184, 203
Heller, Rob, 215, 218–219
Hemingway, Ernest, 114
Henry, Pat, 29, 188

Hepburn, Audrey, 63
Hess, Leon, 58
High Society, 59, 284
Hines, Gregory, 168
Holiday, Billie, 99
honesty, 290
Hootie & the Blowfish, 274–275
Hoover, J. Edgar, 12
Hopper, Edward, 284
Horne, Lena, 263–264
Horowitz, Vladimir, 99
horse racing, 57–58
The House I Live In, 275, 284
"The House I Live In," 151, 275
Houston, Whitney, 167, 216, 257
humanitarian, 114, 271
humidors, 272
Humperdinck, Engelbert, 25, 69–70, 290, 294
Hyde, Stephen, 171–172
Hynde, Chrissie, 263
"I Get a Kick Out of You," 2
"I Will Always Love You," 257
Ianniello, Matty ("the Horse"), 213
"If He Walked into My Life," 191–192
Iglesias, Julio, 69, 235, 254
integrity, 113, 290
International Creative Management (ICM), 52, 104, 215
Internet, 223
Israel, 7–8
Italian-American Civil Rights League, 24–25
Italy, 65–66, 80–82, 84–85, 87–90, 95
"I've Got a Crush on You," 254
"I've Got the World on a String," 73, 253
"I've Got You Under My Skin," 2, 71, 254, 256–257

Jackson, Jesse, 182
Jackson, Michael, 74, 167, 168, 175, 182
Japanese commercial, 208
Jean Hersholt Humanitarian Award, 114
Jenkins, Gordon, 2
Jerry Lewis Labor Day Telethon, 166–167
Jobim, Antonio Carlos, 263
Joel, Billy, 246, 255, 260
John, Elton, 175, 255

John Paul II, 108–112
Jones, Quincy, 72
Jones, Tom, 18, 19, 25, 74
Joubert, Elvina (Vine)
    as assistant, 75, 77, 80–81, 128–130, 240, 242, 265–267, 280
    as beneficiary, 207, 285
    calls from, 248
    folding bills, 188–189
    touring with, 200–202

Kander, John, 64, 120, 197
Kantor, Ed, 166
Kelem, Merrill, 164
Kelley, Kitty, 102, 186
Kelly, Grace, 59–61
Kennedy, Bobby, 158
Kennedy, Jack, 67, 152, 156, 158
Kennedy Center performance, 67–68
Kent, Robert, 172
Kerkorian, Kirk, 104, 200
Kerzner, Sol, 65
King, Alan, 194
King, Larry, 294
King, Martin Luther, Jr., 79, 185
KISS, 131
Kissinger, Henry, 159
Knight, Gladys, 263
Koch, Ed, 170
Kollek, Teddy, 79
Koppelman, Charles, 3, 228–230, 233–236, 239, 245, 262
Korbel champagne, 208, 272
Krieger, Waylon, 222

La Dolce Vita, 4, 242, 243, 248
L.A. Is My Lady, 3, 229
LaBelle, Patti, 263, 275
Labriola, Gary, 47–48, 64
Lady Blue Eyes (Sinatra, B.), 149, 280
"Lady Is a Tramp," 254, 275
Lawford, Peter, 123, 158
Lawrence, David, 191–192
Lawrence, Michael, 191
Lawrence, Steve
    bookings and, 7, 174, 176, 292
    Diamond Jubilee Tour and, 194–195, 200–203

Duets II and, 263
eightieth birthday show and, 274
management of, 52–53
as pallbearer, 282
Sinatra, T., on, 192–193, 200
talent of, 190–191
tours of, 220
legacy, 1–3, 107, 237, 262
"Let Me Try Again," 75
Liberace, 25
Lifetime Achievement Award, 190–191, 257
Lincoln, Abraham, 114
Little Richard, 274
"Lonely Boy," 74
Losapio, Billy, 22–23
love songs, 2
loyalty, 50, 290
Luft, Lorna, 64, 216

MacLaine, Shirley, 123, 228, 231, 294
Madison Square Garden comeback concert, 75
Mahler, Gustav, 99
Manchurian Candidate, 284
Mar-a-Lago club, 176
Marson, Tommy, 31, 34, 38
Martin, Billy, 147
Martin, Dean
death of, 276–277
health of, 127–130
last conversation with, 276
in own world, 182
photos of, 2
in Rat Pack, 123
roast show, 67
shows with, 26, 44
on stage, 20
tours with, 104, 117, 123–130, 135
Martin, Dean Paul ("Dino"), 126
Martocci, Michael, 216
Marx, Bobby, 60, 80, 92–93, 102–105, 280–284, 288
Marx, Zeppo, 27
Maselli, Rocco, 146–149
MasterCard, 272
May, Billy, 2, 72
Mayfield, Curtis, 257
Mays, Willie, 159

McCartney, Paul, 246
Meadowlands Arena, New Jersey, 117–122
Medal of Freedom, 281
Meir, Golda, 78–80
Michelangelo, 114
Miguel, Luis, 263
Miller, Bill, 3
Minnelli, Liza
booking deals and, 7, 43, 174
at Carnegie Hall, 236, 237
dog of, 140–141
duets with, 194
ending management of, 238
film work, 53, 131
as icon, 63
management of, 37–38, 47–48, 64–65, 69
at Meadowlands Arena, 117–122
meeting pope, 108–111
"New York, New York" and, 197–199, 251
in rehab, 64, 113
Rudin and, 238, 252–253
star quality of, 64
tours with, 132–133, 160–161
Ultimate Event and, 137–142, 160–163, 190
Minnelli, Vincente, 63, 132, 228
Mitchell, Edgar, 156
mob affiliations, 12, 33, 43, 74, 158, 289
Moore, Roger, 194
Moreno, Rita, 63
Morgan, Lorrie, 263
Mottola, Tommy, 236
"Mr. Bojangles," 161
Mukasey, Michael, 40, 46
Murphy, Eddie, 167
musical charts, 116, 118–119
"The Music of the Night," 160–162
My Father's Daughter (Sinatra, T.), 280
"My Way," 73–75, 169, 254–255, 263, 273–274

Neckties, 208, 272
Neiman, LeRoy, 262
Nelson, Willie, 263
Nevada Gaming Control Commission, 33–34
"New York, New York," 132, 194, 197–199, 238, 251, 253, 275

New York Times, 7, 65, 199
Newhart, Bob, 194
newspaper reader, 50
Newton, Isaac, 114
Newton-John, Olivia, 65
"Nice Work If You Can Get It," 73
Nixon, Richard, 159

Oakland Coliseum, 124–125
Oakley, Barry, Jr., 222
O'Donnell, Rosie, 276
Ol' Blue Eyes is Back album, 284
Onassis, Aristotle, 26
Onassis, Jackie, 27–30
"One for My Baby," 71, 246–247
100th anniversary, 289–295
Oppedisano, Tony, 225, 227, 266, 267, 276, 280, 282
organized crime, 12, 30–31, 36, 38
Ostin, Mo, 229–230, 235–236
Ostrow, Norman, 38–39

Pacella, Lou, 26, 34, 38
Palm Springs compound, 151–158, 204, 270, 275–276
Palmer, Arnold, 15
papal audience, 108–112
paparazzi, 29
passionate, 72, 79, 138
Pavaraotti, Luciano, 263, 273–274
Pazienza, Vinny, 171
Peck, Gregory, 113–114, 153, 275, 281
Peck, Veronique, 153
Perez, Willie, 221
perfect pitch, 119
Piccione, Pasquale, 183–184, 267–268
Pippin, 69
Playboy magazine, 114
Porter, Cole, 146
Premier Artists Services, 52, 117
private jet, 77–78
punctuality, 136–137
"Puppy Love," 74
"Put Your Head on My Shoulder," 74

Radio City Music hall, 128, 129, 181, 221, 223, 228, 257
Rainbow Room, 19, 29

Ramone, Phil, 3, 235, 246, 248, 249, 251, 254–255
Rat Pack
    core of, 159
    fading of, 158
    legendary, 257–258
    members, 159, 167, 228
    reputation, 142
    wild days of, 289
Reagan, Nancy, 67–68, 151
Reagan, Ronald, 42, 67–68, 85, 152, 184
Reprise Records, 2, 105, 206, 272
"Restless Farewell," 275
Revaux, Jacques, 74
Reynolds, Burt, 147
Reynolds, Susan, 121, 162, 186, 257, 260–261, 280–281
Rhodes, George, 128
Rhodes, Shirley, 128, 165–166, 181
Rickles, Barbara, 211–213, 215
Rickles, Don
    availability of, 176
    career low point, 7
    death of, 292
    on eightieth birthday special, 275
    friendship of, 194
    management of, 7, 69, 210–219
    as pallbearer, 282
    timing of, 209
Riddle, Nelson, 2, 72, 116, 179
Riklis, Meshulam, 136
"River of Dreams," 260
Rivers, Joan, 69, 215–216
Rizzo, Jilly
    as beneficiary, 207
    as bodyguard, 26–30, 93
    death of, 224–227
    delivering bad news, 180–181
    fraud case and, 200
    friends of, 84
    hanging out with, 119
    ideas from, 230–231
    loyalty of, 86
    with pope, 112
    on tours, 77–81, 88–89, 141–142, 187
    at White House, 85
    wisecracks from, 195
Rizzo, Willy, 225

rock and roll, 256, 258
Rocky the parrot, 155
Rodman, Dennis, 117
Romeo Salta's restaurant, 61–62
Ronstadt, Linda, 263
Roosa, Stuart, 156
Roosevelt, Franklin Delano, 67
Rosenberg, Edgar, 216
Ross, Diana, 22
Ross, Steve, 37
Rubin, Don, 3, 230, 248
Rudin, Mary Carol, 101
Rudin, Mickey
    assistance from, 35, 49–50, 53, 143
    brash style of, 26–27
    calls to, 37
    knowledge of, 39
    lawsuits and, 186
    Minnelli and, 238, 252–253
    mob photo and, 31
    as powerhouse, 6–7
    relationship erosion, 83, 98, 101–103
Rush, 121
Russell, Rosalind, 151

Sands Hotel & Casino, Atlantic City, 163,
    168, 170–171, 175–176, 193, 255
Sayan, Lévon, 95–97
Scandore, Joe, 35, 210–215, 217
Schlatter, George, 153, 167, 208, 266, 274,
    276, 281
Schlatter, Jolene, 153, 276
Schwarzenegger, Arnold, 275
Scorsese, Martin, 197
Secada, Jon, 263
Selleck, Tom, 276
sell-out shows, 26, 30, 56, 190
Separate Tables restaurant, 27–28, 34
Shandling, Gary, 257, 260
Sheffield, 206
Shepard, Alan, 153, 156–157
"She's a Lady," 74
Silbert, Harvey, 204, 207, 211–212, 214, 219,
    279, 285–286
Simmons, Gene, 131
Simon, Carly, 254
Sinatra, Barbara (wife)
    arguments with, 5–6, 243–244

auction by, 276
on blackouts, 160
calls to, 4–5, 241–242, 243
carousing nixed by, 124
Celebrity Invitational Golf Tournament,
    152–155, 270
Center for Abused Children, 152–153,
    270, 274
challenge from, 244
death of, 292
dinners hosted by, 155, 194–195, 228
dislike of Rudin, 101–102
eightieth birthday and, 274
encouragement from, 233
good news from, 256
handling husband, 5–6
husband's funeral and, 281–282
jewelry of, 102, 147, 149
legacy and, 3, 262
loyalty to, 179
marriage to, 30
responsibility to, 206
shopping by, 147–149
traveling with, 59–61, 75, 80–81, 92, 200
will and, 207, 279–285, 288, 292
worry of, 266
Sinatra, Dolly, 126
Sinatra, Frank. See specific topics
Sinatra, Frank, Jr. (son)
    assets to, 101
    concerts and performances, 71–72
    as conductor, 3, 76, 194
    death of, 293
    Duets II and, 263
    at father's funeral, 281
    giving the downbeat, 135–136
    kidnapping of, 164
    rarely around, 70
    will and, 283–284
    worry of, 266
Sinatra, Julie (alleged daughter), 285–288
Sinatra, Nancy (daughter), 70, 272, 274, 280,
    283–284, 287, 292
Sinatra, Nancy, Sr., 30, 101, 179, 207, 260,
    281, 284
Sinatra, Tina (daughter)
    anger of, 287–288
    assets to, 101

Sinatra, Tina (*cont.*)
　dates of, 126
　eightieth birthday party and, 276
　estate and, 206–207
　on father's death, 280–281
　on Lawrence and Gormé, 192–193, 200
　on "My Way," 73–74
　representing children, 283–284
　will and, 288, 292
　writing of, 208
Sinatra 80th: All the Best, 272
Sinatra 80th: Live in Concert, 272
Sinatra: The Song Is You (Friedwald), 272
Smith, Liz, 195
smoking, 100, 126
social media, 223
Solters, Lee, 121
Some Came Running, 228
Somerset Trust, 206
South Pacific, 13
Spatola, Salvatore, 31
Spots, Johnny, 77, 129, 137
Springsteen, Bruce, 255, 263, 274–276
St. John, Jill, 153, 194
stalkers, 164
Stein, Dennis, 111, 136, 153, 298
Steinbrenner, George, 197–199
Sting, 257
Stokowski, Leopold, 99
"Strangers in the Night," 74
Streisand, Barbra, 191, 234, 246, 254, 291
Sugerman, Joseph, 166
"Summerwind," 254
swagger, 60, 200, 258
Swayze, Patrick, 275–276
Sweet, Bob, 40, 45

Taj Mahal casino, 170–172, 175
Tannen, Judy, 190–191, 200–201, 226–227
Taylor, Elizabeth, 136, 151, 179
temperamental, 138
"They Can't Take That Away from Me,"
　254, 269
"This Is It," 74
Together Again Tour, 123–133, 135
The Tonight Show, 214
tours
　American Express, 117–118

　with Davis, S., 124–133, 160–162
　Diamond Jubilee Tour, 194–195,
　　200–203
　Germany, 235–236
　Italy, 80–90, 98, 100–101, 144
　Japan, 268–270
　Jilly on, 77–81, 88–89, 141–142, 187
　of Lawrence and Gormé, 220
　love of, 187
　with Martin, D., 104, 117, 123–130, 135
　with Minnelli, L., 132–133, 160–161
　Monte Carlo, 92–94
　Together Again, 123–133, 135
　Ultimate Event, 134–135, 137–142,
　　160–163, 190
train collecting, 152
Trump, Donald, 169–176
Twain, Mark, 99
Two Clowns Taking a Bow (Hopper), 284
Tyler, Harold, 39–40, 50

U2, 235, 254, 257
Uhleman, Dorothy, 207, 285
Ultimate Event, 134–135, 137–142, 160–163,
　165, 190
Under My Skin: My Father Frank Sinatra
　(Sinatra, J.), 288
unpredictable, 138
Uzi, 78–80, 90

Valoppi, Jennifer, 111, 166–167
Van Heusen, Jimmy, 72
Vandross, Luther, 235, 253
Venetianer, Jay, 175
Vereen, Ben, 69, 294
Victorson, Nifty, 226
Viner, Mort, 104, 127–128, 228
Viscious, Sid, 73
voice problems, 4–5

Wagner, Robert, 153, 194, 195, 275, 281
Warhol, Andy, 132
Warner Brothers, 105, 229
Warner Communications, 37
Washington, Booker T., 99
Washington Post, 37
Webber, Andrew Lloyd, 160
Weisman, Adele, 13, 15–16

Weisman, David, 270–271, 293–294
Weisman, Eliot (manager)
  as accountant, 16–17
  as business manager, 104–107, 143–144,
    173–176
  childhood of, 13–14
  Duets album producer, 3–4, 251–257, 300
  education of, 15–16
  as estate co-executor, 6, 204–208,
    279–288
  with FBI agents, 10–12, 31–35, 45
  imprisonment of, 41–46
  Lawrence and Gormé managed by,
    52–53
  marriage, 16, 95–98
  Minnelli managed by, 37–38, 47–48,
    64–65, 69
  at music fair, 18
  as pallbearer, 282
  prosecution of, 34–39
  Rickles managed by, 7, 69, 210–219
  Westchester Premier Theatre and,
    10–12, 19–25, 33–35, 55, 209–210
Weisman, Eric, 17, 117, 165, 173–174, 293
Weisman, Herman, 20
Weisman, Maria (Chiarella)
  courting of, 66, 69
  first meeting, 58–62
  marriage of, 95–98, 293
  meeting pope, 109–111
  parents of, 177–178
  shopping by, 147–149
Weisman, Maxine (Micky), 10–11, 16–18,
  22–23, 30, 43–44, 46, 292
Weisman, Roy, 6, 17, 220–223, 229, 264, 293
Werblin, Sonny, 58
Westchester Premier Theatre, 10–12, 19–25,
  33–35, 55, 209–210
"What Now My Love," 254
"Where or When," 263
William Morris Agency, 52, 215, 219
Williams, Patrick, 3, 242, 248
Wilson, Woodrow, 99
"Witchcraft," 254
Wonder, Stevie, 167, 263

Yankee Stadium, 21, 198–199
Yormark, Michael, 290–291

"You Make Me Feel So Young," 254
Young at Heart, 284
"Young at Heart," 259
Young & Rubicam, 117

Zadora, Pia, 136
Zappa, Frank, 106
Zylberberg, Régine, 92–94